HONG KONG'S HI~~~~~

Hong Kong's History offers a new perspective on British colonialism in Hong Kong. Challenging the mainstream view that British rule transformed a barely inhabited fishing port on the South China coast to a capitalist metropolis, the book shows that the development of the colony owed very little to the 'good policies' of the colonial state, but was shaped by the actions of, amongst others, the ruling élite, business class, compradors, rural interests, social activists and marginalized groups in their struggle for domination, manipulation of conflicts, as well as in collaboration and compromise.

Rewriting history from the 'bottom up', the chapters investigate hitherto obscured areas of Hong Kong's history such as Chinese collaboration with the colonial regime, legal discrimination and intimidation, rural politics, social movements, government-business relations, industrial policy, flexible manufacturing and colonial historiography. Each chapter shows, from its own special focus, that the nature of British colonial rule was neither 'benevolent' nor 'indirect'. By highlighting the roles played by a variety of social actors in Hong Kong's history, the volume captures the continuity and change of Hong Kong's development from the mid-nineteenth century to the present.

This book is an important contribution to the study of Hong Kong history, differing both from recent celebrations of British colonialism and anti-colonial Chinese nationalism. It contains contributions from historians, sociologists and political scientists, based on new materials uncovered by court cases, colonial archives, government reports, unofficial documents and ethnographic fieldwork. By looking at state–society relations in colonial Hong Kong in a new light, this volume will set the agenda for future research in this field.

Tak-Wing Ngo is Lecturer in Chinese Politics at Leiden University, and currently Fellow of the Netherlands Institute for Advanced Study in the Humanities and Social Sciences at the Royal Netherlands Academy of Arts and Sciences. He is the co-editor of *The Cultural Construction of Politics in Asia*.

ROUTLEDGE STUDIES IN ASIA'S TRANSFORMATIONS
Edited by Mark Selden, Binghamton and Cornell Universities

The books in this series explore the political, social, economic and cultural consequences of Asia's twentieth century transformations and look towards their impact on the twenty-first century. The series emphasizes the tumultuous interplay of local, national, regional and global forces as Asia bids to become the hub of the world economy. While focusing on the contemporary, it also looks back to analyse the antecedents of Asia's contested rise.

This series comprises two strands:

Asia's Transformations aims to address the needs of students and teachers as well as scholars, and the titles will be published in hardback and paperback. Titles include:

1. DEBATING HUMAN RIGHTS
Critical essays from the United States and Asia
Edited by Peter Van Ness

2. HONG KONG'S HISTORY
State and society under colonial rule
Edited by Tak-Wing Ngo

Routledge Studies in Asia's Transformations is a forum for innovative new research intended for a high-level specialist readership, and the titles will be available in hardback only. Titles include:

1. THE AMERICAN OCCUPATION OF JAPAN AND OKINAWA
Literature and memory
Michael Molasky

HONG KONG'S HISTORY

State and society under colonial rule

Edited by Tak-Wing Ngo

London and New York

First published 1999 by Routledge
11 New Fetter Lane, London EC4P 4EE

Simultaneously published in the USA and Canada
by Routledge
29 West 35th Street, New York, NY 10001

Routledge is an imprint of the Taylor & Francis Group

© 1999 Edited by Tak-Wing Ngo

Typeset in Baskerville by Routledge
Printed and bound in Great Britain by
MPG Books Ltd, Bodmin

All rights reserved. No part of this book may be reprinted
or reproduced or utilised in any form or by any electronic,
mechanical, or other means, now known or hereafter
invented, including photocopying and recording, or in any
information storage or retrieval system, without permission in
writing from the publishers.

British Library Cataloguing in Publication Data
A catalogue record for this book is available from the British Library

Library of Congress Cataloging in Publication Data
Hong Kong's History: state and society under colonial rule/edited by Tak-Wing Ngo
p.   cm.–(Asia's transformations)
Includes bibliographical references and index.
1. Hong Kong (China)–History.   2. Hong Kong (China)–Social conditions.   3. Hong
Kong (China)–Politics and government.   4. Great Britain–Colonies–Administration.
I. Ngo, Tak-Wing.   II. Series.
DS796.H757H663   1999
951.25–dc21   99-11838
CIP

ISBN 0–415–20305–8 (hbk)
ISBN 0–415–20868–8 (pbk)

CONTENTS

CONTENTS

LIST OF TABLES

NOTES ON CONTRIBUTORS

John M. Carroll is Visiting Assistant Professor in the Department of History at the College of William and Mary in Williamsburg, Virginia, United States.

Stephen W.K. Chiu is Associate Professor in the Department of Sociology, Chinese University of Hong Kong, Hong Kong.

Alex H. Choi is a Ph.D. candidate in the Department of Political Studies at Queen's University, Kingston, Ont., Canada.

Ho-fung Hung is a Ph.D. candidate in the Department of Sociology at the Johns Hopkins University, United States.

Kim-Ming Lee is a Lecturer in the Division of Social Studies, City University of Hong Kong, Hong Kong.

Tai-lok Lui is Associate Professor in the Department of Sociology, Chinese University of Hong Kong, Hong Kong.

Christopher Munn holds a Ph.D. in history from the University of Toronto.

Tak-Wing Ngo is Lecturer in Chinese Politics at Leiden University and currently a Fellow of the Netherlands Institute for Advanced Study at the Royal Netherlands Academy of Arts and Sciences.

Hui Po-keung is Assistant Professor in the Department of Translation, Lingnan University, Hong Kong.

PREFACE

This book offers neither a conventional account of the history of colonial administration in Hong Kong nor a linear prescription of Hong Kong's development from a barren fishing port to a modern capitalist metropolis. Rather it sets to unveil aspects of state–society relations that are hitherto obscured in Hong Kong's history.

With the transfer to Chinese rule on 1 July 1997, most recent publications on Hong Kong focus on the problem of the transition. A few revisit the historical background leading to the issue of 1997, but typically without questioning the conventional account about the colonial past. The present volume calls into question two underlying assumptions of the dominant scholarship. The first is the one-dimensional view that reduces complex and multi-faceted dimensions of colonial rule to the story of a benevolent colonial state exercising indirect rule over an apathetic society. The second is the static view of colonial rule that slights the agency of such diverse actors as the ruling élite, business classes, compradors, rural interests, social activists, marginalized groups, etc. in shaping colonial rule in Hong Kong.

In response to these problematic assumptions, this book presents an empirically and historically rooted account of state–society relations in the making of colonial Hong Kong that differs from recent celebrations of British colonialism and anti-colonial Chinese nationalism. By highlighting the roles played by a variety of social actors in their struggle for domination, manipulation of conflicts, and collaboration and compromise, the present volume seeks to appraise Hong Kong history from the 'bottom up'.

The idea for this project came originally from my informal discussions with colleagues from Hong Kong about the possibility of organizing a workshop to discuss some missing gaps in the current account of Hong Kong's history and development. With the encouraging support of the Documentation and Research Centre for Contemporary China, a workshop was convened at Leiden University in August 1996. The initiative received a warm response from colleagues who shared the dissatisfaction with the conventional account on Hong Kong history.

The project received generous support from numerous institutions and persons. Financial support came from the International Institute for Asian Studies, Leiden University Fund, the Research School of Asian, African and Amerindian Studies, the Faculty of Arts, and the Sinological Institute at Leiden University. Woei Lien Chong has been an important driving force behind the preparation of the workshop. The workshop papers have been published as a special issue of *China Information*, vol. 12, nos 1&2 (Summer/Autumn 1997). I would like to thank *China Information* for allowing me to include the articles in their revised form in this book.

The original papers have been revised several times, some substantially rewritten, for the present volume. For one reason or another not all the initial papers are included in this volume, but the input of the participants clearly made an impact on the various contributions. We are grateful to those who read and commented on various chapters and drafts. They are Leonard Blussé, Richard Boyd, Timothy Brook, Leo Douw, Florike Egmond, Benno Galjart, Dan Healey, Kees Koonings, Law Kam-yee, Patrick Munn, Derek Roebuck, Mario Rutten, Ming Sing, Eduard Vermeer and Wu Yongping. Gregor Benton and Flemming Christiansen have read the entire script and given suggestions for improvement. In preparing for this publication Mark Selden has offered invaluable advice on sharpening the themes and keeping the project in perspective. His mindfulness provided indispensable help and encouragement for this volume. I thank Victoria Smith at Routledge for her enthusiastic reception of the project and the two anonymous reviewers for their constructive comments. During the final preparation for publication, I gratefully received the assistance of Rebecca Chan, Woei Lien Chong, and Gina Rozario in editing the manuscript.

Finally, a few remarks on the transliteration of Chinese names. As most of the previous works on Hong Kong history have already noted, there is no satisfactory way of transliterating the Hong Kong Cantonese names. In this volume, the Cantonese proper names are given in their official of familiar 'Hong Kong' form. When a proper name has no official or common transliteration, it is given in Pinyin. This complication, and sometimes confusion, over transliteration reflects in a way the ambiguity and complexity of the Hong Kong situation. I hope the style adopted here also reflects the Hong Kong approach to its problems: seeking a compromise that, albeit far from ideal, is nevertheless serviceable in practice.

Tak-Wing Ngo
November 1998, Leiden

1

COLONIALISM IN HONG KONG REVISITED

Tak-Wing Ngo

There are many conflicting accounts of Hong Kong's one-and-a-half centuries of British rule. These accounts affect not only our perception of the past but also that of the present, for history serves a dual and reciprocal function – understanding the past by the present and understanding the present by the past.[1] A revisit of these accounts, and an analysis of those aspects of Hong Kong history that have hitherto been obscured in the dominant narratives, is timely now that the colonial status of Hong Kong has officially ended.

The first set of competing narratives revolves around the question of colonialism versus nationalism. One observer succinctly describes them as 'Hong Kong as apart from China' in contrast to 'Hong Kong as a part of China'.[2] The colonial narrative typically portrays Hong Kong as a 'barren-rock-turned-capitalist-paradise'. Hong Kong is said to have merely been a barren island before the British came; but thanks to the benevolent governance and good policy of the colonial state, this barren rock was transformed into a capitalist metropolis. This barren rock legend, as one critic observes, has been reiterated in one way or the other by every British official and semi-official account of Hong Kong history.[3] Those who uphold the legend imply that, since Britain created Hong Kong out of wilderness, it has contributed more to the development of Hong Kong than anyone else.

In contrast to this colonial narrative, the nationalistic interpretation views the fate of Hong Kong as part of the modern history of China, characterized by invasion and humiliation at the hands of Western powers. This narrative typically begins with the opening sentence: 'Hong Kong has been part of Chinese territory since ancient times'.[4] It stresses the close relationship between mainland China and Hong Kong even during Hong Kong's colonial period, highlights mainland China's contribution to Hong Kong's development (such as providing cheap supplies and maintaining Hong Kong's stability), and underlines the anti-colonial struggles by the indigenous population against British rule. Although critical of British colonialism, the nationalistic account affirms the colony's economic policy and broader socio-economic and legal system. That system is to be preserved, as promised in the Sino-British Joint Declaration and the Basic Law, for fifty years following Hong Kong's hand over to China in 1997.

While these narratives are obviously ideologically driven, there is also another set of narratives which relates to the question of autonomy versus subordination. On the one hand, there are historians and social scientists who claim that Hong Kong did not possess the conventional attributes of a colony, and that late twentieth-century Hong Kong showed little sign of a colonial presence, and even less of a colonial past.[5] It is argued that Hong Kong has thrived under a kind of indirect rule, resulting in the people enjoying increased autonomy. On the other hand there are those who see Hong Kong as squeezed between Britain and China throughout most of its history, behaving like a 'concubine of two masters' who passively accepted its fate that was determined by the 'precarious balance' between Britain and China.[6]

Although seemingly contradictory, all the above-mentioned narratives share a common problem: they ignore the complexity of British colonial rule in Hong Kong. In the words of Bloch, when the passions of the past blend with the prejudices of the present, human reality is reduced to a picture in black and white.[7] It is this danger of gross simplification of the nature of colonialism in Hong Kong that the present volume wants to address. Our aim is to present new empirical evidence that can lead to a more balanced understanding of the multifaceted nature of Hong Kong's colonial past.

Our approach focuses on showing the great variety of social actors who have actively shaped the course of Hong Kong's development in the last century and a half. Much of the existing literature is based on the one-dimensional opposition of 'the ruler' versus 'the ruled'. The colonial ruler is seen as no more than a bureaucratic administrator, while the ruled are depicted as a mass of apathetic market actors, or 'economic animals', whose main attributes are the capacity for hard work among the many and entrepreneurial skills among the élite few.

In contrast to this, the chapters in this volume show, in the first place, that the ruling élite was at various times benevolent, manipulative and oppressive. It was capable of using varied means to reward followers, exclude rivals, neutralize the hostile, and disorganize the dangerous. While the colonial nature of the regime undoubtedly shaped its strategies and policies in certain directions, the imperative of maintaining effective rule was the same as for any other regime.

In the second place, the people of Hong Kong did not confine themselves to hard work and entrepreneurship. There were also collaborators of the ruling regime, compradors of colonial businesses, anti-colonial radicals, marginalized industrialists, revenue farmers, landlords and social activists. They took an active part, not only in economic construction, trading networks and flexible manufacturing, but also in policy making, rural protests and social movements. Far from passive beneficiaries of benevolent rule, they were active agents of Hong Kong's history.

By highlighting the agency of different actors in Hong Kong's history, we hope to avoid the one-sidedness of the established narratives. Without doubt, Hong Kong's development has always been affected by Britain and China, but thanks to the active part played by different actors, the people of Hong Kong also took the initiative in shaping its history. Moreover, while both British rule and Hong Kong's relationship with mainland China had an imprint on Hong Kong society, it was the complex state–society relations that intertwined with the British and Chinese factors which created Hong Kong's unique socio-political landscape.

To elucidate the point, let us look at several issues that are central to our understanding of the nature of colonial rule in Hong Kong: the relationship between the colonial state and the indigenous society, the relationships among the societal actors, the role of colonial rule in promoting as well as constraining Hong Kong's development, and finally, both the impact of colonial rule and the China factor.

The reach of the colonial state

The existing scholarship portrays the colonial state as possessing a limited reach in society as a result of its deliberate policy of indirect rule – a combination of economic *laissez-faire* and political non-intervention. One dominant view sees colonial rule in Hong Kong as characterized by indirect rule carried out by a politically neutral state. The colonial government is seen as an 'administrative state' which imposed an almost complete monopoly of power on an atomistic society.[8] The colonial state disengaged itself from societal affairs, notably by its policy of *laissez-faire*, resulting in a separation of the state from society.[9] The only link between state and society was institutional co-optation of social élites into advisory bodies for the sake of information exchange and public opinion testing.[10]

Others who hold a more critical view of the colonial system agree that society was separated from the state, except for one group of social actors – big business. They argue that the colonial regime secured its basis of support through a coalition of bureaucrats and big businesses. Either they argue that it was a colonial state captured by business interests, or that it was a collusion of bureaucratic and business interests.[11] The situation is figuratively described by the old joke: 'Power in Hong Kong resides in the Royal Hong Kong Jockey Club; Jardine, Matheson & Co.; the Hongkong and Shanghai Banking Corporation; and the Governor – in that order'.[12] The colonial state is thus not regarded as politically neutral, since its economic policy of free market and low profit was aimed at protecting business interests.

Focusing on different aspects of the colonial formation and on different historical periods, the chapters in this volume show that first, the 'reach of the colonial state' was far more penetrating than these portraits suggest; and second, the link between state and society was far more complicated than the polarized views of an administrative co-optation of social élites and a business capture of state power.

In fact, complex state–society relations developed as soon as the Union Jack was raised on Hong Kong Island, and continued to evolve. From the outset, the founding of the colony faced both the co-operation and the resistance from the Chinese inhabitants. This prompted the colonial state to formulate active strategies to enlist the support of collaborators and to pacify the hostility of opponents. As John Carroll argues in Chapter 2, Britain's acquisition of Hong Kong relied not only upon military strength but also upon the indispensable help of Chinese contractors, compradors and other merchants in providing the essential supplies during the Opium War. Furthermore, British business interests had to rely on the pre-existing Chinese trading networks in order to penetrate Asian markets, as Hui Po-keung points out in Chapter 3. In exchange for their collaboration, British authorities rewarded the natives with social and economic privileges so that these collaborators became the first generation of Chinese bourgeoisie in the colony.

This collaborative relationship constituted only one face of colonial state–society interaction. The other face of it was mutual hostility. This hostility came from the indigenous inhabitants of the New Territories who resisted colonial rule. It resulted in a wide range of rural political conflicts discussed by Stephen Chiu and Ho-fung Hung. In order to pacify the indigenous inhabitants of the New Territories who resisted colonial rule, the government instituted rural reforms as soon as peace was secured by military suppression. First, the landownership system was altered to deprive the old landholding élite of their economic base. Then the anti-government voices in the rural representative body Heung Yee Kuk were silenced by declaring the latter illegal and dissolving it. It was then reorganized according to government preference and was filled with pro-government members. Later, a number of state-sponsored rural co-operatives – including the Vegetable Marketing Organization, pig-raising societies, fish pond societies, etc. – were set up to pre-empt anti-government influence (particularly from the pro-Beijing forces) among immigrant farmers. By monitoring the rural economy and society, through a combination of co-optation/exclusion and negotiation/compensation, the colonial state reached down to the very bottom level of the rural community in restructuring its social relations.

An intriguing parallel of state action can be found in the modern sector. Unlike the popular portrait of a non-interventionist government upholding a *laissez-faire* economic policy, the colonial state undertook action to maintain a trade-dominated economy at the expense of industrial upgrading. From the outset, the colonial state was closely tied to trading interests, since British acquisition of Hong Kong was, above all, motivated by trade concern. During the pre-war period, the state delivered a policy verdict that it was unsuitable for Hong Kong to develop industry, for fear of creating tariff protection that would harm trade, and to avoid becoming a competitor of British industry. Later, when Hong Kong industry did expand after the Second World War because of a combination of external geo-political and economic factors, and domestic business strategies, state policy was enacted to prevent industrial upgrading. The reason, as Tak-Wing Ngo and Alex Choi argue in their Chapters, was the dominant position of pro-British trading and banking interests in politics. What is more, as Choi emphasizes, the dominance of trading/banking interests was at the same time maintained by state manipulation to 'domesticate' industrial interests. Analogous to its intervention in rural politics, the state went so far as to marginalize the oppositionist Chinese Manufacturers' Association by creating an obedient Federation of Hong Kong Industries. State co-optation of the industrial élite ensured the latter's acquiescence over the stagnation of industrial upgrading.

The selective co-optation of élites was accompanied by a systematic policy of controlling the working class. One of the instruments to administer such a policy of control was the judicial and criminal law system. This was especially conspicuous in the early years of British colonial rule. In contrast to the widespread belief about the judicial system being fair and protecting individual freedom by the rule of law, Christopher Munn finds that the criminal justice system was taken as a means to police the Chinese inhabitants and to secure easy convictions of suspected members of the populace. The court cases examined by Munn show that the lower classes were closely monitored and systematically intimidated.

The above-mentioned studies highlight the 'strategies of rule' used by the colonial state. These strategies, aimed at maintaining governance, can hardly be conceived as 'indirect rule'. Quite the opposite, the colonial state had painstakingly tried to assert itself in the social fabrics of an alien populace. This was necessary because, the conventional view to the contrary notwithstanding, Hong Kong society was not an apathetic, atomistic entity without political grievances and social conflicts so that the ruler faced little difficulty in governance. In reality, conflicts and social cleavages did exist and were manifested in various forms. These conflicts and cleavages in turn provided the basis for the colonial state to exercise leverage and manœuvre events into the desired directions – in other words, to advance its strategies of rule. In return, state manipulation allowed different social actors to make use of state sanctions to advance their own interests. The result is the unfolding of complex social relationships that formed the backbone of Hong Kong's history.

The manipulation of conflicts among social actors

The existence of complex social relationships and their political implications have hitherto been largely overlooked. We are often told that Hong Kong was a politically apathetic society because of the 'refugee mentality' of its Chinese inhabitants. This apathy was manifested, it is said, in the absence of popular demands on the government as well as the absence of social/political conflicts.[13] A familial ethos supposedly shaped the attitude of individuals, who stayed aloof from and remained indifferent to societal affairs except when events impinged on the well-being of their own families.[14] The circularity of this argument is obvious: the lack of social unrest is taken as evidence of the political aloofness of

5

the Hong Kong Chinese; and this aloofness is in turn used to explain the absence of social conflicts. This social acquiescence is then regarded as the basis of political stability. Notwithstanding its circularity, this argument provides policy makers and supporters of the status quo with a convenient justification for resisting pressures for political and policy change, on the grounds that the existing system worked well in preserving stability.

While it is undeniable that Hong Kong enjoyed a high degree of political stability, especially after the Second World War, this does not mean, first, that social conflicts were absent; and second, that the absence of social unrest was the result of a refugee mentality and political apathy. In fact, as Tai-lok Lui and Stephen Chiu emphasize, while observers were busy explaining the 'political acquiescence' of Hong Kong society, wave after wave of collective actions – from student activism to labour protest and the environmental movement – emerged to shape part of the political life in contemporary Hong Kong. Different groups stood up in different periods to challenge the domination of colonial interests, the unequal distribution of economic resources, and the monopoly of political rights by a few.

What merits special attention is therefore not the absence of conflicts but the management and accommodation of these conflicts by the colonial state. In most cases, the colonial state was not just a neutral arbiter of rival interests. Not only did the state use its power of 'state licensing' to support one party against the other in some conflicts, but sometimes it even deliberately created social cleavages. The conflicts between commerce and industry and among rural factions illustrate the point. The state made use of the division between local clans in the New Territories, namely the 'Yuen Long faction' and the 'Tsuen Wan faction', to launch a 'coup' in the rural representative body Heung Yee Kuk to create supporters for its land resumption policy. Similarly, it sided with British merchants in rejecting the demand for industrial restructuring, by neutralizing the Shanghainese industrialists and marginalizing the small Cantonese producers. In these cases, economic/material conflicts cut across ethnic, regional or even dialectal boundaries, providing multiple bases for manipulation. Hence the conflict between commerce and industry was simultaneously manifested as one between British and Chinese; the conflict between large and small industries as that between Shanghainese and Cantonese; and that between landowners and tenants as one between indigenous and Hakka groups.

'Stability' thus does not mean 'conflict-free'. However, conflicts that might endanger the stability of the colonial regime were pre-empted by the painstaking effort of the colonial state to establish its institutional reach into the urban and rural sectors, the maintenance of shifting alliances between the state and different groups of élite, and the manipulation of cleavages among societal interests. By these political means, the colonial state created power brokers who became mutually dependent. As a result, conflicts could be pacified by negotiation and compensation of material resources, thereby preventing them from escalating to moral, anti-colonial platforms. This view is advanced by Tai-

6

lok Lui and Stephen Chiu, who suggest that anti-colonialism was originally the root of social movements after the 1967 riots. However, collective action originating in the early 1970s as a response to national identity formation was gradually transformed from a manifestation of 'identity politics' to a 'secular' movement centred on resource allocation.

At the same time, social actors were not politically ignorant, passively subjected to state manipulation. They, in turn, made use of state power to mediate relations among themselves. This active agency was indeed part of the colonization process, since oppression and exploitation were not a prerogative of the colonizers alone. In such a process, some social actors – including the Chinese compradors, the commercial and banking élites, the rural landlords, etc. – prospered by subjecting others to subordination, and became an indispensable part of colonial domination. The most extreme case of domination by one social actor over another can be found in the coolie and opium trade. As Hui Po-keung argues in Chapter 3, many Chinese merchants obtained their 'first tank of gold' from participating in the coolie trade – by shipping their fellow countrymen as contracted labour to Southeast Asia and North America. Working closely with colonial authorities and the British business interests in exploiting other social groups, these Chinese compradors eventually surpassed their British partners in terms of wealth and social power. In the course of such a domination/exploitation process, they also helped turn Hong Kong into a major commercial and trade centre.

In sum, the multilateral and politically constructed relationships between social groups remind us that state–society relations in Hong Kong should not be characterized simply as a one-dimensional link between a bureaucratic polity and an atomistic, homogeneous and apathetic society. Stability and the avoidance of widespread, open confrontations rested not just on cultural ethos or collective psychology, but on the painstaking process of state–society interactions in accommodating, dissipating, marginalizing or even suppressing the conflicts.

The role of colonial rule in modernization

Having highlighted the colonial state's strategies of rule and manipulation of social conflicts, it would be wrong to suggest that colonial rule in Hong Kong merely rested upon political manipulation. Many people have indeed applauded the colonial state as being an agent of modernization. There is a high degree of consensus that the benevolent policy of the colonial state was the major determinant of Hong Kong's developmental success.[15] Although a small number of sceptics argue that government non-intervention is over-stated, most agree that the liberal economic policy of free trade and free market under a fair legal system and stable political environment was responsible for Hong Kong's prosperity. The colonial regime has thus acquired legitimacy by virtue of what is called its 'correct policy' and 'superior politico-economic system'.[16]

Here we caution against an over-simplification which views colonial policies and measures as either totally positive or totally negative. Evidence shows that colonial policies both advanced and constrained Hong Kong's development. The most obvious case of positive intervention, as noted earlier, is the colonial state's contribution to Hong Kong's commercial and trade development. But at the same time, it played a negative role in discouraging industrialization before the Second World War, as well as blocking the opportunity for industrial upgrading in the 1960s. The connection between colonial rule and economic modernization is further complicated by the fact that the policy bias was not only upheld by the colonial state, but also sanctioned by the dominant commercial and financial interests, as well as by some fractions of the industrial interests and organized labour, in view of different calculated self-interests.

Notwithstanding such policy sanctions and bias, Hong Kong's past economic performance has been rather satisfactory. This suggests that equating policy input or 'non-input' (in the sense of a *laissez-faire* policy) to an aggregate economic outcome is not very helpful in understanding the actual processes that took place in between the input and the outcome. Again there is the need to bring in the agency of different actors in the development process. For instance, in regard to trading, Hui Po-keung argues that Hong Kong's entrepôt economy exhibited a high degree of transnationality that formed an integral part of East Asian regional economy dating back to the nineteenth century. Although colonial expansion was a crucial factor in creating the geo-economic and political context, the most indispensable element in Hong Kong's rise as a trading centre was the establishment of a business network linking Chinese merchants from Hong Kong and China to Southeast Asia and beyond. In regard to the industrial economy, Kim-Ming Lee in Chapter 9 attributes Hong Kong's economic performance to the 'guerrilla tactics' of industrialists in maintaining a flexible strategy of production in small-sized labour-intensive units. Such a strategy was not an outcome of positive colonial policy, but an unintended response to the constraints of government discouragement and financial hostility towards industrial upgrading.

In retrospect, given the ambiguous role of the colonial state in development, why is there still such a wide consensus that state policy positively contributed to Hong Kong's development? Part of the answer is to be found in the ideological sphere. In Chapter 7 Tak-Wing Ngo argues that the policy bias against industrial development was legitimized by the construction of a unilinear economic history. In this dominant historiography, economic activities other than entrepôt trade were excluded from historical memory, so that the policy bias against industry was concealed. Industry hardly entered historical records at all until the 1950s. In addition, the policy of *laissez-faire* that originally served to administer economic privilege to a few was rationalized *post hoc* as being instrumental to the growth and expansion of the industrial economy.

However, we should not rashly conclude that the positive attitude towards colonial rule in Hong Kong was merely a result of colonial consciousness buttressed by dominant historiography and rhetoric. The effectiveness of the dominant belief did not rest on a totally hypocritical construction of benevolent rule. Also important was the enormous resources put into infrastructural projects, public housing, and social services, leading many to conclude that the government's care for social needs was genuine and not merely undertaken for manipulative reasons.[17] Probably it was a mixture of positive as well as negative policy measures, and the intended and unintended outcomes of progress and development, that allowed the ruling authorities to convey the belief among many Hong Kong citizens that colonial policies were for the most part benevolent in nature.

The colonial factor versus the China factor

The penetrative reach of the colonial state into Hong Kong society and the active part played by both state and societal actors in shaping Hong Kong's underlying socio-economic structures lead us back to the questions raised in the beginning of this Chapter. As will be shown in this volume, it is simply not true that the colonial presence was hardly felt in Hong Kong.

While it is often stated that British rule brought the rule of law to Hong Kong, it is, ironically, precisely in this area that colonial power was most strongly applied to oppress the local population. As Christopher Munn argues, for the great majority of the Chinese population, English justice in Hong Kong meant intrusive policing, racial and class discrimination, and periodic campaigns of repression. Indeed, some of the features that put the Chinese-speaking community and the lower class in a disadvantageous position remained unchanged throughout the colonial period. For instance, until the very last few years of British rule, all legislation and all court proceedings were in English, while residents were required to be able to speak English in order to serve as jurors, thereby excluding the majority of residents. This remained unchanged although Chinese was recognized by the colonial authorities as an official language in the 1970s, under severe pressure from social movements.

It is also often stated that Hong Kong owed its free economy to colonial rule. However, the persistence of labour-intensive manufacturing and the dominance of trade over industry were essentially the by-products of British colonialism. Hong Kong was acquired by Britain with the aim of conducting East Asian trade, and the colonial authorities never changed their conviction that this was the colony's overriding if not exclusive purpose. Not only was there no attempt to industrialize Hong Kong during the first century of colonial rule, but the development of colonial industry was even discouraged for fear of competing with British industry. After the Second World War, Hong Kong's financial reserve was used to support British sterling rather than to finance industrial expansion and upgrading, as revealed by Alex Choi in Chapter 8. The resulting trade-oriented economy, commonly seen as a 'natural' result of the free market, was in reality the outcome of hidden colonial intervention, or what Tak-Wing Ngo calls the 'artifice of *laissez-faire* capitalism'.

It is interesting to note that even official and semi-official Chinese writings have either overlooked or chosen to ignore these areas of 'colonial oppression'. While denouncing the colonial political system, they praise British economic policies and the legal system for bringing prosperity to Hong Kong. But perhaps this is not surprising. Paradoxical as it appears to be, the colonial dimension is intimately related to the China dimension, as a closer look at the trading economy reveals. The trading network flourished as a result of British colonial expansion in East and Southeast Asia. At the same time, Hong Kong would not have been so successful as a trading centre had its ambivalent status not provided it with access to the China market. This benefited not only the British empire, but also China. Up to the present day, Beijing has always been eager to maintain Hong Kong's intermediary role. Hong Kong's competitive edge as a regional business centre lies in its middleman role between China and the West – a kind of 'middleman capitalism', as Hui Po-keung calls it, that can be traced back to the unique connections between British colonialism and Chinese trade interests since the Opium War.

As a result, compradors who manipulated both the colonial and the Chinese authorities thrived, taking advantage of their bilateral connections. This kind of middleman capitalism is not something of the past, but still survives today. During the last decade of colonial rule, many of the British co-opted business élite who once defended colonial rule turned their allegiance to Beijing. Not unlike their comprador predecessors, they have taken an active part in the politics of transition, playing one sovereign power against the other. As one critical observer has rightly commented, Governor Chris Patten and British officials should not be too harsh in their condemnation of Beijing's preference for plutocracy in the Hong Kong Special Administrative Region government, because many of those whom they criticized as Beijing's lapdogs were originally groomed and nurtured by the colonial authorities.[18]

Politically, colonial rule was even more closely linked to the China factor. Colonial intervention in rural politics was basically aimed at pre-empting pro-Beijing organizations from taking root in the New Territories. Social movements originated as patriotic, anti-colonial struggles searching for a Chinese identity. Later, this quest for identity was replaced by a democratic movement against the domination of both British and Chinese authorities in determining the fate of Hong Kong. In all these cases, the reactions of the colonial authorities were prompted by the China factor, and vice versa.

It is important to remember this intricate relationship between the British and the Chinese factors in Hong Kong's history. Over the years, the Beijing government has consistently upheld a policy of maintaining the status quo of colonial Hong Kong. As a result, it is inaccurate to regard Hong Kong either as apart from China, as a part of China, as fully autonomous, or as a subordinate actor. Rather, it is the complex state-society relations in Hong Kong, combined with the British and Chinese dimensions that created Hong Kong's unique socio-political landscape.

Conclusion

Our conclusion from this revisiting of Hong Kong's colonial past is modest: the existing scholarship has overlooked the complexity of colonial rule in Hong Kong. Indirect rule, non-interventionism, and political acquiescence are far from accurate descriptions of the colonial formation. Part of the complexity of coloniality is reflected, as this volume shows, in the combination of different strategies of rule and the reach of the state (through co-optation/exclusion, coercion/consensus, etc.); the delicate manipulation of social conflicts and the maintenance of regime stability; the mixed roles of colonial rule as an agent of modernization and a hindrance to development; and the colonial-cum-China dimension in shaping state–society relations.

Admittedly, this hardly scratches the surface of the complexity of coloniality. But by highlighting the agency of both dominant and subordinate actors in shaping Hong Kong's history, we hope that the present volume can still contribute to the much needed investigation of this neglected field. By apprehending the complexity of coloniality, we believe that it will open up new and fruitful avenues of research for those who want to probe into colonial history. Borrowing Prakash's words, we hope to shake colonialism loose from the stillness of the past, and to unsettle the calmness with which colonial categories and knowledge were instituted as the facts of history.[19]

NOTES

1 Marc Bloch, *The Historian's Craft*, Manchester, Manchester University Press, 1954, pp. 32–9; E.H. Carr, *What is History?*, 2nd edn, London, Penguin Books, 1987, pp. 107–8.
2 Gordon Mathews, 'Heunggongyahn: on the past, present, and future of Hong Kong identity', *Bulletin of Concerned Asian Scholars*, 1997, vol. 29, no. 3, p. 5.
3 Chan Kai-cheung, 'History', in Choi Po-king and Ho Lok-sang (eds), *The Other Hong Kong Report 1993*, Hong Kong, Chinese University Press, 1993, p. 457.
4 See, for example, Liu Shuyong, 'Hong Kong: a survey of its political and economic development over the past 150 years', *China Quarterly*, 1997, no. 151, September, p. 583; Yu Shengwu and Liu Cunkuan (eds), *Shijiu shiji de Xianggang* (Nineteenth-century Hong Kong), Beijing Zhonghua Shuju, 1994, p. 69 (n.7), p.180 (n.27).
5 Frank Welsh, *A History of Hong Kong*, London, HarperCollins, 1993, p. 3; Peter Harris, *Hong Kong: A Study in Bureaucracy and Politics*, Hong Kong, Macmillan, 1988, p. 12.
6 Caroline Courtauld and May Holdsworth, *The Hong Kong Story*, Hong Kong, Oxford University Press, 1997, p. 1. See also the discussion in Ming K. Chan, 'Introduction: Hong Kong's precarious balance – 150 years in an historic triangle', Ming K. Chan with John D. Young (ed.), *Precarious Balance: Hong Kong Between China and Britain, 1842–1992*, Hong Kong, Hong Kong University Press, 1994.
7 Bloch, *The Historian's Craft*, p. 116.
8 The term is used by Harris, *Hong Kong*, p. 1.
9 Lau calls this a 'minimally integrated socio-political system'. Lau Siu-kai, *Society and Politics in Hong Kong*, Hong Kong, Chinese University Press, 1982.

10 King calls this 'administrative absorption of politics'. Ambrose Y.C. King, 'Administrative absorption of politics in Hong Kong: emphasis on the grass roots level', in Ambrose Y.C. King and Rance P.L. Lee (eds), *Social Life and Development in Hong Kong*, Hong Kong, Chinese University Press, 1981.

11 See John Rear, 'One brand of politics', in Keith Hopkins (ed.), *Hong Kong: The Industrial Colony*, Hong Kong, Oxford University Press, 1977; S.N.G. Davies, 'One brand of politics rekindled', *Hong Kong Law Journal*, 1977, vol. 7, no. 1, pp. 44–84; Benjamin K.P. Leung, 'Power and politics: a critical analysis', in Benjamin K.P. Leung (ed.), *Social Issues in Hong Kong*, Hong Kong, Oxford University Press, 1990.

12 Quoted in Richard Hughes, *Borrowed Place Borrowed Time: Hong Kong and Its Many Faces*, 2nd rev. edn, London, André Deutsch, 1976, p. 23. The interlocking directorate and policy networks is documented in Davies, 'One brand of politics rekindled', while the connection between economic power and political office of the actors mentioned in the joke is vividly summarized by Gilbert Wong, 'Business groups in a dynamic environment: Hong Kong 1976–1986', in Gary Hamilton (ed.), *Business Networks and Economic Development in East and Southeast Asia*, Hong Kong, Centre of Asian Studies, University of Hong Kong, 1991, p. 136.

13 There are a few exceptions to the apathy thesis. For example, Turner argues that the low incidence of labour protest is better explained by an absence of channels for expressing discontent rather than an absence of dissatisfaction. H.A. Turner *et al.*, *The Last Colony: But Whose?*, Cambridge, Cambridge University Press, 1980.

14 Lau calls this 'utilitarianistic familism'. Lau Siu-kai, 'Utilitarianistic familism: the basis of political stability in Hong Kong', CUHK Social Research Centre occasional paper no. 74, Hong Kong, Chinese University of Hong Kong, 1978.

15 Among the few exceptions are writers from the Marxist tradition who argue that Hong Kong's economic growth (or capital accumulation) was achieved by a low-wage, labour-intensive production strategy made possible by the state-sanctioned practices of labour exploitation. See Jon Halliday, 'Hong Kong: Britain's Chinese colony', *New Left Review*, 1974, no. 87–8, September–December, pp. 91–112.

16 As mentioned earlier, some writers have actually questioned the appropriateness of describing Hong Kong as 'colonial'. See Harris, *Hong Kong*, p. 12.

17 In regard to the phenomenal expansion of social services since the late 1960s, Castells even describes Hong Kong as a 'colonial version of the welfare state'. Manuel Castells, 'Four Asian tigers with a dragon head: a comparative analysis of the state, economy, and society in the Asian Pacific rim', in Richard P. Appelbaum and Jeffrey Henderson (eds), *States and Development in the Asian Pacific Rim*, Newbury Park, Sage, 1992, p. 45. Another writer argued, in a somewhat over-stated manner, that local demand for government action never preceded the government's own initiatives to provide public services. Catherine Jones, *Promoting Prosperity: The Hong Kong Way of Social Policy*, Hong Kong, Chinese University Press, 1990, p. 283.

18 Ming K. Chan, 'The legacy of the British administration of Hong Kong: a view from Hong Kong', *China Quarterly*, 1997, no. 151, September, p. 579.

19 Gyan Prakash, 'After colonialism', in Gyan Prakash (ed.), *After Colonialism: Imperial Histories and Postcolonial Displacements*, Princeton, NJ, Princeton University Press, 1995, p. 6.

2

CHINESE COLLABORATION IN THE MAKING OF BRITISH HONG KONG

John M. Carroll

Social scientists have long been impressed by the political stability of Hong Kong, especially the amicable relationship between an alien colonial state and the overwhelmingly larger Chinese population.[1] Lennox Mills, an American political scientist who visited the colony on the eve of the Second World War, attributed this stability to the colonial government's 'consistent policy of conciliation and co-operation'.[2] More recently, free-market economists have cited the *laissez-faire* policy of the colonial government.[3] Sociologists Lau Siu-kai and Kuan Hsin-chi have stressed the 'vested interests' that colonial rule created in Hong Kong society. Furthermore, Lau and Kuan argue, the government's policy of *laissez-faire* and social non-interventionism combined to minimize the integration of state and society, thereby reducing the potential for conflict.[4] Others have stressed the delicate economic, political and strategic relationships between Hong Kong, China and Great Britain. Norman Miners, for example, emphasizes the importance of the economic factor to all three parties involved. Miners also cites the traditional political apathy of the Chinese and the local Chinese élite's support for the colonial regime.[5]

Another frequently cited explanation for the colony's political stability is that Hong Kong realities do not fit classical patterns of colonialism. For example, Lau Siu-kai argues that most theories of colonialism tend to emphasize the coercive power of the state or the importance of 'segmentation' by race or ethnicity, none of which applies very well to Hong Kong. Since Hong Kong was obtained for trade rather than for territorial control, Westernization or civilization, and has no significant natural resources, its acquisition cannot be explained in terms of extracting resources for the metropole.[6] Other scholars have argued that Marxist theories of colonialism hardly apply better to Hong Kong. As sociologist Chan Wai Kwan argues in his study of early Hong Kong society, the Marxist, bipolar division of society into the exploitative colonizer and the exploited colonized oversimplifies social relations in Hong Kong. It also explains the social development of Hong Kong as solely 'related to, if not explained by, events in China or Britain'.[7]

In spite of their many strengths, these explanations have several limitations. First, by downplaying the colonial nature of Hong Kong, they overlook important aspects of the colony's history and society. For example, although brute force was not used as extensively in Hong Kong as in other European colonies, coercion and military strength were used to wrest the island from China. The Hong Kong government did not enforce separate residential, occupational and legal status for Chinese and foreigners as rigidly, for example, as the Spanish government did in colonial Mexico[8], but as Christopher Munn's contribution in this volume clearly shows, legal discrimination existed at every level of Hong Kong society. Racial or ethnic segregation and discrimination were by no means unique to European colonialism[9], but in Hong Kong they were both tolerated and encouraged to a much greater extent than a government that prided itself on administering impartial British justice would care to admit.[10] Hong Kong may not have been obtained for territorial gain or the extraction of resources, but it acted as a base for market penetration and extraction. And although the British did not attempt to convert the Chinese to Christianity as the Spanish and Portuguese colonial governments did their Latin America subjects, early colonial administrators certainly saw their mission in South China as promoting civilization. Second, although these theories explain how the relationship between state and society was maintained, they do not explain how this relationship came about in the first place. Finally, they tell us little about the Chinese involved in the making of British Hong Kong or about what the colonial situation had to offer these Chinese.

This Chapter traces the historical roots of the relationship between the Hong Kong Chinese bourgeoisie and the colonial government. It argues that, at least from the standpoint of the forerunners of the Chinese bourgeoisie – contractors, compradors and other businessmen – the colonial regime was not a conquest state. As Ronald Robinson observes in his work on British West Africa, imperialism was not simply a function of European expansion. Rather, it was as much a function of the collaboration of indigenous peoples, who co-operated to build the new economic, social and political infrastructures. Without indigenous collaboration, European colonists, who often had only questionable support from their metropoles, could never have built their empires.[11]

The first Chinese merchants of the British empire's eastern outpost, the island of Hong Kong, were not passive victims of colonialism. Like the African traders in what later became British West Africa, many of the successful early Chinese businessmen in Hong Kong came from a long tradition of co-operating and trading with foreigners, either in South China or in other European colonies in Southeast Asia. Colonial expansion was made possible by Chinese co-operation throughout the early history of the colony – during the Opium War (1839–42), which led to the cession of the island to Britain, and in the building of the infant colony during the early 1840s.

Although the Hong Kong colonial government did not attempt to create a local bourgeoisie as actively, for example, as the Japanese colonial government did in Korea, the making of the Chinese business class was inseparably linked with the colonial nature of the island.[12] By rewarding these men with privileges such as land grants and offering important lucrative monopolies, the government helped foster the growth of a Chinese business élite in Hong Kong. By enforcing separate business and residential districts for Chinese, the colonial government unwittingly provided them with a domain in which to flourish.

British interest in a trading post

Little is known about the island of Hong Kong before the British occupation in 1841. The island is rarely discussed in Chinese historical records before the Qing dynasty (1644–1911), though Kowloon is frequently mentioned as the place where the Song emperor sought refuge after the Mongol conquest in 1276. During the Yuan dynasty (1276–1368) the island is said to have been inhabited by fisherfolk and pirates, many of them Song loyalists. Throughout the Ming dynasty (1368–1644), settlers from Dongguan County in southern Guangdong and Fujian migrated to Kowloon. Some of these settlers moved across the harbour to Hong Kong, but the island remained mostly unpopulated, with only a few villages scattered along its southern coast. The Tang family was the most powerful on the island, and seems to have owned most of its arable land. In the early Qing, settlers complied with the Kangxi emperor's famous decree to clear the Chinese coast, returning after the order was lifted. The 1830 gazetteer for Xin'an County, to which the island belonged, mentions several areas of the island, including a Hong Kong Village, but the island did not get its name until the late 1830s. An assistant magistrate (*kunfu*) visited the island occasionally to collect land taxes and register fishing vessels, but local government was mainly left to the local headmen or village elders (*tepo*). In the early years of the nineteenth century, the island was the stronghold of the notorious pirate Zhang Baozai, who used the island's peak as a lookout for his buccaneering exploits. When the British arrived in the late 1830s, however, the island was little more than a barren rock, speckled with a few tiny fishing villages.[13]

However, this rocky island is part of the larger Canton delta region, a commercial centre with a long tradition of transnational and intra-Chinese trade.[14] For centuries, Chinese merchants from Canton, Chaozhou, and Fuzhou had used the port of Canton for shipping goods between China, Southeast Asia and, eventually, the West. Western merchants made their début in the delta in 1557 when the Portuguese began trading in Canton from their permanent base in Macao. In 1654 the Portuguese allowed the British East India Company to land in Macao. British merchants used this base to trade in Whampoa, the harbour near Canton. Though the 1729 Xin'an gazetteer noted that both Chinese and foreign merchants had been trading in the area for many years, it was not until 1771 that the East India Company was allowed to open a post in Canton. By 1844, almost 100 foreign *hongs* (trading houses) were trading on the South China coast. Half of these were British and one-quarter Indian, mainly Parsee. Jardine,

Matheson & Co. was the largest *hong*, followed by another English firm, Dent & Co., the American firm of Russell & Co., and D. and M. Rustomjee, a Parsee firm from British India.[15]

British interest in a trading base on the China coast dated back almost as far as the British presence in the Canton delta region, although neither the choice of Hong Kong nor the idea of a colony was seriously considered until the early nineteenth century. In the early eighteenth century, traders for the East India Company discussed the idea of an island base off the coast of South China. In 1815, a Company official in Canton called for Britain to establish a base on the eastern coast of China, as close as possible to Peking. George Staunton, translator of the Qing Code and an East India Company employee, reiterated the need in 1833 (though he may have meant trading factories rather than a colony). In August 1834, Lord Napier, British Superintendent of Trade, suggested that a small British force should take possession of the island of Hong Kong in order to secure European trading rights in China. James Matheson, then in Canton, echoed to commercial groups back in Britain his fellow merchants' desire to protect British trading interests.[16] Although Chusan, Ningbo and Formosa were usually considered the most attractive choices, British traders in Canton preferred Hong Kong, with it deep-water harbour, sheltered from typhoons and easily accessible from both China and the open sea. On 25 April 1836, the *Canton Register* declared:

> If the lion's paw is to be put down on any part of the south side of China, let it be Hongkong; let the lion declare it to be under his guarantee a free port, and in ten years it will be the most considerable mart east of the Cape. The Portuguese made a mistake: they adopted shallow water and exclusive rules. Hongkong, deep water, and a free port for ever.[17]

The beginning of collaboration during the Opium War

The British lion's paw was eventually put down on Hong Kong island during the Opium War, and its traders won their coveted deep harbour and free port. After war broke out between Britain and China in 1839, Foreign Secretary Lord Palmerston declared his intention to seize the island. On Monday, 25 January 1841, in accordance with the Convention of Chuenpi (20 January 1841), Captain Edward Belcher landed with a small group on the northern shore of the island and raised the Union Jack at what would be known as Possession Point (now the west end of Hollywood Road). The next day, the naval commander of the British expeditionary force, Gordon Bremer, took formal possession in the name of the British crown.[18]

Bremer's action merely staked royal claim to a rocky island; it did not guarantee a prosperous port and colony. Chinese co-operation assisted both the British victory in the Opium War, which led to the cession of the island, and the early development of the infant colony. Chinese sources from this period often mention the Chinese 'traitors' (*gan*) who made the growth of early Hong Kong possible – guides, provisioners, builders, carpenters and artisans. Some Chinese officials even attributed Britain's strength not to its military might, but to its treacherous use of 'Han traitors' (*hongan*).[19] There is some reason in their views, for the British had great difficulty in obtaining supplies in the early part of the Opium War, especially on the island of Chusan, where the local Chinese refused to co-operate.[20] The important role played by these 'traitors' can also be seen from the British acknowledgement of Chinese co-operation. In June 1841, shortly after the British occupation, the British superintendent of trade, Captain Charles Elliot, argued that the British crown had an obligation to retain Hong Kong, not just for commercial and strategic interests, but 'as an act of justice and protection to the native population upon whom we have been so long dependent for assistance and supply'.[21]

Many of these natives were Tankas, outcasts who had been prohibited since 1730 from taking the civil service examinations or settling on land. From the earliest days of the foreign presence in Canton, Tankas had traded with foreign merchants and served as middlemen, even though the Qing government prohibited this at the risk of death. Working from bumboats (small boats used for peddling goods to ships anchored in the harbour), the Tankas provided British naval and merchant vessels with fuel and other supplies. After the settlement of Hong Kong, the British rewarded the Tankas with land in the new town of Hong Kong.[22]

Such was the case with Loo Aqui, an influential Tanka merchant and land-owner in early Hong Kong. Little is known of Loo's background, except that he was a bumboatman who rose to prominence through piracy and provisioning foreign vessels. In 1841, during the Opium War, the Guangdong authorities secretly invited Loo to Canton, offering him an official feather and button of the sixth rank to help stir up trouble in Hong Kong. As leader of several secret societies, Loo promised to provide support from within Hong Kong. Instead, he returned to Hong Kong, where he was rewarded for provisioning the British forces with a large lot of valuable land in the Lower Bazaar, the area where much of the Chinese population would eventually settle. Soon Loo became one of the colony's wealthiest and most powerful Chinese residents.[23]

Like Loo Aqui, many of the colony's early compradors also received their early business experience dealing with the British or other foreigners in South China. These compradors soon became Hong Kong's most important businessmen. Kwok Acheong was another Tanka bumboatman who supplied provisions to the British forces during the Opium War. After the British takeover of Hong Kong, Kwok settled in the colony. He joined the Peninsular and Oriental (P&O) Steam Navigation Co. in 1845 and soon became its comprador. In the 1860s, Kwok started a fleet of steamships that competed with the European-owned Hong Kong, Canton and Macao Steamboat Co. In 1876,

Kwok was the third largest property taxpayer in the colony, paying a total of HK $:6,909.36. Only the European firms of Douglas, Lapraik & Co. (a shipping giant) and Jardine, Matheson & Co. paid more than Kwok. By 1877, Kwok owned thirteen steamships, making him not just a successful local Chinese businessman but a regional shipping magnate. Kwok Acheong was a frequent advisor to the colonial government until his death in 1880.[24]

Chinese contractors and the building of Hong Kong

While Hong Kong was founded with help from the Chinese, the building of the colony continued a network of co-operation between British and Chinese. More than just cultural, political, economic and social control over non-European societies, European expansion and colonialism was also a process of physical construction – from government, residential and commercial buildings to entire cities and towns.[25] As in many other Southeast Asian colonies, this construction was carried out by Chinese workers and contractors.

When the British took control on 26 January 1841, the north shore of the island was for the most part unoccupied. There was a small settlement in Sai Ying Pun, next to present-day lower Pokfulam Road. To the east, in Wong Nai Chung, was the largest settlement on the north side of the island, perhaps the largest agricultural area on the island. There were two smaller villages at Soo Kun Po and Hung Heung Loo, along with some rice paddies. Further east, in Shau Kei Wan, was a small village of fisherfolk and quarry workers. On the southern side of the island were smaller settlements at Tai Tam, Chek Chu (later called Stanley), Heung Kong Tsai (Little Hong Kong), Shek Pai Wan (later Aberdeen) and Pokfulam. The island's Chinese land and water population was probably under 5,000.[26]

Elliot's proclamation on 2 February 1841 that Hong Kong would be a free port, however, attracted 'a great influx of natives' from Guangdong, who settled mainly in huts on the beach and on the overlooking hillsides.[27] That month shiploads of foreign merchants and missionaries began to arrive from Macao. Jardine, Matheson & Co. built a temporary godown on the north shore of the island. By the end of March, an array of shanties, matsheds, makeshift godowns and residences began to punctuate the northern landscape of the once barren rock.[28] A British engineer recalled how:

> ...in the course of two months, the native town, Victoria, which had before presented to the eye scarcely anything but streets and rows of houses, formed of the most crazy, perishable, and inflammable materials, now boasted at least a hundred brick tenements, besides a spacious and commodious market-place...a stone jail, a wide, excellent road, drains, and bridges, wherever necessary, and an official residence for the presiding magistrate.[29]

In the summer of 1841, after the first official land sales, godowns and houses were built on the new lots, forming the town's water esplanade, the *Praya*, named after that of Portuguese Macao. Military facilities were mainly at West Point and on the hillside. By late 1841 the island had over fifty permanent houses and buildings.[30] A French naval official compared the island to a busy anthill, observing that 'the [Chinese] cafés, eating and drinking shops, gambling houses, opium booths, &c., have already fully occupied the space allotted by the authorities'.[31] The *Canton Press* wrote in early December that 'The bazaar is well supplied at cheap rates, and workmen and artisans as well as the materials for building are plentiful...'.[32] In February 1842 Henry Pottinger, plenipotentiary and superintendent of trade, moved the Superintendency of Trade from Macao to Hong Kong. Pottinger soon reported that:

> ...the impetus given by the removal...has been quite remarkable, even within the last week or ten days; that highly respectable and affluent Chinese Merchants are flocking from Canton and Macao to settle here, or at least form branches of their trading firms, that it is moderately estimated that there are not less than twenty-five thousand souls in the Colony; that extensive and solidly built warehouses, wharves, jetties, &c., besides private dwelling houses, are springing up in every direction, and that the early receipt of the intentions and commands of Her Majesty's Government connected with the Island is most desirable.[33]

The *Canton Press* observed in the same month 'great bustle and preparation' for building along the waterfront. Sturdy brick and granite godowns had been built, and granite piers for landing goods extended into the harbour. New government buildings included a magistracy, post office, land and record office, jail and 'several other barracks either finished or building'.[34] The new town also boasted numerous shops, brothels, gambling houses and tailors, linked by a few rough roads. In March, the total island population was over 15,000, with 12,361 Chinese, mainly artisans and labourers. Soon the first Chinese market was built in the Lower Bazaar. The *Canton Press* wrote that 'the Chinese shopkeepers have evinced much good taste in their buildings', predicting that 'the bazaar will soon surpass China Street in Canton, indeed...the China town at Hongkong will be among the most striking features of the new settlement'.[35] The Europeans settled in the main town, in what is now Central District, and along the waterfront from Central Market to Causeway Bay.

By mid-1843, Hong Kong had twelve large English firms, ten smaller ones, six Indian ones (mainly Parsee), some godowns and houses, a few shipwrights, three newspaper offices, some floating offices and houses in the harbour, and about six English opium firms. Warehouses dotted the waterfront, and present-day Central District was already becoming the commercial centre of the island.[36] A foreign visitor noted in June 1843 how most of the Chinese shopkeepers in Macao had moved to Hong Kong, 'flying like rats from a falling house'.[37] Robert Fortune, an

English botanist who visited the island in 1843 and 1845, wrote that 'a very large proportion of the [Chinese] Macao shopkeepers have removed their establishments to Hong Kong; the former place being useless since the English left it'.[38]

When Robert Fortune returned to Hong Kong in December 1845, he was surprised at the colony's progress, marvelling at how 'new houses and even new streets had risen, as if by magic'. He found:

> Some noble new government buildings...excellent and substantial houses...for the [foreign] merchants...a large Chinese town...a beautiful road, called the Queen's Road...lined with excellent houses, and many very good shops. Many of the Chinese shops are little inferior to those in Canton, and certainly equal to what used to be in Macao.... The bazaar or market is also a most excellent one. Here we find all the natural productions of China...and in fact every luxury which the natives or foreigners can possibly require.[39]

All this development did not happen 'by magic'. As it was in European colonies across Southeast Asia, all major construction work was completed by Chinese contractors, builders and labourers.[40] In the summer of 1841, site clearance and building construction for the new town had to be delayed because of a lack of labourers and craftsmen.[41] In April 1846, Governor John Francis Davis wrote Colonial Secretary William Gladstone that the construction of private and public works in Hong Kong 'could not have taken place except for the ready command of the cheap and efficient labour of the Chinese'.[42] Many Chinese contractors also came to the island, eager to profit from the building boom. Few, however, were familiar with Western building techniques, and they often submitted estimates that were far too low. When the contractors could not complete the projects as agreed, they were imprisoned for not fulfilling their contracts; others, realizing how much money they would lose and fearing imprisonment, simply fled the island.[43] The situation became so desperate that in January 1845 plans were discussed for the establishment of a contractors' combination or union.[44]

As was the case in other Southeast Asian colonies, the contractors who did well in early Hong Kong were those who had prior experience working with foreigners. Tam Achoy, one of the more successful of these contractors, was generally considered among the most prominent members of the Chinese community in the early years of the colony. Originally from Hoi Ping in Guangdong, Tam came to Hong Kong in 1841 from Singapore, where he had been a foreman in the government dockyards. Tam built some of the most important buildings in the colony, including the P&O Building and the Exchange Building for Dent & Co. (one of the largest European *hongs*), which the government later bought in November 1847 for use as the colony's first Supreme Court.[45]

Wealth and power of the collaborators

Chinese co-operation was instrumental, both in the founding and the building of the new colony. But why were men such as Loo Aqui, Kwok Acheong and Tam Achoy willing to help the British in these processes? European historians have generally seen the Chinese in early Hong Kong at best as sojourners, and at worst as the 'scum of Canton'. Chinese historians, on the other hand, have tended to view the Chinese in Hong Kong and elsewhere in Southeast Asia as either helpless victims duped by the foreigners or as unfilial scoundrels who abandoned their families and homeland.[46] This rhetoric, however, masks the more important and interesting question of what the colonial situation offered to the Chinese who chose to live under alien rule. If, as Robinson argues, from the perspective of the 'collaborators or mediators the invaders imported an alternative source of wealth and power which, if it could not be excluded, had to be exploited in order to preserve or improve the standing of indigenous élite in the traditional order',[47] what were these sources in early colonial Hong Kong?

Land grants, used by the new government to reward those Chinese who had helped the British secure and develop the island, constituted one important source. For his services rendered during the Opium War, Loo Aqui received a plot of valuable land in the Lower Bazaar. He was later able to obtain, through other grants or purchases eased by his connections to the colonial regime, many more lots in the Lower Bazaar. Building upon this wealth, Loo was soon running a gambling house, a theatre, and several brothels. Rev. George Smith, who later became Bishop of Victoria, recalled a visit to Loo's home in November 1844: 'He possesses about fifty houses in the bazaar, and lives on the rent, in a style much above the generality of Chinese settlers, who are commonly composed of the refuse of neighbouring mainland'.[48]

As it did for Loo Aqui, working for the British helped make Tam Achoy a leader of the local Chinese business community. In return for his services to the British crown in both Singapore and Hong Kong, Tam was also granted land in the Lower Bazaar. Using the income from this land, Tam soon bought up the land of his neighbouring landholders, blocking off a significant piece of waterfront property for himself. Tam quickly expanded these holdings to include a very profitable market in the Lower Bazaar. The transition from landholder to large businessman was an easy one for Tam. When Hong Kong became the major port of departure to North America and Australia in the late 1840s and 1850s, he was one of the main brokers and charterers of emigrant ships. Tam also ran a general merchants' company.[49] In 1865 he leased a wharf to the new Hong Kong, Canton and Macao Steamboat Co. Earlier in 1857 the *Friend of China* called Tam 'no doubt the most creditable Chinese in the Colony'.[50] Because of his wealth, Tam was known to foreigners in the colony as the 'Nabob of Hong Kong'.[51]

Apart from providing the basis for considerable wealth through land grants, the early colonial regime introduced other measures that made the colony attractive to Chinese willing to live there. Colonial officials and British historians have generally stressed the role of free trade in Hong Kong's economic development. In the early years, however, the production, preparation and retail of commodities such as opium and salt were highly regulated by a system of monopolies and farms, usually offered for sale by public auction, while the sale of such goods as liquor and tobacco was licensed and taxed.[52] Ownership of these monopolies offered powerful financial rewards. Thus when Loo Aqui acquired the opium monopoly from his partner Fung Atae he guarded his new possession carefully, to the point of relying on intimidation.[53] Rev. Smith wrote that:

> A-quei...by the rights which he has acquired as the purchaser of the opium-farm, wields an instrument of oppressive exaction and extortion over the rest of the Chinese settlers. At one period he was in the habit of visiting the native boats and private houses, in order to seize every ball of opium suspected of being sold without his license.[54]

Until the 1850s, the main Chinese markets were also run by monopolies leased for five-year periods. In 1844, when the government relocated the Chinese residents of the Middle Bazaar to the hillside of Tai Ping Shan, Loo Aqui petitioned the government for permission to open a market in the new settlement and purchased the management of the market for five years. A similar situation existed for salt. In September 1845, for example, a merchant named Losin secured the salt monopoly; Kam Teen Sze won the stone quarry farm. In March 1845 the government announced a short-lived plan to invite tenders to operate sedan chairs in Victoria, and in June it offered tenders to operate the ropewalk in the Wong Nai Chung valley area near the free hospital.[55] Although not all monopolies were as lucrative as the one on opium, they provided an invaluable means of enhancing wealth in the new colony.

The growth of a Chinese business élite was also helped indirectly by the colonial government's efforts to reserve lucrative real estate exclusively for Europeans. In the first years of the colony, most of the Chinese lived in the Lower Bazaar, the Upper Bazaar (sometimes called the 'Middle Bazaar') or on the hillside at Tai Ping Shan. In September 1841, A.R. Johnston, acting plenipotentiary, made land grants at rates below market price to Chinese who had supplied the British fleet before and during the Opium War. Though the early land sales had been designed to keep Chinese away from the valuable waterfront properties, the Chinese were able to stay in the Lower Bazaar. Chinese were also encouraged to settle in the Upper Bazaar, where land was again sold at modest rates. By 1843, however, colonial officials had decided that the more ramshackle Chinese shops and houses were taking up valuable land. In July 1843, Land Officer A.J. Gordon proposed the construction of a European-style town in the Wong Nai Chung valley area. Only European and Parsee shops would be allowed in the main section of the new town, with a smaller Chinese town to the south. European warehouses would be given marine access while bazaars for 'paltry Chinese shops', for whom sea frontage would be 'far too valuable,' would be permitted at certain locations.[56] These plans never materialized as Johnson had envisioned, but in 1844 the government proceeded with a plan for relocating Chinese residents of the Upper Bazaar to the hillside at Tai Ping Shan to make room for the construction of a European-style town. The area was to be exclusively Chinese, and no Europeans, except for police officers, could live there. An unintended result of the relocation was that it allowed the development of a local leadership independent of the colonial government. The government had a hard time administering the area, where official regulations such as registration of land sales went unchecked. As we have seen, the more successful landowners such as Loo Aqui were able to buy up the properties of others, producing a small group of wealthy property owners.[57] Thus, by rewarding the Chinese with privileges such as land grants and monopolies and enforcing separate business and residential districts for the Chinese, the colonial government helped foster the growth of a Chinese business élite in Hong Kong and gave it a domain in which to flourish.

Not only did the colonial situation help the growth of a Chinese business élite, it enabled the members of this élite to recreate aspects of the traditional order from which they had been excluded in China. As Tanka outcasts, both Loo Aqui and Kwok Acheong were barred from assuming any gentry functions in China. By working for the British in Singapore, Tam Achoy had violated Qing prohibitions against overseas emigration.[58] In British Hong Kong, however, these prohibitions meant nothing. The colonial government, which neither understood its new Chinese constituents nor took much interest in their welfare, did not attempt to fill the vacuum left by the departure of the old gentry class after the British takeover in 1841.[59] So new landowners and merchants were able to fill the old gentry functions. In 1847 Loo and Tam built the Man Mo Temple on Hollywood Road, in the heart of the Chinese community.[60] Although its ostensible purpose was to worship the Gods of Literati and War and to observe religious festivals, the Man Mo Temple served other important functions. It soon became the main social centre for Hong Kong's Chinese population, regardless of their regional or occupational affiliation.[61] By controlling the centre of Chinese religious and social life, men such as Loo and Tam became leaders of the colony's Chinese community. Perhaps even more important, the Man Mo Temple soon evolved into the self-managed, informal government of the Chinese community. According to a later source, soon after its establishment, Loo and Tam used the temple as an informal courtroom, resolving legal disputes and generally managing the affairs of the Chinese community in Hong Kong.[62]

Thus, in early colonial Hong Kong, outcasts could become respected leaders of the local Chinese community. Apart from being trustee at the Man Mo Temple, Tam was also trustee at two other temples and a well-known philanthropist. In 1847, he donated £185 to the colonial treasury for the building of a Chinese school in the Lower Bazaar. In September 1852, Tam was again one of the chief donors to a subscription for the building of a Chinese hospital, an earlier one having been destroyed by fire the previous winter.[63] In 1856, after several particularly damaging fires along Queen's Road, Tam helped form a Chinese fire brigade, later named the Tam Achoy Engine Co. No. 1.[64] In 1861, he led the Chinese community in contributing to a retirement fund for A.L. Inglis, the colony's harbour master.[65]

In the new colonial environment, Tam's friend Loo Aqui, who hailed from a dubious background, also became a prominent member of the Chinese community. Although Loo seems to have not changed his spots (he was widely rumoured to be involved with Triad groups and pirates, and to encourage corruption among the police force),[66] he was also known about town for helping 'those who were in distress, in debt or discontented'.[67] He too was a chief contributor to the Chinese hospital fund. Dr. Henry Julius Hirschberg of the London Missionary Society, who organized the fundraising, recorded a meeting with Loo Aqui in 1852, during which he asked Loo for a contribution:

> Loo Ah-qui...received me most friendly, and in very good english [sic] said to Lee-Kip-Yye, a Chinese broker who went with me to collect the money, 'Do not trouble that gentleman to come here again, I send you the money (fifteen dollars) to your house to-morrow morning', and then turning so to me he said: 'a very good cause, Sir, a very good cause', and then took my hands and shook them most heartily according to english [sic] fashion.[68]

When the *China Mail* published a list of all the subscribers to the hospital fund, along with their occupations, Loo Aqui, formerly a lowly bumboatman, was now listed simply as a 'Gentleman'.[69]

Conclusion

When trying to explain Hong Kong's stability and the relationship between state and society, there is no better place to start than at the beginning. On the Chinese side of the harbour, in Kowloon and neighbouring Canton, the loss of Hong Kong provoked great animosity and resentment, with the island seen as the 'citadel of British imperialism' – a sentiment that survived well into this century.[70] But although British military might was used to secure the island from China, from the perspective of the forerunners of the Chinese bourgeoisie – the landowners, contractors, compradors and merchants we have seen – colonialism in Hong Kong was not imposed upon a passive Chinese population. Colonial expansion in Hong Kong was made possible with Chinese co-operation throughout the early history of the colony. Many of the prominent Chinese businessmen in early Hong Kong came from a long tradition of co-operating with foreigners. Loo Aqui and Kwok Acheong had helped the British during the Opium War, which led to the cession of the island. Contractors such as Tam Achoy were instrumental in the building of the infant colony. Indeed, without their help, there could well have been no colony for the British to rule. For the Chinese who helped found and build the colony, colonialism provided invaluable opportunities. By rewarding these men with privileges such as land grants, offering lucrative monopolies and trying to enforce separate business and residential districts for the Chinese, the colonial government helped foster the growth of a Chinese business élite in Hong Kong. Finally, the colonial nature of Hong Kong enabled the members of this élite to join the traditional order from which they had been excluded in China. Thus the making of a Chinese business élite was inseparably linked with the colonial nature of the island.

Rather than downplaying the role of colonialism in Hong Kong's history simply because Hong Kong realities may not fit classical models of colonialism, we need to ask exactly what type of colony Hong Kong was and what role colonialism may have played. Recent works have expanded the colonial framework to examine how a colonial regime both exploits and co-operates with its subjects, often as rulers try to compensate for the weaknesses of the colonial state. Challenging the common notion of an all-powerful colonial state, Nicholas Dirks has suggested that colonial rule was 'predicated at least in part on the ill-coordinated nature of power', and that colonial rulers were always aware of the limitations of colonial power. Carter Eckert has shown how, by fostering the growth of a Korean bourgeoisie, the Japanese in colonial Korea were 'both agents of socioeconomic change and oppressors at one and the same time'. According to Erik Zürcher, partnerships based on 'mutual dependence and advantage' developed between Chinese and foreigners in colonies and semi-colonies such as Hong Kong and the Chinese treaty ports. Alison Gilbert Olson has recently shown how American interest groups were able to help shape British policy toward the American colonies. John Coatsworth has argued that in colonial Mexico the strength of the Spanish state was dependent on the special power and economic privilege enjoyed by the Spanish-American élite, granted in exchange for loyalty to the state, and that in all areas other than financial extractions the state was quite weak.[71]

Re-examining the role of colonialism should not be confused with defending colonialism, European or otherwise, in Asia or anywhere else. The point is simply that when we look at the relationship between the colonial state and Chinese society, we must take into careful account the choices and alternatives that the colonial setting offered and China did not. This is, after all, what the forerunners of the Hong Kong Chinese bourgeoisie were doing.

NOTES

1 For critiques of this notion of stability, see Chapter 5 by Stephen W.K. Chiu and Ho-fung Hung, and Chapter 6 by Tai-lok Lui and Stephen W.K. Chiu in this volume.
2 Lennox A. Mills, *British Rule in Eastern Asia: A Study of Contemporary Government and Economic Development in British Malaya and Hong Kong*, London, Oxford University Press, 1942, pp. 413–14.
3 For example, Alvin Rabushka, *Hong Kong: A Study in Economic Freedom*, Chicago, IL, University of Chicago Press, 1979.

4 Lau Siu-kai and Kuan Hsin-chi, *The Ethos of the Hong Kong Chinese*, Hong Kong, Chinese University Press, 1988, pp. 19–22.

5 Norman J. Miners, *The Government and Politics of Hong Kong*, Hong Kong, Oxford University Press, 1975, pp. 3–14, 23, 29, 185–94.

6 Lau Siu-kai, *Utilitarianistic Familism: An Inquiry into the Basis of Political Stability in Hong Kong*, Hong Kong, Chinese University of Hong Kong Social Research Centre, 1977, pp. 21–4; and *Society and Politics in Hong Kong*, Hong Kong, Chinese University Press, 1982, pp. 7–9. For a more recent and critical argument, see Jung-fang Tsai, *Hong Kong in Chinese History: Community and Social Unrest in the British Colony, 1842–1913*, New York, Columbia University Press, 1993, p. 6.

7 Chan Wai Kwan, *The Making of Hong Kong Society: Three Studies of Class Formation in Early Hong Kong*, Oxford, Clarendon Press, 1991, pp. 4–6.

8 John H. Coatsworth, 'The limits of colonial absolutism: the state in eighteenth century Mexico', in Karen Spalding (ed.), *Essays in the Political, Economic and Social History of Colonial Latin America*, Newark, DE, Latin American Studies Program, University of Delaware, 1982, pp. 27–9.

9 Anthony D. King, 'Colonial cities: global pivots of change', in Robert Ross and Gerald J. Telkamp (eds), *Colonial Cities: Essays on Urbanism in a Colonial Context*, Leiden, Martinus Nijhoff, for Leiden University Press, 1985, p. 22.

10 Chen Qian, 'Xianggang jiushi jianwen lu (1)' (Recollections of old Hong Kong, Part 1), *Guangdong wenshi ziliao* (Studies in Guangdong Literature and History), 1984, vol. 41, pp. 8–11; Henry J. Lethbridge, 'Caste, class, and race in Hong Kong before the Japanese occupation', in Marjorie Topley (ed.), *Hong Kong: The Interaction of Traditions and Life in the Towns*, Hong Kong, Royal Asiatic Society, Hong Kong Branch, 1975, pp. 42–64; Peter Wesley-Smith, 'Anti-Chinese legislation in Hong Kong', in Ming K. Chan (ed.), *Precarious Balance: Hong Kong Between China and Britain, 1842–1992*, Armonk, NY, M.E. Sharpe, 1994, pp. 91–105; Wu Hao, *Huai jiu Xianggangdi* (Longing for Old Hong Kong), Hong Kong, Boyi, 1988, p. 46.

11 Ronald Robinson, 'Non-European foundations of European imperialism: sketch for a theory of collaboration', in Roger Owen and Bob Sutcliffe (eds), *Studies in the Theory of Imperialism*, London, Longman, 1972, pp. 117–42; and 'European imperialism and indigenous reactions in British West Africa', in H.L. Wesseling (ed.), *Expansion and Reaction: Essays in European Expansion and Reactions in Asia and Africa*, Leiden, Leiden University Press, 1978, p. 143. This argument is applied to the case of both indigenous (Indonesian) and non-indigenous (Chinese) collaborators in Batavia by Leonard Blussé in *Strange Company: Chinese Settlers, Mestizo Women and the Dutch in VOC Batavia*, Dordrecht, Foris, 1986, especially Chapter 4.

12 For more on the Japanese colonial government in Korea, see Carter J. Eckhart, *Offspring of Empire: The Koch'ang Kims and the Colonial Origins of Korean Capitalism, 1876–1945*, Seattle, WA, University of Washington Press, 1991, especially Chapter 2.

13 Great Britain, Public Record Office, *Colonial Office Records*, CO 129, Dispatches from the Governor of Hong Kong, CO 129/12, 24 June 1845, pp. 305–6; Cheng Zhi, 'Xianggang jianshi' (Brief history of Hong Kong), in Li Jinwei (ed.), *Xianggang bainianshi* (Centenary History of Hong Kong), Hong Kong, Nanzhong chubanshe, 1948, p. 7; E.J. Eitel, *Europe in China: The History of Hong Kong from the Beginning to the Year 1882*, London, Luzac & Co., 1895, p. 127; Great Britain, Public Record Office, *Foreign Office Records*, FO 233, Records of letters between the Plenipotentiary and the High Provincial Authorities, and proclamations by H.E. the Governor and Chief Magistrate, 1844–9, F.O. 233/185/2, 6 January 1845; Lu Yan, *et al.*, *Xianggang zhanggu* (Hong Kong Anecdotes), vol. 1, Hong Kong, Guangjiaojing chubanshe, 1977, pp. 111–14; William F. Mayers, N.B. Dennys and Charles King, *The Treaty Ports of China and Japan: A Complete Guide to the Open Ports of those Countries, Together with Peking, Yedo, Hongkong and Macao*, Hong Kong, A. Shortrede, 1867, p. 2; Joseph Sun Pao Ting,

'Native Chinese peace officers in British Hong Kong, 1841–1861', in Elizabeth Sinn (ed.), *Between East and West: Aspects of Social and Political Development in Hong Kong*, Hong Kong, Centre of Asian Studies, University of Hong Kong, 1990, p. 148; Yu Lou, 'Xianggang chuqi haidaoshi' (Piracy in early Hong Kong), in Li Jinwei, *Xianggang*, pp. 12–14; Zhang Yueai, 'Xianggang, 1841–1980' (Hong Kong, 1841–1980), in Lu Yan *et al.*, *Xianggang zhanggu*, vol. 4, pp. 2–4.

14 Luo Xianglin, *Yiba sier nian yiqian zhi Xianggang jiqi duiwai jiaotong* (Hong Kong's Overseas Relations before 1842), Hong Kong, Zhongguo Xueshe, 1959, ch. 1; Tsai, *Hong Kong in Chinese History*, pp. 1, 17.

15 Colin N. Crisswell, *The Taipans: Hong Kong's Merchant Princes*, Hong Kong, Oxford University Press, 1981, pp. 4–5, 11, 27; Peter Y.C. Ng and Hugh D.R. Baker, *New Peace County: A Chinese Gazetteer of Hong Kong Region*, Hong Kong, Hong Kong University Press, 1983, p. 77.

16 Eitel, *Europe in China*, pp. 53–7; John King Fairbank, *Trade and Diplomacy on the China Coast: The Opening of the Treaty Ports, 1842–1854*, 2 vols, 1953, repr. (2 vols in 1), Cambridge, MA, Harvard University Press, 1964, p. 123. James Matheson graduated from Edinburgh University and went to Calcutta to work for his uncle's firm, MacIntosh & Co. After an unsuccessful stint there, he joined a partnership in Canton in 1819. In 1821 he was working for a Spanish firm, Yrissari & Co., and shortly after became Danish consul in Canton. Matheson's partner, William Jardine, was born in Scotland in 1784. He joined the East India Company as a ship's surgeon in 1802. Jardine left the East India Company in 1819 to work for several powerful Bombay Parsee firms. He also maintained close connections with Howqua, one of the largest Canton Co-hong houses. By the 1830s, Jardine and Matheson controlled approximately one-third of foreign trade with China, mostly in opium. See Crisswell, *The Taipans*, pp. 3–4, 20–2.

17 Cited in Eitel, *Europe in China*, p. 60.

18 Dafydd Emrys Evans, 'The foundation of Hong Kong: a chapter of accidents', in Topley, *Hong Kong*, pp. 12–13; Fairbank, *Trade and Diplomacy*, p. 123.

19 Joseph Sun Pao Ting, 'Xianggang zaoqi zhi huaren shehui, 1841–1870' (Early Chinese Community in Hong Kong, 1841–1870), Ph.D. dissertation, University of Hong Kong, Hong Kong, 1989, pp. 146–8.

20 Christopher Munn, 'The Chusan episode: Britain's occupation of a Chinese island, 1840–46', *Journal of Imperial and Commonwealth History*, 1997, vol. 25, no. 1, pp. 89–90.

21 CO 129/1, Elliot to Auckland, 21 June 1841, p. 206.

22 CO 129/25, Inglis to Caine, 10 August 1848, pp. 144–46; Eitel, *Europe in China*, pp. 168–9; Dafydd Emrys Evans, 'Chinatown in Hong Kong: the beginnings of Taipingshan', *Journal of the Hong Kong Branch of the Royal Asiatic Society*, 1970, vol. 10, p. 70; Carl T. Smith, *Chinese Christians: Elites, Middlemen, and the Church in Hong Kong*, Hong Kong, Oxford University Press, 1985, p. 110.

23 CO 129/12/306, 24 June 1845; *Friend of China*, 6 May 1846; Yen-p'ing Hao, *The Comprador in Nineteenth Century China: Bridge between East and West*, Cambridge, MA, Harvard University Press, 1970, p. 195; *Qingdai chouban yiwu shimo, Daoguang* (Complete Account of our Management of Barbarian Affairs, Daoguang Reign), vol. 58, pp. 39b–42b, cited in Fairbank, *Trade and Diplomacy*, p. 88; Smith, *Chinese Christians*, p. 109; Rev. G. Smith, *A Narrative of an Exploratory Visit to Each of the Consular Cities of China and to the Islands of Hong Kong and Chusan, In Behalf of the Church Missionary Society in the Years 1844, 1845, 1846*, London, Seeley, Burnside & Seeley, 1847, p. 82; *Yingyi ruyue jilue* (The English Barbarians' Invasion of Guangdong), Yazheng (Opium War) section, vol. 3, pp. 25–6, cited in Ting, 'Xianggang zaoqi', pp. 204–9.

24 *Hong Kong Daily Press*, 23 April 1880; Hong Kong Government, *Administrative Report, 1880–81*; Smith, *Chinese Christians*, pp. 124–5; Yuan Bangjian, *Xianggang shilue* (A Brief History of Hong Kong), Hong Kong, Zhongliu chubanshe, 1988, p. 130.

25 Gerard J. Telkamp, *Urban History and European Expansion: A Review of Recent Literature Concerning Colonial Cities and a Preliminary Biography*, Leiden, Leiden Centre for the History of European Expansion, 1978, p. 1.

26 Evans, 'The foundation of Hong Kong', p. 13; and 'Chinatown in Hong Kong', p. 69; Carl T. Smith, 'The Chinese settlement of British Hong Kong', *Chung Chi Bulletin*, 1970, vol. 48, pp. 26–7; Yuan, *Xianggang shilue*, p. 10.

27 Edward H. Cree, *The Cree Journals: The Voyages of Edward H. Cree, Surgeon R.N., as Related in His Private Journals, 1837–1856*, edited by Michael Levien, Exeter, Webb & Bower, 1981, p. 78.

28 G.B. Endacott, *A History of Hong Kong*, rev. edn, Hong Kong, Oxford University Press, 1973, p. 28; Mayers *et al.*, *The Treaty Ports of China and Japan*, p. 3; Smith, *A Narrative of an Exploratory Visit*, p. 68.

29 John Ouchterlony, *The Chinese War: An Account of All the Operations of the British Forces from the Commencement to the Treaty of Nanking*, London, Saunders & Otley, 1844, pp. 216–17.

30 Ding You, *Xianggang chuqi shihua* (Early Hong Kong), Beijing, Lianhe chubanshe, 1983, p. 76; Eitel, *Europe in China*, pp. 167, 184; Evans, 'The foundation of Hong Kong', p. 62; China Mail, *The Hong Kong Almanack and Directory for 1846*, Hong Kong, China Mail, 1846; Zhang, 'Xianggang', p. 12.

31 *Friend of China*, 8 June 1843, p. 50.

32 *Canton Press*, 4 December 1841.

33 FO 17, China Correspondence, FO 17/56, Pottinger to Aberdeen, 8 February 1842, pp. 111–12.

34 *Canton Press*, 19 February 1842.

35 *Canton Press*, 19 February 1842.

36 *Historical and Statistical Abstract of the Colony of Hong Kong, 1841–1930*, Hong Kong, Noronha, 1932, p. 3; Yuan, *Xianggang shilue*, p. 111.

37 Arthur Cunynghame, *The Opium War; Being Recollections of Service in China*, London, Saunders & Otely, 1844, p. 216.

38 Robert Fortune, *Three Years' Wanderings in the Northern Provinces of China, including a Visit to the Tea, Silk, and Cotton Countries: With an Account of Agriculture and Horticulture of the Chinese, New Plants, etc.*, London, J. Murray, 1847, p. 14.

39 Fortune, *Three Years' Wandering*, pp. 14–15.

40 T.N. Chiu, *The Port of Hong Kong: A Survey of Its Development*, Hong Kong, Hong Kong University Press, 1973, p. 19; Smith, *Chinese Christians*, p. 114. On the Chinese in other European colonies, see, for example, Blussé, *Strange Company*, pp. 52, 63 and 80.

41 *Canton Press*, 24 July 1841, cited in Smith, 'The Chinese Settlement', p. 27.

42 CO 129/16, Davis to Gladstone, 15 April 1846, p. 224.

43 CO 129/2/142, Gordon to Malcolm, 6 July 1843, pp. 139–40; CO 129/3, Treasurer's Report, 1847, cited in Smith, *Chinese Christians*, p. 114; Yuan, *Xianggang shilue*, p. 111.

44 *Friend of China*, 18 January 1845.

45 *China Mail*, 23 September 1852; Eitel, *Europe in China*, p. 220; *Friend of China*, 5 January 1856; Smith, *Chinese Christians*, p. 114.

46 Blussé, *Strange Company*, p. 49.

47 Robinson, 'Non-European foundations', pp. 120–1.

48 Smith, *A Narrative of an Exploratory Visit*, p. 82.

49 *The China Directory for 1867*, Hong Kong, A. Shortrede, 1867, p. 39A.

50 Cited in Smith, 'The Chinese Settlement', p. 29, n. 12.

51 Smith, *Chinese Christians*, pp. 114–15, 123–4; William Tarrant, 'History of Hong Kong', *Friend of China*, 23 November 1860.

52 FO 233/185: Opium, 17 and 19 November 1844, 19 and 24 December 1844, 7 March 1844, 2 July 1845; FO 233/185: Salt, 9 and 11 July 1845; FO 233/185: Liquor, 17 July 1845; FO 233/185: Tobacco, 17 July 1845.
53 CO 129/12, Davis to Stanley, 13 June 1845, pp. 182–3; *Hong Kong Register*, 27 January and 31 March 1846; Smith, 'The Chinese Settlement', p. 26, n. 3; Smith, *A Narrative of an Exploratory Visit*, pp. 82–3.
54 Smith, *A Narrative of an Exploratory Visit*, p. 513.
55 FO 233/185, 17 March 1845, 16 June 1845.
56 CO 129/2/142, Gordon to Malcom, 6 July 1843, pp. 142–8.
57 Evans, 'Chinatown in Hong Kong', pp. 69–76; Smith, 'The Chinese Settlement', p. 31.
58 June Mei, 'Socioeconomic origins of emigration: Guangdong to California, 1850–1882', *Modern China*, 1979, vol. 5, no. 4, p. 477.
59 Elizabeth Sinn, *Power and Charity: The Early History of the Tung Wah Hospital, Hong Kong*, Hong Kong, Oxford University Press, 1989, pp. 3–4.
60 Ting, 'Xianggang zaoqi', p. 184; China Mail, *China Review, 1873*, Hong Kong, China Mail, 1873, vol. 1, p. 333, cited in Smith, *Chinese Christians*, p. 109.
61 Ting, 'Xianggang zaoqi', p. 185.
62 *China Review 1873*, vol. 1, p. 333, cited in Smith, *Chinese Christians*, p. 109.
63 *China Mail*, 23 September 1852.
64 *Friend of China*, 27 February 1856, p. 66; *China Mail*, 8 April 1857, p. 111; *Friend of China*, 25 July 1857, p. 234.
65 From Carl T. Smith's unpublished list of philanthropy in Hong Kong. I am grateful to Rev. Smith for sharing this list.
66 William Tarrant, 'History of Hong Kong', *Friend of China*, 9 November 1861; Smith, *A Narrative of an Exploratory Visit*, p. 82.
67 'The districts of Hong Kong and the name Kwan Tai Lo', *China Review 1873*, vol. 1, pp. 333–4.
68 Great Britain, SOAS Library, South China and Ultra Ganges, Box 5, London Missionary Society/CWM, 1843–72, Hirschberg to Tidman, 5 September 1853 (courtesy of C. Munn).
69 *China Mail*, 23 September 1852.
70 Ming K. Chan, 'All in the family: The Hong Kong–Guangdong link in historical perspective', in Reginald Yin-Wang Kwok and Alvin Y. So (eds), *The Hong Kong–Guangdong Link: Partnership in Flux*, Armonk, NY, M.E. Sharpe, 1995, pp. 32–4, 42.
71 Coatsworth, 'The limits of colonial absolutism', pp. 25–51; Nicholas B. Dirks, 'Introduction: colonialism and culture', in Nicholas B. Dirks (ed.), *Colonialism and Culture*, Ann Arbor, MI, University of Michigan Press, 1992, p. 7; Eckert, *Offspring of Empire*, p. 6; Alison Gilbert Olson, *Making the Empire Work: London and American Interest Groups, 1690–1790*, Cambridge, MA, Harvard University Press, 1992; Erik Zürcher, '"Western expansion and Chinese reaction" – a theme reconsidered', in Wesseling, *Expansion and Reaction*, p. 76.

3

COMPRADOR POLITICS AND MIDDLEMAN CAPITALISM

Hui Po-keung

Long before the return of Hong Kong to China, the colony had already firmly established itself as a regional business centre. The proportion of Hong Kong's trade, foreign investments, and banking and financial services to other Asian countries accounted for a significant part of the colony's economic activities, and was rising.[1] Not only had the colony attracted the regional headquarters of a number of Western and Japanese transnational corporations, but many overseas Chinese businesses from East and Southeast Asia also established regional headquarters or subsidiaries in the territory.[2] Apart from manufacturing firms, international financial institutions and commercial enterprises have also established bases in Hong Kong.[3]

This 'transnationality' of Hong Kong's economy is not a recent phenomenon. Hong Kong has long been regarded as a haven for Chinese capital taking refuge from mainland China and Southeast Asia.[4] This process of transnationalization began as soon as Hong Kong was declared a free port by British colonizers. Less than twenty years after the British acquired the colony, the island of Hong Kong had grown from a fishing village to a major commercial centre. With that achievement, the Governor of Hong Kong, John Bowring, proudly stated in 1858 that 'Hongkong presents another example of elasticity and potency of unrestricted commerce'.[5]

The account given by Bowring and subsequent historians attributes Hong Kong's rise as a trading and business centre to its free trade policy and stable government under colonial rule. Without denying the role of the free trade policy, this Chapter argues that such a single-factor account slights the geo-political context in which Hong Kong emerged as a trading entrepôt and the agency of Chinese business élites in the process. Taking advantage of the geo-political location of Hong Kong as the gateway to the China market, Chinese merchants – the so-called compradors – in Hong Kong actively sought investment and trading opportunities both within and without the colony, by serving as middlemen between the Europeans and the indigenous population in both China and Hong Kong. The compradors succeeded in forging partnerships with both the colonial and the Chinese authorities, and in doing so, they turned

Hong Kong into a territory of 'middleman capitalism' in the East Asian and Asian–Western trade.

European expansion and the rise of Chinese business

From the outset, the rise of Hong Kong as a trading centre was closely related to the incorporation of the East Asian region into the world market as a result of European colonial expansion. This process of incorporation began in the nineteenth century when the European colonizers expanded their colonial territories in East and Southeast Asia. With the arrival of the steamship and the opening up of the Suez Canal in the 1860s, integration accelerated rapidly.[6]

A direct consequence of Western expansion was the rapid growth of East Asian economies and trade from the mid-nineteenth century onwards, which transformed East Asia into the world's main source for such raw materials as rubber, tin and sugar.[7] Another result of Western expansion was the massive influx of Chinese and Indian labourers and merchants into Southeast Asia.

By far the most significant merchants in East Asia were the Chinese. European colonial expansion in the region in the nineteenth century was instrumental to the further expansion of Chinese merchants. Chinese merchants, who had long controlled the East Asian regional trading networks, now tapped into global networks through the colonial powers. The overseas Chinese had a long history as sailors, interpreters and/or traders, who had actively participated in both the tribute and private trade between China and Java, Siam, Malacca and the Ryukyuan Kingdom. As Chang states:

> At all major trade ports in Southeast Asia itinerant Chinese traders would therefore find resident Chinese merchants to deal with in business transactions. Chinese became the *lingua franca* in the business world of East Asia.[8]

The establishment of this extensive business network was based on the fact that the Chinese, unlike the Europeans, could speak local languages and were familiar with domestic customs and business practices. Moreover, the Chinese were willing and able to penetrate into villages in every corner of the region to collect and distribute goods.[9] Above all, Chinese merchants had the 'China-links' which allowed them to obtain resources and to have access to the markets of mainland China. This provided them with an unassailable monopoly status. When the politically and militarily stronger Europeans came to Southeast Asia, they quickly realized the value of encouraging the regional trade already firmly controlled by Chinese merchants.[10]

Chinese merchants were highly mobile both within and outside China.[11] To better carry out their work, they established residences in important port cities all over East Asia. With their extensive business networks in the region and their

China-links, the Chinese compradors in East Asian port cities were able to assist Western merchants in establishing business-bases in the region.[12] Foreign merchants were closely tied to the Chinese middlemen through contracts in every important East Asian port city.

The dominant position of the Chinese merchants in Asian trade was further strengthened when the European powers destroyed indigenous trading communities in Makassar, Malacca, Aceh, Johore and Banten.[13] The Europeans discriminated more against Southeast Asian traders because of their stronger political connections with the indigenous states. The overseas Chinese, in contrast, were 'lost children' of their imperial court and a marginal trading minority in Southeast Asia. Not only did they present no serious political or military threat, but the colonial powers saw in them a means to deflect anger that might otherwise be directed against the colonial power, and to control anti-colonial movements centred in conquered peoples. While the loss of independence for indigenous states meant that indigenous traders lost military and political support for their trading activities, as well as access to key trading commodities such as pepper and weapons for long distance trade[14], the Chinese, by contrast, were regarded as suitable partners.

With the presence of strong Chinese business networks in East Asia, European businesses could not succeed without the collaboration of the overseas Chinese. As Carroll succinctly argues in Chapter 2, the establishment of the British colony of Hong Kong was predicated upon the collaboration of Chinese businessmen. In order to satisfy the demand for Chinese raw silk and silk products, tea, porcelain and foodstuffs, the European powers had to participate in intra-Asian trade, exchanging Southeast Asian goods (including opium) for Chinese products. The Europeans needed not only Chinese commodities for intra-Asian trade and trade between Asia and Western countries, but also Chinese goods for the survival of their colonial empires in the East Asian region. European settlers in the region needed Chinese foodstuffs, products and services of daily use, military-related products, as well as silk and tea for their daily consumption. In order to penetrate East Asian markets, Western merchants had to overcome a number of hurdles, including the problems of language. They also had to come to grips with the different and complicated monetary units, learn the appropriate methods of collecting relevant information, and adapt to the commercial practices and regulations of the region.[15] These difficulties were compounded by the fact that only the Chinese had access to inland markets, whereas Western merchants were only allowed to operate in the treaty ports. In addition, by paying tariffs and other taxes, Chinese merchants provided the Europeans with a major source of income to support their colonial expansion in East Asia. The dependence of the Europeans on the Chinese and their commodities further promoted the development of Chinese business networks in East Asia. As a result, the Chinese in Hong Kong profited significantly from the growth of both the wholesale and retail trade.

Hong Kong's role as a regional trade centre

Since the 1840s, Hong Kong, along with other important East Asian cities, has been a regional centre where capitalist activities have been concentrated. When it became a major trading port in the first half of the nineteenth century, the overseas Chinese in East Asia were provided with a centre facilitating long distance trade, both legal and illegal. Since long distance trade has been a key area of capitalist development, Hong Kong's location on a major trade route of the region, and close proximity to China (while at the same time being free from its direct political intervention), allowed it to become one of the centres of commercial activity in the region.[16] The advantageous geo-political context guaranteed Hong Kong business a good position to participate profitably in the regional and world economy.

Despite the fact that Hong Kong was a British colony, 'much of [its] importance lay not in distributing British goods in Asia, but in redirecting and reallocating Asian goods within Asia'.[17] Because of its key location within intra-Asian trade, hooking up with Hong Kong became inevitable not only for East Asian countries, but also for Western nations and merchants. In the rice trade, for instance, Hong Kong had long functioned as a redistribution centre for Southeast Asia and China. Similarly, Chinese millers in Bangkok dealt directly with Chinese merchants in Hong Kong, instead of using British merchant houses as middlemen. As early as 1875, about 60 per cent of Siamese rice exports went to China and Hong Kong, with another 27 per cent going to Singapore. Most of Bangkok's foreign trade (not only rice) was through either Hong Kong or Singapore, and it was only via these two overseas Chinese business centres that British manufactures could find their way to East Asian markets. For Western powers and merchants, hooking up with Hong Kong was the most convenient way to integrate into the intra-Asian trading network.[18]

In this context, Hong Kong was primarily an outlet for the China trade. For most of the nineteenth century, it was a major opium trading and smuggling centre.[19] As soon as China prohibited the import of opium in 1800, Hong Kong became a base for opium smuggling by Western merchants.[20] By 1880, about 45 per cent of opium flowing into China was smuggled through Hong Kong, and the opium trade did not end until 1909.[21]

After the 1850s, trading activities became more diverse. In addition to the opium trade, Hong Kong also benefited from the booming emigration business or the 'coolie trade'.[22] Thereafter, Hong Kong was a major outlet for Chinese emigrants until the abolition of the coolie trade in the early twentieth century. Although the Chinese coolie trade – promoted first by the Portuguese and then by the Dutch – started as early as the beginning of the sixteenth century, it was only after the 1840s that a significant number of Chinese 'contract labourers' began to leave China, and emigration peaked in the years between 1851–75. This was largely the result of the high tide of colonial expansion in the mid-nineteenth century, when the European colonial empires needed enormous numbers of labourers to run the large-scale rubber plantations and tin mining in Southeast Asia, the construction of railroads in North America, and gold mining in North America and Australia.

About two-thirds of the 'contract labourers' were shipped to Southeast Asia in the period from 1801–1925.[23] Of those who went to the Americas, Australia, Europe and Africa, many were transported through Hong Kong.[24] The economic prosperity of Hong Kong in the nineteenth century was, to a large extent, supported by this coolie trade.[25]

There were two sources of profit from the coolie trade. The first was the direct sale of coolies, where the profit rate usually exceeded 100 per cent. The second was the transportation of coolies, where profit rates could sometimes be as high as 1,000 per cent.[26] Most of the coolie trade was controlled by Chinese secret societies based in Hong Kong and other major ports of China and Southeast Asia.[27] Transportation, on the other hand, was in the hands of European shipping companies. Many famous Western companies and prominent Chinese merchants in Hong Kong obtained their 'first tank of gold' from participating in the coolie trade.[28]

The outflow of nearly two million Chinese via Hong Kong in the second half of the nineteenth century not only provided good business opportunities for Chinese merchants, but also turned Hong Kong into the major shipping centre of South China. The economy began its rapid growth as a result of the development of shipbuilding, ship-repairing industries and related economic activities.[29] Moreover, coolie remittances to their families in China, routed through Hong Kong, provided a powerful stimulus to Hong Kong finance and banking.

In addition to the opium and the coolie trade, Hong Kong was also an important entrepôt for Chinese silk, tea and porcelain, as well as British manufactures.[30] The significance of the China trade to Hong Kong is shown in Table 3.1.

Table 3.1 Hong Kong's share of China's foreign trade (1871–1921)

Years	China's Imports from Hong Kong (%)	China's Export to Hong Kong (%)
1871–73	32.5	14.7
1881–83	36.2	25.4
1891–93	51.2	39.3
1901–03	41.6	40.8
1909–11	33.9	28.2
1919–21	22.4	23.8

Source: Yan, Zhongping *et al.*, *Zhongguo jindai jingji shi tongji ziliao xuanji*, (Selection of Statistical Data on the Economic History of Modern China), Beijing, Kexue chubanshe, 1955, pp. 65–6.

Its significance in the China trade decreased after the early twentieth century, as a result of the rise of ports in northern and central China.[31] China was Hong Kong's most important partner both in terms of imports and exports from the late nineteenth century to the early twentieth century, as shown in Table 3.2.

Hong Kong also had a strong trade connection with Southeast Asia, though not as strong as Singapore's. Merchants from Amoy and Swatow (the Hokkien and Teochew merchants) were the key traders in the Hong Kong-Southeast Asian trade. They handled most of the rice, sugar and other products imported from Southeast Asia to Hong Kong, while the Cantonese and Western merchants handled the shipment of these products to America and other continents. As a result, Hong Kong became one of the centres of trade and communication in Southeast Asia.[32]

Large Hong Kong-based firms were maintained for cross-border business activities, such as Kin Tye Lung (founded by the Lee family in 1851) and Yuen Fat Hong (established by the Ko family in 1853), which had business connections

Table 3.2 Hong Kong's trading partners, 1877–1913 (% of value traded)

Trading partners		1877	1880	1890	1900	1910	1913
UK	M	17.63	19.40	10.57	10.78	10.73	11.66
	X	12.55	8.51	4.28	4.43	1.94	1.98
China	M	22.13	23.55	32.92	36.22	40.98	45.28
	X	54.85	59.63	65.32	64.73	75.28	76.15
Singapore	M	3.89	4.68	6.72	5.91	3.24	3.96
	X	10.72	11.48	8.84	15.87	12.62	14.51
Australia	M	0.85	1.26	1.59	1.41	1.94	2.19
	X	2.25	3.07	2.43	1.17	0.79	1.07
French Indo-China	M	8.06	4.52	7.68	7.25	5.23	5.42
	X	-	-	-	-	-	-
Bangkok	M	4.16	2.49	6.44	4.23	8.17	7.30
	X	1.98	2.18	2.71	2.84	3.74	3.27
India	M	43.24	44.06	27.95	19.69	22.08	13.78
	X	17.62	15.09	13.16	6.44	4.99	2.30
Japan	M	-	-	6.09	14.46	6.96	8.74
	X	-	-	3.24	4.48	0.22	0.38
Philippines	M	-	-	-	-	0.63	1.62
	X	-	-	-	-	0.38	0.31

Source: Latham, A.J.H., 'The dynamics of intra-Asian trade 1868–1913: the great entrepôts of Singapore and Hong Kong', in A.J.H. Latham and H. Kawakatsu (eds), *Japanese Industrialization and the Asian Economy*, London and New York, Routledge, 1994, pp. 160, 162.

Note:
M = imports to Hong Kong
X = exports from Hong Kong

all over Southeast Asia. Many prominent Southeast Chinese merchants and bankers also expanded their businesses to Hong Kong.[33] This was particularly true in the sphere of revenue farming. A revenue farm was a franchise with a license to collect state revenue – a monopoly right to practice a certain business. Such a monopoly was granted by a state to a 'farmer' for a limited period of time and in a locality (a city, district or province) strictly defined by the government. In return, the farmers (bidders) had to pay the government, in advance, an agreed fixed sum to maintain their monopoly status.[34]

Major revenue farms included, at various points of time in the nineteenth century, the opium farm, the gambling farm, farms for the sale of liquor, salt, pork, pawnbroking, fishing, farms to run markets, as well as farms which could impose duties on goods in transit along roadways and in seaports. Most of these were run by Chinese farmers.[35] It was common for prominent Chinese revenue farmers to form transnational syndicates on a considerable scale. In fact, the success of the opium farmers was largely based on their international connections. For example, the opium firm Yan Wo Hong of Hong Kong was able to out-compete its main rival Wo Hang Hong in most of the years in the period 1858–87 because it had better connections with the markets of Macao, California and Australia.[36] The formation of this kind of farming syndicate was based on the pre-existing social bonds among the Chinese, including membership of the same clans or same dialect groups, families, relatives and friendship connections, as well as through intermarriages.[37] Many of these revenue farmers and their family members were involved in opium farming in Hong Kong, as were Ban Hap of Saigon in 1879–82, Cheang Hong Lim of Singapore and Lee Keng Yam of Malacca in the late nineteenth century, and Loke Yew of the Malay States in the early twentieth century.[38]

In sum, it can be stated that many early Chinese businessmen in Hong Kong, in their role of middlemen merchants, accumulated their wealth through participation in the opium trade and the emigration business, which were direct consequences of European colonial expansion. By the 1870s, they were able to challenge the predominance of the British merchants. The expansion of East Asian regional trade benefited the Chinese compradors/merchants more than the British, because the former had better connections with dealers from Southeast Asia and China, and had greater knowledge about these markets. The success of the Chinese businessmen in the nineteenth century was based on their transnational connections in the context of the expansion of European colonization and the growth of the regional trade. However, the success of this élite group was, to a large extent, achieved at the expense of other groups both inside and outside the colony, most notably the coolies and the opium consumers.

The emergence of a Chinese comprador class

In the process of colonial expansion, Chinese businessmen played the role of middlemen. They served as intermediaries between European importers/exporters and native consumers/producers. This was due to the fact that the Chinese traders, lacking political support from China, in turn relied on the Europeans to explore and protect new business opportunities. Whenever the Europeans established a new colony in the region, the Chinese immediately moved in. The overseas Chinese in East Asia thus developed steadily along with the expansion of the European powers. As Jansen argues, '[m]uch of the activity we have parochially thought of as the "expansion of Europe" was European participation in the expansion of [overseas Chinese in] East Asia'.[39] As middlemen between the West and the local people in the region, Chinese businessmen created a chain of complex credit arrangements which linked up the whole process of export/import to local producers/consumers. They also established multiple networks of Chinese agents and petty traders which penetrated every corner of the region, resembling the role of Hong Kong business firms today who act as experienced guides bypassing the often time-consuming process of building relationships in China. As middleman merchants, the Chinese were compradors of Western banks and firms, revenue farmers, financiers, rice merchants and millers, junk-owners, shopkeepers, petty industrialists, dealers in land, etc.

Chinese business in nineteenth-century Hong Kong was characterized by the development of the comprador. Throughout the second half of the century, compradors were among the richest and most prominent Chinese in the colony as well as in China and throughout Asia.[40] The word 'comprador' stems from the Portuguese *comprar*, meaning 'to purchase': a comprador is a purchaser. The Chinese equivalent term *maiban* originally referred to the official broker who purchased supplies for the Chinese government in the Ming dynasty (1368–1664). Thereafter the term, translated as 'comprador', was used to describe the staff of the *cohong* of Canton from around 1720 to the early nineteenth century, who were licensed agents assisting foreign merchants to procure daily supplies and manage servants and money.[41] After 1842, the monopoly status of the *cohong* system was abolished under the Treaty of Nanking, but the term 'comprador' was still used to identify the middleman between Western (and later Japanese) merchants and Chinese markets.

After the First Opium War, in the early 1840s, Chinese compradors, especially those from Canton, developed very rapidly in line with the dramatic increase of the number of foreign trading firms in China, which also diversified from mere trading to shipping, insurance, finance, dockyards, warehouse construction and even industry and mining.[42] The activities of the Chinese compradors expanded accordingly, although their basic role of promoting foreign goods in Chinese markets and purchasing Chinese products for foreign firms remained intact. In 1845, only two compradors were identified in Hong Kong, but the situation changed significantly in the 1850s. As a result of the Taiping rebellion and the Sino-British War, many foreign firms, with their compradors, moved to Hong Kong from Canton. By the second half of the 1850s, the number of compradors recorded in Hong Kong had increased to twenty-seven, and by the end of the

1860s, a group of prominent Chinese compradors had emerged to become leaders of the Chinese community in Hong Kong.[43] Already in late nineteenth-century Hong Kong, compradors such as Ho Tung, Ho Fuk, Ho Kam Tong, Wei Yuk, Fung Wah Chuen, Lau Chu Pak and Lo Koon Ting were among the wealthiest Chinese in the colony.[44] According to data published in the *Government Gazette* in 1876, eight of the twenty highest ratepayers in Hong Kong were Chinese. Five years later, this number increased to seventeen, of which seven were from comprador families while another six were merchants.[45] In 1877, 90 per cent of the Hong Kong government's revenue came from ethnic Chinese. In 1881, among the eighteen richest property owners, who paid HK$4,000 per year in land tax, only one was British (Jardine), the rest (seventeen) were ethnic Chinese.[46]

The notable economic status of these compradors meant that they were not always subordinate to their Western counterparts. Ho Kai, a famous Hong Kong comprador, stated in the 1890s that compradors could earn as much as Western merchants. One author even argues that Ho Kai's claim was too conservative, and that the compradors actually earned more than their Western bosses.[47] Quite often, the comprador still enjoyed economic well-being even when his boss went bankrupt. This was primarily a result of the fact that employing compradors was very expensive for foreign firms, in terms of commission and 'squeeze'. The Chinese compradors, on the other hand, having learned the techniques of 'modern' Western business and international trade from their Western bosses, were able to develop their own businesses very successfully. They had the advantage of not having to pay commissions and they were not subject to 'squeeze'. These advantages allowed them to accumulate a significant capital for further development, in spite of the constraints set by the Western powers.[48] In fact, some British *hongs* were forced to shift to other activities in order to survive the Chinese competition, but many failed and went bankrupt.[49]

As the profits of Western merchants continuously increased thanks to the assistance from Chinese compradors and other middlemen, a rich and powerful business élite arose in Hong Kong.[50] The fact that many compradors also became increasingly independent of their Western bosses and began to develop their own businesses is illustrated by the following account:

> When the P&O Steam Navigation Co. disposed of their shipwright and engineering department in 1854, it was taken over by Kwok Acheong [its former comprador]. He developed a fleet of steamships in the 1860s which provided keen competition for the European-controlled Hong Kong, Canton and Macao Steamboat Co. In addition to his shipping interests, he operated a bakery, imported cattle into the colony and operated as a general merchant under the firm name Fat Hing. In 1876, he was the third largest ratepayer in Hong Kong, and the first among the Chinese.[51]

The further development of Chinese compradors' businesses was, to a large extent, the result of their joint investment with foreign firms in shipping, insurance, banking, real estate and industry. Many of the major Chinese stockholders of these companies were compradors, who controlled a significant share of these China-based foreign investments.[52] This co-investment practice reflected the mutual dependence of the Chinese merchant and foreign capital – the former needed the protection and connections with the West, while the latter needed the capital and domestic connections of the Chinese.

Complementary enemies

Purely economic connections were not sufficient for business success. The Chinese comprador also had to strengthen his business through 'political investments', such as buying official status from the Chinese government or cultivating informal political connections with the colonial authorities. Situated between the mainland Chinese authorities and the British colonial regime, the Hong Kong compradors sometimes needed protection from the latter against the former. This is one reason why the Chinese were willing to become the official or unofficial agents of the colonial government (from being opium farmers to members of the Legislative Council) in managing local communities, in order to prevent their businesses from being 'squeezed' by the mandarins, a common practice in mainland China. For instance, it was reported that during the Second Sino–British War, Chinese officials had 'squeezed' HK$2,000 out of Ho Asek, a prominent Chinese merchant and the first gambling monopoly holder in 1871.[53]

Their political weakness, however, put Chinese businessmen at a disadvantage when competing with their Western counterparts, who were granted a more privileged status by the colonial government. As a result, Chinese merchants/compradors sometimes had to play a double-sided game, trying to maintain good relationships with both the Western powers and the Chinese government. A typical example in the 1840s was Loo Aqui, who had not only received a large piece of land in Hong Kong as a reward from the colonial government for providing the British navy with various supplies, but was also awarded an official degree by the Canton government.[54] This strategy was possible because since the 1860s, the policy of the Qing court turned in favour of the overseas Chinese, allowing them to buy official positions and honorary titles. The change in the Qing court's policy was mainly a result of a combination of factors. The Qing government was experiencing financial difficulty caused by war reparations, loans, balance of trade deficit, military expenditures to suppress the Taiping Rebellion, as well as natural disasters, which forced it to turn to overseas Chinese for financial support. In addition, anti-Qing forces such as the Taiping and Sun Yat-sen revolutionaries were very active in overseas Chinese communities. This also forced the late Qing government to become more positive towards overseas Chinese and contend for their support.[55]

As a result, many Hong Kong compradors purchased Chinese official titles to enhance their reputation and social status, which helped consolidate their leadership in domestic Chinese communities, a crucial factor in their business success. These official positions also secured protection for their relatives and property in China, and enabled them to gain access to the arms trade and government loan business.[56] However, their double affiliation was also the cause of tensions with both the native and Western powers. As Tsai notes, the seeking of Chinese official titles

> made various demands on them [Hong Kong's prominent Chinese merchants] (such as assistance in fund-raising for reliefs in China) and treated them as Chinese subjects under Chinese jurisdiction. This in turn incurred the displeasure of the colonial government, which insisted on its sole jurisdiction over all Chinese in Hong Kong. Thus, gentrification paradoxically brought élite members under mandarin control, which they resented; they therefore turned to the colonial government for protection against excessive mandarin demands. The colonial government needed the élite's co-operation in the maintenance of local community order, but the government also looked with a suspicious eye on the élite's connections with the mandarin in Canton.[57]

Consequently, the colonial government always kept a close surveillance over the Chinese residents and adopted discriminating measures against them.[58] For example, it did not allow Chinese merchants/compradors in Hong Kong to step into the field of public utilities, which were strategically and economically crucial to the Hong Kong economy.[59]

Even so, the colonial authorities could not stop the continuous advancement of Chinese businessmen, due to the 'thinness' of the colonial administration, which forced it to continue its reliance on Chinese middlemen to manage and rule the domestic community. Many of the founders and/or leaders of social and charity organizations, such as the Tung Wah Hospital, Po Leung Kuk, neighbourhood (*kaifong*) associations and temple committees, were Chinese compradors. For example, five out of the twelve founders of the Tung Wah Hospital, the most important civic centre for the Chinese community in late nineteenth-century Hong Kong, were compradors.[60] Moreover, bribes made to the colonial government also eroded the effectiveness of its discriminating policies.[61] In return for their assistance, the Chinese middlemen received benefits from monopolies such as opium farming as well as political protection.

For the Chinese middlemen, the Western business circles and political authorities were simultaneously partners and rivals, friends and enemies. Sometimes they co-operated, while at other times they engaged in severe competition and conflict. From the mid-nineteenth century to the early twentieth century, the relationship between the Western merchants and the colonial government on the one hand, and the Chinese businessmen in Hong Kong on the other, is best characterized by the term 'complementary enemies'.[62] Each needed the other to strengthen their own position and solve certain problems. In particular, the compradors and Western merchants often co-operated to promote their common interests against their common 'foes' – the labourer and the peasant.[63] At the same time, the colonial authorities and merchants also regarded the Chinese merchants as competitors and a potential threat to their prestige, and repeatedly constrained the development of Chinese businesses.

The Chinese comprador declined and finally disappeared in the early twentieth century.[64] The reasons, according to Hao, were numerous, and included the increasing independence of Western merchants as they became familiar with Chinese markets. Direct investment in China also played a role, as did the increasing independence and experience of Chinese merchants in foreign trade, who could now work alone without reliance on foreign merchants. Finally, the development of the 'modern' Chinese banking system also contributed to the demise of the comprador. But the comprador phase had greatly stimulated the growth of Hong Kong-based Chinese commercial and financial interests and these continued to grow. Even with the disappearance of comprador, Chinese middlemen were not entirely eliminated. They reappeared as independent brokers, managers and commission agents.

Conclusion

Colonialism no doubt played a major role in the rise of Hong Kong as a trading centre in the nineteenth century. This role, however, is more complicated than just the benevolent free trade policy under British rule. In the first place, it was colonial expansion into the East and Southeast Asian region that created the socio-economic context for trading business. And in this context, Hong Kong was strategically located in the centre of the flourishing trade routes.

Without such a strategic location, the agency of Hong Kong Chinese businessmen in capturing the trading opportunities could not have occurred. The success of Hong Kong Chinese businesses was, and still is, largely a product of the excellent regional and geo-political context: the China-link and the booming regional trading activities, which were mainly a result of Western colonial expansion. This regional context – being at the centre of the vital currents of trade and near to the core of decision-making – provided businessmen with golden opportunities. Chinese businessmen in Hong Kong were 'both sufficiently informed and materially able to choose the sphere of [their] action'.[65] Their flexible loyalties to different national regimes also put them closer to the centre of decision-making, thus allowing them to advance their wide ranging business interests despite being politically marginalized.

The role of Chinese business under colonial rule further reveals the complexity of colonialism. Rather than viewing colonialism exclusively as a process through which one country dominates another, it is more fruitful to look at the interplay of different social forces in establishing a colonial regime. In the case of

Hong Kong, we can clearly see that the Chinese middlemen, that is the compradors, were indispensable actors making possible colonial domination. Far from being simply subordinate partners of the European powers and merchants, the compradors played a very active and lucrative role in this collaboration, often benefiting more in economic terms than the imperialist powers and foreign merchants. Chinese compradors prospered, particularly in terms of the coolie and opium trade, by manœuvring effectively in local and regional markets and exploiting other social groups in the community. In the process they became partners as well as competitors of colonial interests, and some eventually surpassed the British in terms of wealth and social power.

NOTES

1 In terms of trade, according to the Hong Kong Trade Development Council, over 60 per cent of Hong Kong's total trade was within the East Asian region in 1992. From 1980 to 1995, the average annual growth rate of Hong Kong's trade within the Asia-Pacific region was 21 per cent. By 1989, in terms of foreign investments, Hong Kong accounted for 25 per cent to 28 per cent (10 per cent if China is excluded) of total investment flows to Asia. *Hong Kong Financial Times*, 28 November 1990, p. 3. According to a survey conducted by the Trade Development Council, Hong Kong's companies employ eleven times more workers overseas than they employ within Hong Kong. Most of these workers are located in underdeveloped Asian countries, including China. Hong Kong Government, Hong Kong Trade Development Council, *Survey on Hong Kong Domestic Exports, Re-exports, and Triangular Trade*, 1991, p. 3.

2 According to an official survey conducted in 1995, 22.8 per cent of the overseas companies operating in Hong Kong identified themselves as regional headquarters, and another 37.5 per cent identified themselves as regional offices. Calculated from Hong Kong Trade Development Council data, http://www.tdc.org.hk, 6 July 1996.

3 In 1995, 85 of the world's top 100 banks established branches or offices in Hong Kong. Hong Kong Trade Development Council data, http://www.tdc.org.hk, 6 July 1996.

4 Chen Qiaozhi, 'Dongnanya huaren ziben de tedian yu dongxiang' (The characteristics and directions of Southeast Asian Chinese capital), in Wang Muheng (ed.), *Dongnanya huaren jingji* (The Economy of the Chinese in Southeast Asia), Fuzhou, Fujian renmin chubanshe, 1989, pp. 6, 15; Henry Sender, 'Inside the overseas Chinese network', *Institutional Investor*, 1991, vol. 25, no. 10, September, p. 40.

5 Great Britain, Public Record Office, *Colonial Office Records*, CO 129, Dispatches from the Governor of Hong Kong, CO 129/73/54, Bowring to Lytton, 29 March 1859, pp. 296–7.

6 David Joel Steinberg, *In Search of Southeast Asia: A Modern History*, Honolulu, University of Hawaii Press, 1987, p. 219.

7 D.J.M. Tate, *The Making of Modern South-East Asia*, Kuala Lumpur, Oxford University Press, 1979, pp. 429, 497.

8 Chang Pin-tsun, 'The first Chinese diaspora in Southeast Asia in the fifteenth century', in Roderich Ptak and Dietmar Rothermund (eds), *Emporia, Commodities and Entrepreneurs in Asian Maritime Trade, C. 1400–1750*, Stuttgart, Franz Steiner Verlag, 1991, pp. 23–4.

9 Zhuang Guotu, *Zhongguo fengjian zhengfu de huaqiao zhengce* (The Chinese Feudal Government's Policies Towards Overseas Chinese), Xiamen, Xiamen daxue chubanshe, 1989, p. 38.

10 Zhuang Guotu, 'Lun Ming ji haiwai Zhongguo sichou maoyi (1567–1643)' (On China's overseas silk trade during the late Ming period (1567–1643)), in Xiamen daxue nanyang yanjiusuo (ed.), *Nanyang yanjiu lunwenji* (Anthology of Nanyang Studies), Xiamen, Xiamen daxue chubanshe, 1992, p. 280.

11 According to Thomas Knox, a nineteenth-century American merchant engaged in East Asian trade, 'the Chinese comprador was active in Japan, Cochin China, Bangkok, Rangoon, Penang, Malacca, Singapore, Java, and Manila, and [that] his influence was even felt in India'. Hao Yen-p'ing, *The Comprador in Nineteenth Century China: Bridge between East and West*, Cambridge, MA, Harvard University Press, 1970, p. 55. See also Naosaku Uchida, *The Overseas Chinese*, Stanford, Hoover Institution, Stanford University, 1959, p. 48.

12 Hao, *The Comprador in Nineteenth Century China*, pp. 54–9.

13 Rajeswary Ampalavanar Brown, *Capital and Entrepreneurship in South-East Asia*, New York, St. Martin's Press, 1994, p. 17; Anthony Reid, 'The seventeenth century crisis in South-East Asia', *Modern Asian Studies*, 1990, vol. 24, pp. 652–4.

14 Syed Husein Alatas, *The Myth of the Lazy Native: A Study of the Image of the Malays, Filipinos and Javanese from the 16th to the 20th Centuries and Its Function in the Ideology of Colonial Capitalism*, London, Frank Cass, 1977, pp. 196–9; Philip D. Curtin, *Cross-Cultural Trade in World History*, Cambridge, MA, Cambridge University Press, 1984, pp. 162–8.

15 Nie Baozhang, 'Yang hang maiban yu maiban zhichan jieji' (Foreign companies, compradors, and comprador bourgeoisie), in Sun Jian (ed.), *Zhongguo jingji shi lunwen ji* (Collection of Articles on China's Economic History), Beijing, Zhongguo renmin daxue chubanshe, 1987, p. 164; Chen Shijun, 'Lun yapian zhanzheng qian de maiban he jindai maiban zhichan jieji de chansheng' (On the compradors before the Opium War and the origin of the modern comprador bourgeoisie), in Ning Jing (ed.), *Yapian zhanzheng shi lunwen zhuan xuanbian* (A Collection of Articles on the History of the Opium War), Beijing, Renmin chubanshe, 1984, p.61.

16 For more on capitalist development and long distance trade, see Karl Polanyi, *The Great Transformation*, Boston, MA, Beacon Press, 1957; Fernand Braudel, *The Wheels of Commerce*, New York, Harper & Row, 1982; and *The Perspective of the World*, New York, Harper & Row, 1984.

17 A.J.H. Latham, 'The dynamics of intra-Asian trade 1868–1913: the great entrepôts of Singapore and Hong Kong', in A.J.H. Latham and H. Kawakatsu (eds), *Japanese Industrialization and the Asian Economy*, London and New York, Routledge, 1994, p. 145.

18 Francis E. Hyde, *Far Eastern Trade 1860–1914*, London, Adam & Charles Black, 1973, p. 86; Latham, 'The dynamics of intra-Asian trade 1868–1913', pp. 146 and 163.

19 T.N. Chiu, *The Port of Hong Kong: A Survey of Its Development*, Hong Kong, Hong Kong University Press, 1973, pp. 27–8; Zhu Zongyu, Yang Yuanhua and Dou Hui, *Cong Xianggang gerang dao nuwang fanghua* (From the Loss of Hong Kong to Her Majesty's Visit to Hong Kong), Fuzhou, Fujian renmin chubanshe, 1990, p. 24.

20 Chiu, *The Port of Hong Kong*, pp. 16–17.

21 C.P. Lo, *Hong Kong*, London, Belhaven Press, 1992, p. 11.

22 Yuan Bangjian, *Xianggang shilue* (A Brief History of Hong Kong), Hong Kong, Zhongliu chubanshe, 1987, p. 114.

23 Chen Zexian, 'Shijiu shiji shengxing de qiyue huagong zhi' (The prevailing 'contract labour' system in the nineteenth century), in Cuncui Xueshe (ed.), *Zhongguo jin sanbainian shehui jingji shi lunji* (A Collection of Articles on the Socio-Economic History of China in the Last Three Hundred Years), vol. 2, Hong Kong, Chongwen shudian, 1972, pp. 349–51.

24 Zheng Youkui, 'Zhuzai de luesuo ji qi lirun' (The seizure of 'coolies' and the resulting profits), in Chen Hansheng (ed.), *Huagong chuguo shi ziliao huibian* (Anthology of

Materials Concerning the Export of Chinese Labour), vol. 4., Zhonghua shuju, 1981, p. 242.

25 Chen, 'Lun yapian zhanzheng qian de maiban', pp. 336, 339; Peng Jiali, 'Shijiu shiji xifang qinluezhe dui Zhongguo laogong de lulue' (The seizure of Chinese labour by western invaders in the nineteenth century), in Chen Hansheng (ed.), *Huagong chuguo shi ziliao huibian*, vol. 4, Beijing, Zhonghua shuju, 1981, 181–94.

26 Peng, 'Shijiu shiji xifang qinluezhe', pp. 196–200; see also Zheng, 'Zhuzai de luesuo ji gi lirun', pp. 242–4; Lin Yuanhui, and Zhang Yinglong, *Xinjiapo Malaixiya huaqiao shi* (History of Overseas Chinese in Singapore and Malaysia), Guangzhou, Guangdong gaodeng jiaoyu chubanshe, 1991, p. 173.

27 Lin and Zhang, *Xinjiapo Malaixiya huaqiao shi*, p. 173.

28 Peng, 'Shijiu shiji xifang qinluezhe', p. 151.

29 Tsai Jung-fang, *Hong Kong in Chinese History: Community and Social Unrest in the British Colony, 1842–1913*, New York, Columbia University Press, 1993, p. 26.

30 Chiu, *The Port of Hong Kong*, p. 28.

31 Tsai, *Hong Kong in Chinese History*, p. 33.

32 Tsai, *Hong Kong in Chinese History*, pp. 29–30.

33 Brown, *Capital and Entrepreneurship in South-East Asia*, pp. 129–39, 140, 160–71; Tsai, *Hong Kong in Chinese History*, pp. 73–4.

34 James Rush, *Opium to Java*, Ithaca, NY, Cornell University Press, 1990, pp. 1 and 25; Anthony Reid, 'The origins of revenue farming in Southeast Asia', in John Butcher & Howard Dick (eds), *The Rise and Fall of Revenue Farming*, New York, St. Martin's Press, 1993, p. 69; John Butcher, 'Revenue farming and the changing state in Southeast Asia', in Butcher & Dick, *The Rise and Fall of Revenue Farming*, p. 21; Howard Dick, 'Fresh approach to Southeast Asian history', in Butcher & Dick, *The Rise and Fall of Revenue Farming*, p. 3.

35 Reid, 'The origins of revenue farming in Southeast Asia', p. 72; Carl A. Trocki, *Opium and Empire: Chinese Society in Colonial Singapore, 1800–1910*, Ithaca, NY, Cornell University Press, 1990, p. 73; Rush, *Opium to Java*, p. 2.

36 Cheung Tsui Ping, 'The opium monopoly in Hong Kong, 1844–1887', unpublished M.Phil. thesis, University of Hong Kong, Hong Kong, 1986, p. 36.

37 David Brown, *The State and Ethnic Politics in Southeast Asia*, London and New York, Routledge, 1994, pp. 144–50, 182; see also Carl A. Trocki, 'The collapse of Singapore's great syndicate', in Butcher & Dick, *The Rise and Fall of Revenue Farming*.

38 Cheung, 'The opium monopoly in Hong Kong, 1844–1887', pp. 48–51; Trocki, *Opium and Empire*, p. 178; John Butcher, 'Loke Yew', in Butcher and Dick, *The Rise and Fall of Revenue Farming*, pp. 257–8.

39 Marius B. Jansen, *China in the Tokugawa World*, Cambridge, MA, Harvard University Press, 1992, p. 25.

40 Steinberg, *In Search of Southeast Asia*, pp. 225, 232, 235; Tate, *The Making of Modern South-East Asia*, pp. 338, 415, 456, 463, 539, 543.

41 Chen, 'Lun yapian zhanzheng qian de maiban', pp. 54–5; Zhuang Wenqing, 'Ming Qing Guangzhou zhongxi maoyi yu Zhongguo jindai maiban de qiyuan' (Sino–Western trade in Ming-Qing Canton and the origin of modern Chinese compradors), in Guangdong lishi xuehui (ed.), *Ming Qing Guangdong shehui jingji xingtai yanjiu* (A Study of the Social and Economic Situation in Ming-Qing Guangdong), Guangzhou, Guangdong renmin chubanshe, 1985, pp. 313–14, 324–6.

42 For the development of the comprador, see Hao, *The Comprador in Nineteenth Century China*, pp. 48–53; and Wang Jingyu, *Shijiu shiji xifang ziben zhuyi dui Zhongguo de jingji qinlue* (The Nineteenth-Century Western Capitalist Economic Invasion of China), Beijing, Renmin chubanshe, 1983, pp. 106–7.

43 Carl T. Smith, *Chinese Christians: Elites, Middlemen, and the Church in Hong Kong*, Hong Kong, Oxford University Press, 1985; Chan Wai Kwan, *The Making of Hong Kong*

Society: Three Studies of Class Formation in Early Hong Kong, Oxford, Clarendon Press, 1991, p. 77.
44 Tsai, *Hong Kong in Chinese History*, p. 87.
45 Smith, *Chinese Christians*, p. 105.
46 Yuan, *Xianggang shilue*, p. 130.
47 Hao, *The Comprador in Nineteenth Century China*, pp. 110–19.
48 Ibid.
49 Chan, *The Making of Hong Kong Society*, pp. 106–7.
50 Colin N. Crisswell, *The Taipans: Hong Kong's Merchant Princes*, Hong Kong, Oxford University Press, 1991, pp. 101–2, 119–20.
51 Smith, *Chinese Christians*, p. 124.
52 Tsai, *Hong Kong in Chinese History*, pp. 87–8.
53 Smith, *Chinese Christians*, p. 123.
54 Tsai, *Hong Kong in Chinese History*, p. 43.
55 Lin and Zhang, *Xinjiapo Malaixiya huaqiao shi*, pp. 180–3.
56 Huang Yifeng, 'Diguo zhuyi qinlue Zhongguo de yige zhongyao zhizhu – maiban jieji' (The comprador class – an important support for the imperialist invasion of China), in Cuncui Xueshe (eds), *Zhongguo jin sanbainian shehui jingji shi lunji* (A Collection of Articles on the Socio-Economic History of China in the Last Hundred Years), vol. 4, Chongwen shudian, 1974, pp. 251–2; Tsai, *Hong Kong in Chinese History*, p. 63; Lin and Zhang, *Xinjiapo Malaixiya huaqiao shi*, pp. 183–90.
57 Tsai, *Hong Kong in Chinese History*, p. 82.
58 Tate, *The Making of Modern South-East Asia*, p. 22.
59 Tsai, *Hong Kong in Chinese History*, p. 90.
60 Chan, *The Making of Hong Kong Society*, p. 108; see also Smith, *Chinese Christians*, pp. 120–7; Tsai, *Hong Kong in Chinese History*, p. 67.
61 See for instance Cheung, 'The opium monopoly in Hong Kong, 1844–1887', pp. 81–4.
62 This concept was originally used by Germaine Tillion in 1962 to describe France and Algeria during the Algerian War. Braudel uses the term to describe the specific relations between the Netherlands and Spain in the late sixteenth century. Braudel, *The Perspective of the World*, pp. 208–10.
63 Chan, *The Making of Hong Kong Society*, pp. 134–6.
64 Hao, *The Comprador in Nineteenth Century China*, pp. 59–63; Uchida, *The Overseas Chinese*, p. 48.
65 Braudel, *The Wheels of Commerce*, pp. 400, 402; Braudel, *The Perspective of the World*, p. 622.

4

THE CRIMINAL TRIAL UNDER EARLY COLONIAL RULE

Christopher Munn

'It is of the highest importance,' remarked Governor Sir John Bowring (1854–59) on a suspected miscarriage of justice in 1856, that

> the native population especially should know that the administration of justice is held by us to be a sacred and responsible duty, and that every man's life and liberty on British soil is intended to be most reverently protected by every security against wrong which legislation can provide.[4]

The 'rule of law' supplanting the arbitrary justice of indigenous regimes has long been a staple of British colonial rhetoric. Nowhere, perhaps, has the claim been more keenly advanced than in Hong Kong, this 'little miniature representative of Great Britain, its laws, its manners, its institutions' set against a backdrop of oriental despotism.[1] Early officials in the colony were convinced of the importance of the rule of law in legitimating British rule. A year or so after the conclusion of the Opium War, the governor-designate, John Francis Davis, predicted that 'the protection of equal laws' would be one of the 'miracles of peace' that would draw wealthy Chinese merchants to the new colony.[2] 'The right to a due and even-handed administration of the English laws', Chief Justice Hulme (1844–59) informed Hong Kong's leading Chinese inhabitants four years later, was 'one of the greatest privileges' they could enjoy.[3]

Hong Kong's standard colonial histories have swallowed these claims almost without question. In their discussions of the early judicial system, E.J. Eitel and G.B. Endacott dwell on the narrow controversies between the bibulous Chief Justice Hulme and the unpopular Governor Davis, portraying them as a simple struggle between the rule of law and executive encroachment. Endacott stresses Hulme's popularity among European colonists as an impartial judge and defends the severity of measures taken to control the Chinese population by noting that 'the Chinese proved to be difficult and not readily amenable to British ideas of law and order'. Frank Welsh similarly admits the early colonial government's insensitivity towards Chinese residents but asserts, quite erroneously, that 'in capital cases the laws and the penalties were equal for all. Europeans were tried, flogged and even hanged, in public, in the same way and for the same offences as Chinese'.[5]

The only work to contain any sustained account of the colony's judicial system is Norton-Kyshe's *History of the Laws and Courts of Hong Kong*, which, after blaming problems in establishing the rule of law on the Chinese, proceeds to a detailed narrative designed to prove that 'the Chinese acquiesce in our laws and fully admit their beneficence'.[6] The myth that Norton-Kyshe had access to a large body of records since destroyed has persuaded even the most anti-colonial of historians to invest his work with the status of a primary text.[7] Yet the newspapers, ordinances and public documents to which Norton-Kyshe had access reveal a dysfunction between the colony's early legal system and the mostly Chinese defendants and witnesses who came before it that goes far deeper than his account seems to suggest. An extensive, and now public, government correspondence enables us to trace the process by which early governors of the colony transformed a failing criminal justice system founded on English principles into an instrument designed for what Governor MacDonnell (1866–72) described as the '*self-preservation* and protection' of a beleaguered European colonial élite against 'the migratory refuse of many millions of Chinese'.[8] A reassessment of justice in nineteenth-century Hong Kong is long overdue.

In this Chapter I attempt a contribution to that reassessment by examining some aspects of the criminal justice system in the first twenty-five years of British rule in Hong Kong. My discussion focuses on the criminal trial in the Supreme Court, the fountain-head of English justice in the region. I first explore the political background of Hong Kong's Supreme Court, and then examine the caseload and sentencing of the Court. This is followed by a discussion of the problems with Chinese witnesses and the disadvantaged position of Chinese defendants. I then describe how, in response to a succession of crises relating to the credibility of the Supreme Court, the Hong Kong government embarked on a radical reorganization of the colony's criminal justice system to enable it to police the Chinese inhabitants and secure convictions more easily. I make 1866 the closing year for this discussion because it marks the culminating point at which these reforms were consolidated into a system that was to serve the colony for the rest of the century and beyond.

English criminal law in early British Hong Kong

The sudden extension of English law to the non-European population of Hong Kong in 1844 was something of an anomaly. It was at variance both with the more gradual application of English law in Britain's other Asian possessions and with the intentions of Hong Kong's earliest rulers.[9] Hong Kong's first governor, Sir Henry Pottinger (1841–4), had initially negotiated with the Chinese authorities a divided jurisdiction, in which Chinese accused of committing serious crimes in the colony would be handed over to a Chinese magistrate for trial by Chinese law.[10] Chinese officials continued to claim such jurisdiction until well into the 1860s. In 1843, however, the British government abruptly decided to apply the full apparatus of English law equally to all inhabitants on the island regardless of nationality or race. Rationalized by claims that English justice would attach Chinese people to British rule, this decision was motivated equally by a desire to extend British sovereignty unequivocally over the new colony. Pottinger's successor, Sir John Francis Davis (1844–8), summarized the position when he observed that the colony's first hanging of a Chinese together with an Englishman in June 1845 'for ever established the once disputed British jurisdiction over Chinese in capital cases, and demonstrated to Her Majesty's Chinese subjects at Hongkong the perfect equality of British Law'.[11]

The British courts in Hong Kong were established primarily to control British subjects in the colony and along the China coast. The Supreme Court that opened in Hong Kong in 1844 exercised full jurisdiction over such people. Admiralty jurisdiction (for a brief period administered in a separate Vice-Admiralty Court before its absorption by the Supreme Court in 1850) extended the reach of English law into the China Seas. In theory, this was intended to control and protect British trade. In practice, the majority of those who appeared as defendants in the courts were Chinese, sometimes for offences against Europeans, but more usually for crimes committed against other Chinese in Hong Kong, on the high seas, and often within Chinese waters. What had originated in a plan to provide the British in China with their own judicial machinery quickly developed into a system in which Europeans tried Chinese for crimes against other Chinese committed in and often well beyond the colony.

The ordinances introducing English law into the Hong Kong region allowed variations where local conditions required them.[12] The most substantial differences between English and Hong Kong practices appeared in the structure and procedures of the Court. The Hong Kong system made no use of the grand jury, the panel of jurors who in England decided whether prosecutions should proceed to trial. This function was vested in the Attorney General, who also became the public prosecutor in all criminal cases: in early nineteenth-century England most prosecutions were still conducted privately by the complainants themselves.[13] A third important difference came in the composition of petty juries. Made up of only six men, these were half the size of juries in England and were composed of European colonists. This made nonsense of the claim in the legislation that a prisoner who pleaded not guilty was 'deemed to have put himself or herself upon the country for trial'; it also conflicted with the practice in some other Asian possessions.[14] While it naturally set jurors apart from the majority of defendants and witnesses, it did not necessarily ensure that they were familiar with English judicial procedure or even competent in the English language.[15] Finally, most trials in Hong Kong required the services of interpreters, who exerted an enormous if immeasurable influence on the course of the trial. European observers naturally imputed corruption and incompetence to the Chinese interpreters who came into the Court in the mid-1850s. The greatest scandal, however, may have been in the fact that, up to that period, most trials were interpreted by Daniel Caldwell, who in his capacity of assistant police superintendent frequently doubled as principal prosecution witness. In the late 1850s Caldwell was exposed as the central figure in a web of piratical and corrupt connections.

If the differences between Hong Kong and English practices were substantial, those between English and Chinese law were greater. British observers dwelt on the wholesale butchery under a judicial system which, in the disorder then prevalent in southern China, was rapidly breaking down. While it might be difficult to make out a case for the benevolence of Chinese justice as administered in the late Qing period, it would also be a mistake to draw too many contrasts between it and the English justice dispensed by Hong Kong's Supreme Court.[16] The crimes for which defendants were tried in Hong Kong were in nearly all cases also crimes under the Qing Code. The significant differences between Chinese justice and English justice in Hong Kong were to be found more in the process than in the substance of law. Chinese justice was more summary in its procedures and more certain in its results. English justice, hedged in by protections for the accused and governed by the presumption of innocence, made conviction far less certain. The Chinese trial was inquisitorial and depended more on the confession of the offender, sometimes under torture, than on the evidence of witnesses. The English trial was adversarial, relied on evidence from witnesses on oath, and was scrupulous to avoid any possibility of self-incrimination by the defendant. Chinese law took the status and relationship of individuals as the basis for defining crimes and determining punishments. English law, in theory at least, regarded all before the courts as equals. Above all, the Chinese system discouraged litigation: magistrates were distrustful of those who brought accusations and wary about false accusations.

People in imperial China had little contact with the formal apparatus of law. Most disputes were dealt with by the overlapping structures of informal power, such as clans, villages, guilds and secret societies, which organized people's lives.[17] In contrast, the Hong Kong government's urge to regulate an alien, rapidly increasing, and often unco-operative population brought thousands of people into contact with the law. The number of people who appeared before the lower courts between 1846 and 1866 merely *as defendants* was nearly 134,000: in annual terms, this is equal to between 8 and 10 per cent of the population, rising to more than 12 per cent in some years. The vast majority of these defendants were Chinese, many convicted of offences unheard of in English law, such as failing to carry registration tickets, walking the streets after curfew or being a 'suspicious character'. Fewer than a third of those who appeared before the lower courts left them without some form of punishment or restraint: the main punishments were short prison sentences, public floggings, queue cutting, deportation and exposure in the cangue (or 'Chinese stocks').

Despite the caseload of the lower courts, the early colonial government had only a feeble grasp of what was happening in the colony. Chinese society in

Hong Kong organized itself around villages, lineages, bazaars and secret societies. Some of these structures gained power and recognition from the government through its *tepo* or headman schemes, compradorial links and trade monopolies. Some, like the Triad Society, were outlawed at an early date. Others, like the bazaars at Sheung Wan and East Point, became centres both of an embryonic bourgeois Chinese society and of piratical enterprises and trade in stolen goods. The colony became notorious as a centre of crime and as the place at which crimes committed elsewhere were plotted. The British complained that they were the targets of this crime, but the main victims were the ordinary Chinese inhabitants and sojourners: the small traders who received scant protection against the pirates waiting outside colonial waters; the foot-travellers robbed of their clothes along the island's isolated bridleways; the dupes of extortionists who could claim or counterfeit some association with the colonial power; or the women and children abducted by traffickers in human beings. Though frequently exploited as a tool in the extortions and petty quarrels that went on in the colony, the Supreme Court operated almost in a political vacuum: it possessed only a vague understanding of the people who came before it and exerted little or no deterrent effect on crime. In 1848 the Court's conviction rate was as low as 25 per cent. Only in 1851 did the conviction rate pass 50 per cent, and even after that date it rarely reached the 70 per cent conviction rate usually achieved by its equivalents in England.

The criminal jurisdiction of the Supreme Court

The magistrates' limited sentencing powers ('Chinese punishments' and a maximum of three months' imprisonment, increased to six in 1849) required them to commit defendants accused of serious offences for trial by jury in the Supreme Court, which could impose sentences ranging from death or transportation to imprisonment or fines. Just over 4,000 defendants appeared before the Supreme Court in criminal trials in the twenty-two years between 1844 and 1866: more than half of them were convicted. Most official trial records for this period have disappeared. Beginning in 1848, however, the Supreme Court produced annual returns summarizing the number of defendants tried, convicted and sentenced for each offence. It is possible to fill out these returns in a rough but revealing manner by consulting the extensive reports of cases in the colony's three main newspapers. The thoroughness of the newspaper coverage varies from year to year and begins to decline in the late 1850s, when other concerns, such as regional rebellion and the hostilities between Britain and China, begin to take precedence. The discussion in this section relies mainly on an exhaustive survey of 566 reported criminal cases involving 1,132 defendants tried by the Supreme Court in the ten years between 1848 and 1857. The defendants represent about 85 per cent of all defendants (1,334) reported in the official returns for those years.

A little over 86 per cent (977) of these 1,132 defendants were Chinese, fewer than 6 per cent (66) were European or American, and slightly more than 7.5 per cent (87) came from other places in Asia.[18] Almost 98 per cent (1,108) of defendants were men. The social position of most defendants, where it can be identified, was low: most were described as coolies, boatmen, stone-cutters or hawkers, or as having no profession. About 73 per cent (338) of complainants in the 462 cases in which they can be identified were Chinese, 22 per cent (101) were European, and 5 per cent (23) were from elsewhere; 90 per cent were men and 10 per cent women. The most striking result of this survey is that, while Europeans figure disproportionately large as complainants, more than 70 per cent of the Court's business concerned cases brought by Chinese complainants against Chinese defendants.

About 70 per cent of the defendants in the survey were tried for property offences, more than 74 per cent of these for offences, such as robbery or piracy, which also involved violence. According to official returns, out of the 722 defendants convicted by the Supreme Court between 1848 and 1857, 430 were sentenced to periods of transportation ranging from seven years to life, or to 'death recorded', in which mandatory death sentences were commuted automatically to life transportation. With the closing of most of the Australian colonies to transports, this punishment had nearly died out in England. The Hong Kong government, however, was able to secure destinations in other colonies in the region, such as Singapore, Penang, Labuan and Sind, which were willing to accept Chinese and other Asian convicts from Hong Kong to labour on their public works. In the eyes of Hong Kong's officials this was an ideal punishment, since it relieved the colony of a large financial burden and was understood to be almost as dreaded by Chinese offenders as the death penalty. But transportation was rarely secured without great difficulty, since other colonies became increasingly unwilling to take Hong Kong's often rebellious transports. By 1858, when the last destination, Labuan, finally closed its doors, the only alternative was to replace transportation with long periods of penal servitude.[19]

Imprisonment, usually with hard labour, was a poor alternative to transportation. Despite the unsanitary and overcrowded conditions and the high death rate, it became axiomatic among colonists that Chinese convicts found prison enjoyable because it offered better food, shelter and clothing than that available to the average labourer.[20] The prison regime was insecure, so that escapes, sometimes with the connivance of turnkeys, were frequent. Only 242 defendants convicted by the Supreme Court between 1848 and 1857 were given prison sentences, which averaged at around eighteen months. To these, however, should be added the large numbers of short-term prisoners sentenced by the lower courts, prisoners on remand and convicts awaiting transportation. Pressure on accommodation became particularly severe in the colony's troubled years of 1856 and 1857, when the number of prisoners was sometimes more than double the capacity of the prison. Faced with a threefold increase in the prison population in the early 1860s, Governor Robinson (1859–65) purchased a hulk for the temporary accommodation of convicts and commissioned the construction of a large but ultimately unnecessary prison on Stonecutters' Island.

Although the official statistics for the period 1848 to 1857 reveal forty-three sentences of death, only nineteen of these sentences appear to have been carried out, all for offences involving murder: twelve of those hanged were Chinese, six were Filipinos, and one was a Malay. Half of these were found guilty of crimes against Europeans. Of the twenty-four not hanged, two were pardoned by the Governor-in-Council when evidence collected after the trial proved that they had been the victims of malicious prosecutions; and twenty-one had their sentences commuted to transportation, usually on the ground that they had a lesser degree of guilt than the principal murderers but also, in the case of nine convicted pirates, because the offence had concerned only Chinese.[21] Although severe deterrents were considered necessary, governors were anxious not to allow too many hangings to take place, particularly where convictions were unsafe. The English system traditionally depended on a measured balance between terror and mercy.[22] Too sanguinary a regime would anyway undermine the claims that English law was more humane than Chinese: mass hangings were, in the words of Governor Bonham (1848–54), 'contrary to the spirit of the present age'.[23] Given that at least seven of these nineteen hangings were badly bungled and that some were carried out against fears of last-minute rescue attempts by Triad bands, the impression that hangings made on the thousands of Chinese who attended them is open to question. Certainly, the effects of Bowring's attempt in 1858 to advertise the 'equal justice' of 'the authority of British law' by inserting a Chinese proclamation in the *Government Gazette* announcing the execution of the first two Europeans convicted of murdering a Chinese are impossible to assess, despite reports that more than 2,000 people, including the Chinese military commander from Kowloon, turned out for the execution.[24]

European and Chinese differences

Fourteen of the prisoners in the survey sentenced to transportation and twenty-two of those sentenced to imprisonment were Europeans. Do conviction rates and sentencing patterns reveal any great differences in the treatment of Europeans? The answer is no. The conviction rates are about the same (63.5 per cent for Europeans and 62.5 per cent for Chinese). The average prison sentences are slightly higher for Chinese convicts (seventeen months compared with fifteen). Chinese prisoners sentenced to transportation, on average, did better: 64 per cent of European transports were sentenced for life, compared with only 42 per cent of Chinese transports.

These figures ought to provide resounding confirmation of the claims made for even-handed justice. Looked at more carefully, however, they do nothing of the sort. Out of the sixty-six Europeans committed for trial in the Supreme Court, forty-three were tried for offences against the person (mainly murder, manslaughter, wounding and assault) or offences against authority (such as assaulting a policeman or revolt on board ship). Four out of the forty-three were tried for crimes against Chinese. Two of these were acquitted on technicalities. The third, George Luscombe, an American ship's mate, was sentenced to life transportation for strangling a Chinese tailor over a quarrel about payment for a flannel shirt.[25] The fourth, Denis Griffin, the carpenter of another American ship, was tried for the murder of a Chinese caulker, who fell into the sea and drowned when Griffin cut the rope of a work stage hanging over the side of the ship after the Chinese working on it refused to stop working during the rain. The jury acquitted Griffin after his counsel convinced them that the incident had been nothing more than a 'harmless joke'.[26] Given the numerous reports in the newspapers of violence by Europeans against Chinese, we can only conclude that most other cases of this kind were either not brought to trial or dealt with in the lower courts.

In the regime of intimidation that prevailed in early Hong Kong, cases of violence by Chinese against Europeans, at least within the colony itself, were rare. Of the nine Chinese defendants in our survey tried for the murder or manslaughter of Europeans, eight were found guilty: three were hanged, three were sentenced to death recorded and one received life transportation; the eighth, a pregnant woman who had allegedly assisted her husband in the murder of an American traveller in 1854, had her death sentence commuted to life transportation and was pardoned just under a year after conviction. None of these defendants appears to have had a fair trial. The authorities offered large rewards to informants and deployed all the police resources at their disposal to capture the suspects, despatching gunboats to seize three of them from Chinese territory. The trials were rushed, the court ignored important questions of jurisdiction and evidence, and legal counsel was provided to only one defendant. The single defendant to be acquitted, an old man tried with one other on very dubious evidence for the murder of the government auctioneer during the panic of early 1857, was, on his acquittal, dragged back to gaol through the streets, chained to the convicted murderer.[27]

Other contrasts reveal themselves in the handling of lesser offences. William Wallace and John Bradley pleaded guilty in July 1855 to plundering the captain's cabin on the ship on which they worked and to throwing overboard the sextant and ship's papers. The Chief Justice sentenced them each to two years' imprisonment and told them they were lucky that the acting Attorney General (W.T. Bridges) had prosecuted them on an indictment for simple larceny rather than larceny on board a ship, which would have earned them transportation for ten years.[28] Immediately after this case came the trial of the servant Choi Aluk, who pleaded guilty to stealing a watch from his master, an English publican.[29] The Chief Justice sentenced him to seven years' transportation. When, in January 1855, William Clark and Thomas Sinclair were convicted of armed robbery at a Chinese house in the west end of the colony, the *China Mail* observed that this was the first time that the court had tried Europeans for robbery, but added that 'it is believed that such and worse robberies have been frequently perpetrated, especially afloat'. In sentencing them to three years' imprisonment with hard labour, the acting Chief Justice, Paul Sterling, remarked that 'circumstances prevented his passing sentence of transportation, which the crime well merited'.[30] The usual sentence for Chinese defendants convicted of armed robbery was transportation for at least fifteen years.

Sterling was referring to the impossibility of finding destinations for European transports. This placed the colonial government in a peculiar dilemma. On the one hand, temperate destinations were no longer available to civilian transports, and officials considered it inhumane to transport Europeans to the tropical colonies deemed acceptable for Chinese convicts. On the other hand, incarceration in the unsanitary gaol of semi-tropical Hong Kong was an injustice to prisoners awarded what was considered in England to be a more lenient sentence than prolonged imprisonment. Of the fourteen Europeans in our survey sentenced to transportation none was actually transported: one died in prison; one (the American, Luscombe) escaped and was never recaptured; and eight were pardoned. These pardons, like the more expensive rations, greater trust and spacious rooms extended to European prisoners, were a quite admirable application of mercy to men who were usually outside the pale of respectable colonial society and sometimes sentenced more harshly than they would have been at home. The same consideration was not extended to Chinese prisoners. At least thirty-two Chinese prisoners in the survey *did* receive pardons but in most cases the executive granted these pardons because it considered the convictions to be unsafe. If the highly critical accounts of trials in the newspapers are reliable, the number of Chinese defendants convicted on doubtful grounds was far higher than this.

The problem with witnesses

One of the greatest difficulties for the early Supreme Court was the unreliability of many Chinese prosecution witnesses. Witnesses would often vanish during the weeks that elapsed between committal by the magistrate and trial in the Supreme Court. They were vague about details and tended to exaggerate evidence in order to 'make a strong case'. They frequently withdrew evidence they had previously given in the magistrate's court. The court could rarely be entirely sure that a prosecution had not been brought out of malice. More than 100 out of the 380 recorded defences in the survey contained counter-charges of false accusations: while juries usually dismissed what the Chief Justice called 'this stereotyped defence', some of them must have been valid.[31] European observers usually put these problems down to the inability of the oaths on which English trials relied to bind the 'carnal conscience' of the heathen Chinese.[32] But the reasons perhaps derived more from the incompleteness of British rule, the tensions within the inchoate Chinese communities, and the confusing procedures and assumptions of the court. Informal networks of power tangled with the English legal system with complex results. Those who 'understood English customs' or had connections with the colonial authorities frequently used threats of prosecution to extort money from the ignorant.[33] Disputes over unpaid bills or access to resources often escalated into accusations of robbery. Pirate and Triad groups had ample resources to manipulate witnesses with little fear of detection by the authorities. The breakdown of attempts by elders, compradors or other prominent figures to resolve conflicts sometimes resulted in unfathomable prosecutions in the Supreme Court. A case of this kind in December 1850 so baffled the court that it was compelled to acquit the defendant Chung Ayee of assault. The explanation, according to the *China Mail*, was 'simply as follows':

> In the beginning of October last, a brass gun was stolen from someone in Shek-pai-wan, and as information was given to the European Police Constable there that it was in the possession of the present prosecutor, he sent several lucongs [or Chinese policemen], among whom was the prisoner, to Sow-ke-wan, to search the premises. This the prosecutors refused to permit, and the consequence was that they had a fight, and were all taken before the Tepo, where they were advised to arrange the matter quietly. This was ultimately done by the prosecutor agreeing to pay the sum of 59 taels for the gun, which he had sold, the elders of his village becoming securities for the amount; but next day, he altered his mind, and came with a petition to the Magistrate, on learning which, the prisoner brought in a counter-petition, and was apprehended and charged with assaulting the prosecutors. The jury however found him *not guilty*.[34]

The working of Hong Kong's early criminal justice system encouraged these processes. Prosecutions were easy to bring. With the exception of the occasional perjury charge, complainants had no fear of punishment by the authorities if their accusations failed, as they had under the Chinese system. Even if the defendant was finally acquitted, the spell in prison between committal and trial, which was often two months or longer, was sometimes enough to teach him a lesson. During the lapse between committal and trial witnesses often changed their minds. The authorities attributed this to bribery or intimidation, which was undoubtedly often the case.[35] Leong Ahoan, an old man whose house at West Point was burgled in January 1856, refused to heed warnings made by the friends of two of the defendants committed for trial to:

> make his testimony as mild as possible, so as to get them only a slight punishment, as 6 months, or a year of imprisonment with hard labour; but that if he so spoke...as to cause them to be transported they would settle his business...meaning murder him'.[36]

The two defendants were found guilty and sentenced to ten years' transportation. A few days after the trial, Leong and his wife were beaten with stones on the beach near their house: Leong died and his wife was badly wounded. Other cases suggest that complainants and defendants often came to terms before the main trial. Reporting on a failed piracy prosecution heard on the same day as Leong Ahoan's case, the *China Mail* noted that before the magistrate the complainants:

> swore positively to the Prisoners, but at the trial they professed not to know them, and the jury found them Not guilty. This case had apparently been 'settled out of Court', as both witnesses and prisoners left the Court in company.[37]

Within the trial, the complexities of the proceedings, the frequent badgering by interpreters or defence counsel, and the exacting requirements involved in matching vague evidence to strictly drawn indictments often caused cases to collapse. The greatest problem for the prosecution was the simple non-attendance of witnesses. Prosecutions against at least eighty-five defendants in the survey and against thirty-four (about a quarter) of the defendants in 1848 alone had to be abandoned for this reason.

The predicament of Chinese defendants

While, at least until the reforms of the early 1850s, prosecutions could not go ahead without witnesses, the doubts and contradictions surrounding evidence did not often work in favour of the defendant. Increasingly, juries convicted on thin and often merely circumstantial evidence. The minor cases of highway robbery that led to the conviction of at least fifty defendants in our survey illustrate the problem. The trivial nature of many of these offences, which usually amounted to the taking, with or without violence, of clothes and cash, hardly merited the severe sentences of transportation that were usually handed down: some were clearly no more than private disputes that had got out of hand. Frequently the prosecution evidence rested merely on the unsupported complaint of the victim. Attempts by the defendants to exculpate themselves counted for little.[38] By the mid-1850s, jury indifference to inadequate prosecution evidence produced miscarriages of justice that were glaringly obvious. In December 1855 Foong Achow was tried for attempting to extort $10 from a boatwoman under threat of carrying off her children. Foong was indicted on a charge of robbery. During one of Chief Justice Hulme's extended illnesses, the case was among those tried by a commission, of dubious legality, made up of the acting Attorney General, the Colonial Secretary and the Commander of British Forces. The prosecution evidence contained multiple contradictions and broke down when the acting public prosecutor attempted to prevent a policeman from giving testimony that appeared to exculpate the prisoner. Foong's defence was that he had sold netting to the boat people for $10 and on returning to exchange one of the dollars, which was a counterfeit, he was apprehended. The commission's summing up, by the acting Attorney General, W.T. Bridges, was so prejudiced against the prisoner that it seemed 'more like a pleading than a charge'. Foong was found guilty and sentenced to fifteen years' transportation, which he avoided by hanging himself in the gaol. The *China Mail* asked whether the prosecution evidence would have been 'held sufficient to convict a European, and what weight would have been given to it had it been tendered for the defence instead of the conviction of a Chinaman'.[39]

The quality of justice did not improve when Hulme returned to the bench a few months later. On New Year's night 1856 a gang of about forty armed men attacked the bazaar at East Point, raided a silversmith's shop, and killed one of the Indian policemen employed by Jardine, Matheson & Co. during their escape.[40] Over the next few days the police rounded up suspects from the area and eight local residents were committed for trial in the March sessions. The main prosecution witnesses in the trial were Ching Ahing, the silversmith whose shop was attacked, and his neighbour. The defendants brought forward numerous witnesses to support alibis, vouch for their respectability, and demonstrate that the evidence had been given by the silversmith out of malice. Seven were found guilty and sentenced to death, with a recommendation to mercy for one of them, who had been defended by a barrister.[41] Placards went up in the town accusing Ching Ahing of having extorted money out of his neighbours in return for not accusing them of the crime.[42] Tam Achoy, one of the leaders of the Chinese community, and the missionary James Legge petitioned Governor Bowring about the case. Bowring then used his Executive Council to conduct what amounted to a retrial of the whole case. He commissioned Legge to investigate the alibi of one of the prisoners, which turned out to be correct, and learned that even Ching Ahing now admitted that not all the prisoners had been involved in the crime. Two of the prisoners were eventually pardoned; the remainder had their death sentences commuted to life transportation.[43]

The helplessness of defendants increased in proportion to the gravity of the charge. Barristers were available only to those few who could afford them and were not always effective. At least two cases indicate that defendants were prevented in gaol from writing to friends and family for support.[44] Even if the defendant was able to produce witnesses, the mystifying procedures of an English court, the incomplete interpretation, and the hostility of judge and juries all counted against the defendant. The predicament was nowhere more difficult than in piracy prosecutions, which involved more than a quarter of the defendants in the survey, produced a conviction rate of about 72 per cent, and resulted in transportation for at least fifteen years for most of those convicted. The atrocity of many of these offences is not at issue here. The problem is the manner in which the Court so readily discarded principles of English law in order to secure convictions. The breakdown of authority in southern China in the 1850s gave rise to massive predatory pirate fleets which frequently obstructed trade along the China coast and blockaded the harbour of Hong Kong itself.

The imperative need to produce results was an invasion into the courtroom of the same undiscriminating policy that allowed naval expeditions to burn and sink whole pirate fleets along with their hostages, women and children included.[45] The colonial government needed deterrent examples, particularly since Hong Kong was believed to be the headquarters of pirates, and because of the growing tendency of pirates to attack European or British-registered vessels.

Defendants in such cases faced four disabilities. First, it was usually impossible for them to secure defence witnesses in cases that often took place hundreds of miles away from the colony. Second, many spoke dialects that were incomprehensible to court interpreters. Third, the practice among pirates of taking hostages and prisoners and using them as forced labour made it likely that some defendants were not pirates at all or had committed crimes under duress. Like the countercharge of malicious prosecution, the unsupported defence of duress or mistaken identity made no impression on the court. Fourthly, colonial experts on piracy advised that the crew of any Chinese merchant or fishing vessel would resort to piracy if the opportunity presented itself: the guilt of an individual became less important than the assumption that Chinese seafarers were as a class prone to crime.[46]

The survey supplies many examples of probable mistaken identity in prosecutions for piracy, but none is more disquieting than the case of Wong Awah, sentenced to death for piracy and murder in January 1857. No newspaper reports of this case survive: the colony was in a state of intense panic following an attempt to poison the entire European community in January, and the newspapers were busy with other matters. Our main source is a petition from Wong, forwarded after his sentencing to the Governor-in-Council by two Europeans, both convinced that a miscarriage of justice had taken place and supported by the newly appointed Protector of Chinese, Daniel Caldwell. Wong was from Haifeng, a county a hundred miles to the east of Hong Kong. Ignorant of the Chinese dialects used by interpreters in the Court, Wong had been unaware of most of what had happened during the trial. No counsel had been supplied to him. Nor had anyone advised him to arrange witnesses to testify on his behalf.[47]

In his statement Wong recounts how he was a sailor on board a trading junk that had been attacked by pirates on its return journey from Hong Kong to Haifeng in October 1856. Wounded during the attack, Wong, with his crewmates, was taken on board the pirate ship and forced to work for the pirates. In early December the pirates attacked a junk from Fujian, killing two of its crew. After the fighting was over they brought Wong up from below deck to transfer the plundered cargo. Wong addressed some of the junk's crew in his own dialect and told them that he was not one of the pirates. A month later, Wong, now sick from his wounds, was abandoned on Lingding Island and taken by a passing fishing boat to Hong Kong, where he arrived on 16 January. He then received help from a countryman and did some business on his behalf at a firm known as the Hong-thai-hong. Later in the month he met one of the crew of the same

Fujian junk that had been plundered in early December: the crew member charged him with piracy and handed him over to the police. Wong's trial in the Supreme Court took place on 29 and 30 January. 'On the first day when I was tried', his statement records,

> four witnesses were brought against me, and I was charged with piracy. The next day there were six witnesses and I was accused of murder. I protested against these charges, and requested the interpreter to make known my wish to call the members of the Hong-thai-hong as witnesses to my character, but this was not granted to me and I was told that the Judge had already decided my case.[48]

Having read the Chief Justice's notes of the trial, and seeing no reason to exercise mercy, the Governor-in-Council confirmed the sentence of death. Wong was hanged in the grounds of the gaol early in the morning of 19 February 1857.[49]

Reforms to the criminal justice system

Twelve years' experience of the Supreme Court and a colonial panic probably made it easy for hardened juries to convict men such as Wong Awah. Reforms by the colonial government made it even easier. Most of them were implemented in the ten years covered by the survey during the course of a vigorous public debate on the sad state of justice in the colony. The colony's newspapers seized on the miscarriages of justice that had taken place in the Supreme Court, attacked the technicalities that allowed many clearly guilty criminals to get off, and lamented the poor state of law and order, which the incompetence of the police and the low conviction rates of the Supreme Court were encouraging.[50] They contrasted the poor functioning of Hong Kong's criminal justice system with the simple, summary administration of justice in China and urged modifications to the over-refined English system to suit 'the habits and characters of an insubordinate and semi-barbarous people'. The liberties of the Chinese in Hong Kong, argued one correspondent in 1849, 'are too extended; they find themselves here, too suddenly emancipated – they will require time, and contact with Europeans, to enable them to handle such dangerous weapons with safety'.[51]

The government responded to these concerns with radical reforms intended both to restrict the use of the Supreme Court and to make convictions more easy to secure. These reforms included changes in judicial procedures, an increasing reliance on the lower courts and intrusive policing, and a tendency to hand over difficult cases to the Chinese authorities. Inevitably, the reforms undermined the principles of justice that had been imported along with English law and further criminalized the colony's Chinese population. The result was a transformation of the colony's criminal justice system that retained the institutions of English law but radically modified the way in which they were used.

Ordinance No. 1 of 1849 expanded the powers of magistrates and Justices of Peace by allowing them to try any larceny case up to a value of $50, as well as a variety of other cases normally tried by jury. It also extended their powers of sentencing from three to six months' imprisonment, besides the Chinese punishments allowed by earlier legislation. The number of defendants committed for trial in the Supreme Court declined by more than half within a year (from 167 to 77). A committal rate to the Supreme and Admiralty courts of 20 per cent in 1847 and more than 15 per cent in 1848 gradually settled to around 2 per cent or less by the 1860s and beyond. This process predates a slower, more limited trend towards greater summary justice in England.[52] In Hong Kong it facilitated a higher rate of conviction because the rules of evidence in the magistrates' courts were so lax that defence arguments were often ignored.[53] It also reduced the amount of tampering with witnesses that took place so easily between committal and trial. Although conviction was more certain, defendants benefited also from being relieved of the long wait in prison between committal and trial and from milder sentences.

Within the Supreme Court, four sets of measures loosened the restrictions on evidence and convictions. Several ordinances, some of them modelled on English legislation but most going much further, relaxed the strict rules surrounding indictments so that vagueness about property ownership or names of victims need not be an obstacle to conviction.[54] More radically, Ordinance No. 1 of 1851 allowed written depositions taken at the committal stage to be read as evidence during the main trial in the many cases where the witnesses had absconded. Widely condemned at the time as a breach of the fundamental right of a defendant to an open trial and to cross-examine his accusers, this measure was resisted by juries for a few months, and for longer in cases involving European defendants.[55] English law allowed the use of depositions only in the most extreme cases, such as the death of the witness. A third, arguably more important, measure was the abolition in September 1851 of the requirement that jury verdicts should be unanimous.[56] The measure now allowed conviction on the findings of only four out of six jurors, though capital cases still required unanimity. This naturally enabled juries to convict more quickly: a majority verdict became even easier in 1858 with the decision to increase the number of jurors to seven.[57] Majority verdicts were not normally acceptable in England until 1967.[58] The measures in 1851, combined with the contraction in 1852 of notices of trial, more frequent criminal sessions, and a reduction in the size of the jury panel in 1854, all indicate a desire for quicker trials with less time wasted on scruples and fewer demands made on the services of jurors.[59]

The fourth issue, that of Chinese oaths and the question of perjury, was dealt with more gradually. In the December sessions of 1851 a juror challenged the form of Chinese oath used in the court since 1844 (the burning of strips of yellow paper inscribed with imprecations, taken from the practice in Singapore) and asked whether a Chinese could be convicted of perjury if, as was widely believed, the oath was invalid and in fact laughed at by most Chinese witnesses.

In the debate that followed other jurors declared themselves unwilling to convict a Chinese in future cases of perjury unless a better method of swearing Chinese in could be devised. The sessions collapsed, with more than half of the defendants left untried.[60] The advice of both Caldwell and an 'intelligent Chinese' was sought: both confirmed the prevalent European belief that Chinese, having no conception of an afterlife, were incapable of taking binding oaths.[61] No action, however, was taken until 1856, when Attorney General Anstey proposed that oaths for heathen witnesses be replaced with a severe warning about the penalties attached to telling lies in court. Anstey intended to go even further by making it perjury for an unsworn heathen witness to give false testimony even on issues not material to the case.[62] After objections from the Law Officers in London that such a measure was 'illegal' and 'repugnant to reason and justice', this was disallowed.[63] The removal, however, of the Chinese oath, laughable though it may have been, was a symbolic confirmation of the low value placed by the court on Chinese evidence, just as the warning about punishments reminded juries to expect to hear lies from Chinese witnesses.

An alternative to trying defendants in the Supreme Court was to hand them over to the Chinese authorities. Article 9 of the Sino-British Supplementary Treaty of 1843 allowed for the rendition from Hong Kong of fugitive Chinese criminals from the mainland. The practice of handing over criminals went far beyond this provision. Summary deportation of vagrants and 'suspicious characters' had always been a part of the colony's informal immigration controls: such deportees were reported to have to buy their freedom from the Chinese officials at Kowloon to whom they were delivered.[64] Recognizing that juries would not convict under Davis's draconian anti-Triad legislation, the colonial government also deported Triad society members found in the colony to a more uncertain fate at the hands of Chinese officials.[65] Pirates and sea-robbers, whose depredations crossed international boundaries, fell into a special category. As early as 1844, Davis handed over for summary execution by the Chinese authorities the notorious Chintae and several other pirates alleged to have robbed a British army treasure boat near Stanley because 'there would be no sufficient evidence according to the technicalities of English law to condemn him on the opening of the Supreme Court'.[66] The practice of delivering to the Chinese authorities hundreds of pirates caught by British expeditions became a matter of routine. Chinese officials were reported to be waiting at some Supreme Court trials to apprehend defendants acquitted of piracy.[67] Governor Bonham formalized the rendition procedure by an ordinance of 1850, which vested considerable discretion in the hands of the governor and went far beyond usual rendition agreements.[68] Condemned by some observers, the measure was welcomed by the *Hong Kong Register*, which called it 'giving justice a second chance' and recommended that every Chinese defendant acquitted by the Supreme Court should be presented to the Chinese authorities in such a way.[69]

CHRISTOPHER MUNN

No governor made greater use of deportation and rendition than the liberal-minded Sir John Bowring, who, during the emergency of early 1857 committed two acts that earned him the censure of the home government and condemnation by the *Friend of China* as 'the greatest monster on the face of the earth'.[70] In January, using powers under a new ordinance, he ordered the deportation to Hainan of 121 Chinese minor offenders from the overcrowded gaol and another forty-six Chinese seized on the streets and unable to give satisfactory accounts of themselves.[71] In February, only a few days after the execution of Wong Awah, he decided to bypass the Supreme Court entirely by handing to the Chinese authorities at Kowloon seventy-three men captured by the Royal Navy and charged with the murder of ten of their hostages almost within the boundaries of Hong Kong harbour.[72] Defending himself against a charge from the Colonial Office that in doing so he had flouted 'one of the most important purposes for which the Supreme Court at Hong Kong is established', Bowring pointed to the defective administration of justice in cases of piracy, the difficulties of interpretation, and the practical and political problems that the possible hanging of so many men might present.[73] The seventy-three men, he argued, spoke at least three different dialects among themselves: they were

> to be tried by a Judge and a Jury and prosecuted by an Attorney General who understood no Chinese dialect whatsoever and who had the facts conveyed to them by other Chinese who could not make themselves understood to all the prisoners but required still further interpretations for their own information.[74]

The question of what to do with pirates was considered again in the 1860s, when, after guarantees had been secured from the Chinese authorities that torture would not be used against suspects, the Hong Kong government adopted a formal policy of handing over to the Chinese authorities suspects in piracy cases not involving British ships.[75]

Complementing these judicial and jurisdictional reforms were the numerous policing measures adopted to control the Chinese population. These included the curfew and light and pass regulations, the registration of Chinese inhabitants, considerable increases in police ratios, and the regulation of certain workers, particularly those, such as prostitutes and street coolies, who came into frequent contact with Europeans or their property. The operation of these schemes still awaits a thorough study.[76] From the very earliest years of the colony, governors experimented with successive curfew and registration measures, some of them based on Chinese practices and many of them ineffective. Intensification of these provisions came with Bowring's war measures of 1857 and 1858, enacted to defend a beleaguered European population: these included a short-lived registration scheme modelled on the *baojia* system and an incorporation of the hitherto informal (and technically illegal) system of curfews by proclamation into an ordinance that was to become the basis of the colony's euphemistically termed 'light and pass' system.[77] Such measures were augmented by the registration of chair bearers and cargo boatmen in the early 1860s, and were deepened by a series of policies adopted by Governor MacDonnell in the mid-1860s.[78]

MacDonnell described his policies as 'a social revolution of our relations towards the Chinese population'.[79] He sought to extend surveillance of the Chinese population, to clear the swollen prisons, and to intimidate prospective criminals with a regime of swift justice and corporal punishment. His watchword was 'self-preservation' and his policies explicitly accepted that it was a mistake to attempt to govern the Chinese population with English laws. Those who thought it possible to 'govern the Saxon race of Kent and the Chinese on the same principles' were, he pointed out, mistaken:[80]

> The criminal population does not consist of our own countrymen with all the claims which the latter have on our sympathy and patience, nor even in nine cases out of ten does it consist of residents under the British flag, but simply of the refuse population of the opposite provinces, and piratical banditti, who hang about the town and harbor, kidnapping and robbing when a chance presents itself.[81]

MacDonnell reintroduced the registration of Chinese households abandoned by Bowring in the late 1850s, adding to it provisions for collective responsibility for certain offences and special arrangements for the Chinese servants of Europeans.[82] He extended, for the first time, effective control over Chinese vessels in the harbour.[83] He deepened Bowring's legislation of 1857 for regulating prostitution and attempted a further scheme to license and regulate gambling establishments with the aim of improving police surveillance.[84] Under his government the ratio of police to population became one of the highest in the British Empire; it was augmented by a force of semi-official Chinese detectives managed by Daniel Caldwell, now rehabilitated after his corruption scandal a few years earlier.[85] When the leaders of the Chinese community petitioned to complain that the new policing measures were too severe, MacDonnell replied that they 'should know better than to speak of any Law here as "obstructive" and "oppressive" '.

> You yourselves must have seen that great pains are taken to administer the Law with strict Justice, and that, if it were not for Chinese Thieves, Pirates, and other bad characters, this Government would not have the expense of such a numerous Police, and such extensive Prisons. Fifty Police would suffice to keep the European Population in order.[86]

With the support of a European community more hardened in its racism, and aided by a co-operative judiciary, the government proceeded in the mid-1860s to reorganize justice at the higher levels. Hangings increased and commutations of death sentences decreased. For the first time, public flogging, long the staple of the Magistracy, featured as a punishment in the Supreme Court. The flogging legislation, modelled on an English act of 1861 rather than on Chinese practices and usually applied in cases of robbery with violence, allowed up to three public floggings of up to 50 strokes each to be added to any sentence of imprisonment.[87] In 1865, when the ordinance was first used, 48 of the 200 prisoners convicted by the Supreme Court shared between them nearly 5,000 strokes of the lash, ranging from 20 to 300 strokes per person. When, in April 1866, the acting Chief Justice, Henry Ball, applied the legislation to a European criminal, the colonial community erupted in outrage and petitioned for a pardon. The tendency of English justice to put all men on the same level, the petition argued, was healthy enough in England but had no application to Hong Kong, where a 'small body of exiles' governed 'a large native population by the force in a great measure of our prestige'.

> No impression of Divine justice worked out against all alike would enter into the mind of any Chinaman who might stand by and see this man flogged. It would not be in his Asiatic nature to respect us for being just. He would respect us far more for being strong enough to be unjust towards him.[88]

There is no record of whether a pardon was granted to the prisoner in question, a Polish ex-soldier named John Thompson convicted of using chloroform to stupefy and rob a Chinese woman who happened to be under the protection of several respectable Europeans.[89] It appears, however, to have been the last time the Supreme Court awarded a sentence of flogging to a European, even though it continued to award floggings to Chinese.

A measure that could only be applied to Chinese convicts was MacDonnell's branding and deportation scheme, applied illegally between 1866 and 1870 and then incorporated into legislation in 1872. Under the scheme, convicted felons in the gaol could petition the Governor to be tattooed or branded with an arrow on the left ear lobe and deported to China on the condition that if they returned they would be publicly flogged and sent back to complete their gaol terms. About 60 prisoners were released under this scheme in 1866 and many more came forward the following year.[90] In his despatches to the Colonial Office, MacDonnell stressed that the scheme was entirely voluntary and suggested that the branding would incur no stigma in China, where it merely proved that the bearer had 'infringed the laws of the "barbarians"'.[91] An investigation in 1870, however, during MacDonnell's absence from the colony, revealed that one prisoner had been branded and 'liberated' on a conditional pardon of this kind only one day before the expiration of a sentence of one month's imprisonment for being a 'suspicious character'. The report also estimated that many other Chinese had been branded and deported simply for having been unable to find security to remain in the colony.[92]

MacDonnell believed that his measures were effective in reducing crime in the colony. Referring to statistics that were later found to have been spurious, he reported that crime had declined by about 20 per cent between 1868 and 1869. 'I am not aware', he bragged, 'that the criminal statistics of any British Colony have ever shewn so remarkable a decrease of crime in the same period'.[93] When, in the early 1870s, the Colonial Office ordered an end to the system of regulated gambling and the suspension of branding and deportation, crime figures and the prison population shot up.[94] The branding and deportation scheme was quickly legalized and embodied in Ordinance No. 4 of 1872, which remained on the statute books until the liberal Governor Hennessy removed the branding part in 1881. Hennessy was horrified by the excessive flogging and atrocious treatment of Chinese prisoners he found in Hong Kong. His attempts to reform the system collided with an entrenched and unassailable racism among the European community and largely failed. Even the Colonial Office, which had once protected the colony from some of the more barbaric measures proposed by earlier governors, told him that Hong Kong had always been regarded as a special case and he should not interfere with well-established practices.[95]

It is curious that, in discussing MacDonnell's 'social revolution', Hong Kong's most respected colonial historian, G.B. Endacott, should emphasize vague new policies of inclusion and non-discrimination and the appearance, for the first time, in the Royal Instructions of a prohibition against new legislation that penalized only non-Europeans.[96] In fact, MacDonnell sought and received special permission from the Colonial Office to ignore this prohibition when enacting and implementing his discriminatory laws.[97] It is true that a part of MacDonnell's 'social revolution' consisted of recognizing and supporting Chinese élite organizations. The Victoria Registration Ordinance of 1866 allowed Chinese communities to form neighbourhood police forces. Proceeds from the gambling revenue went towards the construction of the Tung Wah Hospital, which was to become the centre of Chinese power in Hong Kong for the succeeding two or three decades. These measures formed the basis of a new policy of systematic co-operation with the Chinese élites, which replaced the old practice of selective collaboration. But, as Elizabeth Sinn and Jung-fang Tsai have shown, this was a complex and by no means linear process.[98] The greater willingness of the colonial government to co-opt an increasingly powerful Chinese bourgeoisie was balanced by an equally systematic policy of controlling the labouring masses, the 'coolie class' of men and women who made up most of the colony's population.

Conclusion

How much justice was done in the colony during this period? 'The comfort, is' reflected Bowring in February 1858, 'that in no part of China is there *so much* Justice or *so little* venality as here and we do far better than would be expected with the instruments at our Command'.[99] There was really not very much comfort in this. Ye Mingchen, Governor-General of the neighbouring provinces (and a prisoner of war on board *H.M.S. Inflexible* in Hong Kong harbour as Bowring wrote these words) reportedly boasted to his captors 'with a coarse laugh' that he had sentenced to death at least 100,000 people.[100] Bowring, more than any other governor, could claim that wealthy and respectable Chinese were now flocking to the colony to escape the disorders on the mainland and live under the protection of English law. But the assumptions that Bowring so frequently made about the impartiality of English law and the survival of justice in the colony during the trying years of the late 1850s are not borne out by investigation. Given the weak instruments at their command and the troubled state of the region at this time, it is hardly surprising that officials should fail to create the model of good government and equal justice that many had envisaged for the colony. The imperative of protecting European lives and property distorted the colony's criminal justice system into one that gave little consideration to the liberties of the ordinary Chinese people who came before the courts. The language, procedures and assumptions of the English courts systematically disabled Chinese defendants. The belief that Chinese people had been brutalized by their own society gave rise to dual standards of sensibility that demanded heavy punishments and intrusive control for the Chinese but urged consideration and leniency towards Europeans.

A radical reorganization of Hong Kong's criminal justice system, taking place between the late 1840s and mid-1850s, accommodated these attitudes and needs. Trial by jury, the centre-piece of English justice, was, after the reforms of the 1850s, reserved for only a tiny minority of criminal cases, while the remainder were dealt with by the Magistracy or by the Chinese authorities. A mesh of regulatory legislation, consolidated by the mid-1860s, and intended to keep the Chinese labouring masses under control, greatly increased the Magistracy's caseload: most of this relied on what Governor Davis, in his commendation of Chinese law, described as 'preventive justice', which amounted to creating new crimes in order to prevent larger crimes from taking place. By the 1890s, 99.5 per cent of all criminal cases were being decided in the Magistracy, not so much by a system of justice, but by what amounted to a peremptory regime of discipline and punishment. Richer, more 'respectable' Chinese received exemption from some of the system's harsher provisions. A variety of passes could, for example, be obtained to enable their Chinese holders to be on the streets after curfew, on the condition that they carried lanterns: nearly 19,000 quarterly passes were issued for this purpose in 1891.[101] Increasingly, Chinese community leaders identified themselves with colonial views about crime and punishment: some, such as Ng Choy and Ho Kai, recommended English justice as a model for reform in China. For the great majority of the Chinese population, however, English justice in Hong Kong meant intrusive policing, racial and class discrimination, and periodic campaigns of repression.

The repressive measures persisted long after the wars and crises that provoked them were over. The curfew continued until nearly the end of the nineteenth century. Flogging remained a standard punishment until well into the twentieth century. Registration, now in the form of universal identity cards, is still necessary to distinguish the included from the excluded: its absence warrants intrusive police searches, lengthy prison sentences and deportation. Only in the last few decades of British rule did the colonial government shake the habit of resorting to emergency legislation whenever some particularly difficult crisis confronted it.[102] No one, however, would seriously suggest that the abuses and injustices that plagued the early criminal justice system have survived to the present. For once, the claims made for the 'rule of law', so prominent a part of late colonial and post-colonial rhetoric in Hong Kong, carry some conviction. The statutes have now been translated into Chinese. Defendants have recently been given the right to request that their trial be conducted entirely in Chinese, rather than have to experience it at second-hand through interpreters. Juries, although made up of only a small English-speaking fraction of the population and used in a tiny proportion of cases, have survived in Hong Kong while in many other ex-colonies they have been abolished as impractical: for better or worse, the Basic Law guarantees their continued existence.[103] Legal aid has for some years been available to defendants unable to pay for their own counsel. Any perusal of the court pages or visit to a District Court will show, with some exceptions, that justice in the colony is administered impartially and with respect for the rights of defendants. These are, however, recent achievements. The history of criminal justice in Hong Kong during the sluggish century that separates the reforms discussed in this chapter and the reforms of the last few decades remains largely unstudied.

Three conclusions suggest themselves. First, the paradigm of 'non-intervention' or 'indirect rule', so often used to characterize the relations between government and Chinese inhabitants in Hong Kong and usually applied specifically to the early decades of colonial rule, appears to be inappropriate.[104] An intensively policed community whose members were forbidden to walk the streets without a pass after nightfall and statistically stood a one in ten chance in any given year of appearing before an English magistrate can hardly be described as lightly governed. Historians have now begun to explore the workings of a Chinese community that the colonial texts have so readily dismissed as irrelevant or lawless and obstructive. A parallel re-examination of the relationships between that community and the colonial government is now needed to complement these studies. The colonial histories may have had more to say about government and colonial élite than about anything else, but that does not mean that they have said it all. More spadework, using the abundant primary sources now available, is necessary to allow us to question, supplement, modify and, if necessary, reject their bland assumptions.

Second, in our questioning of the colonial interpretation we should be careful not to assume that Hong Kong's early history can only be explained in terms of unrelieved colonial oppression. We need to locate exactly where the oppression took place, how far it was restrained by ideological or practical limitations, foiled by resistance or evasion, and tempered by collaboration or co-operation. This is not an easy task. Apart from scattered petitions and placards, few independent sources exist for this early period outside the massive colonial archive of official correspondence, newspapers and personal accounts. It is, however, possible to subvert the confident colonial narrative by gathering from this archive the fragmented references to the lives of ordinary people and reassembling them in new patterns that more accurately reflect the choices and experiences of those at the receiving end of colonial rule. Carl Smith, in his pioneering work on the early communities of Hong Kong, has shown how fruitful this approach can be in his reconstructions of relationships and neighbourhoods from diverse and seemingly unpromising colonial sources.[105] A reassessment of the machinery of early colonial rule that deploys such methodology to measure and challenge the claims and assumptions of colonial rulers would be highly productive.

Third, a part of this reassessment must allow for the centrality of the criminal justice system, at all levels, as an instrument of colonial government and as an arena in which the preoccupations and contradictions of colonial rule vividly reveal themselves. This Chapter has attempted to show that English justice in early Hong Kong, even at its highest levels, was not the neutral, beneficent institution that some historians have assumed it to be: rather, it was a rickety, unpredictable contraption that failed to deliver justice, systematically handicapped Chinese defendants, and required extensive tinkering before it could begin to offer the security demanded by colonists for themselves and their property. I have suggested that notions of a higher, impartial 'rule of law' do not go very far towards helping us understand this deeply segregated society, in which a colonial government routinely circumvented the courts, enacted discriminatory legislation, and introduced sweeping changes to the judicial system to meet the exigencies of the moment. A critical and extensive study of the history of the institutions of criminal justice in colonial Hong Kong is now needed. The starting point for this study should be the varied experience of the hundreds of thousands of people who have appeared before the colony's courts, and not the complacent myths about equal laws and impartial justice that have so seduced colonial historians.

NOTES

1 Great Britain, Public Record Office, *Colonial Office Records*, CO 129, Dispatches from the Governor of Hong Kong, CO 129/75, Thomas Chisholm Anstey, campaigning against corruption in Hong Kong at a public meeting in Newcastle, *Newcastle Chronicle*, 25 June 1859, p. 228.
2 CO 129/4, Davis to Stanley, 21 December 1843, p. 278.
3 *Hongkong Register*, 4 January 1848, p. 3.
4 CO 129/55, Bowring to Labouchere, 24 April 1856, p. 182.
5 Eitel, E.J., *Europe in China: The History of Hong Kong from the Beginning to the Year 1882*, London, Luzac & Co., 1895, pp. 229–33; G.B. Endacott, *A History of Hong Kong*, Hong Kong, Oxford University Press, 1964, pp. 62–3, 71; and *A Biographical Sketch-Book of Early Hong Kong*, Singapore, Eastern Universities Press, 1962, pp. 66–71; Frank Welsh, *A History of Hong Kong*, London, HarperCollins, 1993, pp. 165–6.

6 J.W. Norton-Kyshe, *The History of the Laws and Courts of Hong Kong, Tracing Consular Jurisdiction in China and Japan, and including Parliamentary Debates, and the Rise, Progress, and Successive Changes in the Various Public Institutions of the Colony from the Earliest Period to the Present Time* (1898), 2 vols, Hong Kong, Vetch & Lee, 1971, vol. 1, p. ix.

7 See for example, the discussion of the Supreme Court in Yu Shengwu and Liu Cunkuan (eds), *Shijiu shiji de Xianggang* (Nineteenth-Century Hong Kong), Hong Kong, Qilin shuye, 1994, pp. 184–9.

8 CO 129/116, MacDonnell to Carnarvon, 23 November 1866, pp. 107–9.

9 For the early Indian experience, see J. Fisch, *Cheap Lives and Dear Limbs: The British Transformation of the Bengal Criminal Law 1769–1817*, Wiesbaden, Steiner, 1983. For the confused and hesitant introduction of English law into Singapore, see A. Boon Leong Phang, *The Development of Singapore Law*, Singapore, Butterworths, 1990, pp. 34–7. For a comparison between the more flexible importation of English law into Ceylon and the rigidity of Hong Kong's courts, see Anton Cooray, 'Asian customary laws through Western eyes: a comparison of Sri Lankan and Hong Kong colonial experience', in Loius A. Knafla and Susan W.S. Binnie (eds), *Law, Society, and the State: Essays in Modern Legal History*, Toronto, Ont., University of Toronto Press, 1995.

10 The negotiations are summarized in G.B. Endacott, *Government and People in Hong Kong 1841–1962: A Constitutional History*, Hong Kong, Hong Kong University Press, 1964, pp. 27–35.

11 Great Britain, Public Record Office, *Foreign Office Records*, FO 17, China Correspondence, FO 17/100, Davis to Aberdeen, 25 July 1845, p. 195.

12 Ordinance No. 15 of 1844, section 3; Ordinance No. 6 of 1845, section 4; and Ordinance No. 2 of 1846, section 3.

13 Ordinance No. 15 of 1844, section 92; and Ordinance No. 8 of 1845, section 1.

14 Ordinance No. 8 of 1845, section 2. The practice in India, in cases in which a native person was tried by jury, was to allow half the jury to be composed of Indians. When, during an early trial in Hong Kong, a native of India claimed this right, the court turned him down. When the first Chinese juror, Wong Shing, appeared on the draft Hong Kong jury list in 1858, the Legislative Council took a vote on whether his name should remain. The Council narrowly approved Wong's inclusion, but the Chief Justice was one of the members who voted against it. CO 129/12, Davis to Stanley, 16 July 1845, p. 312; CO 131, Minutes of Executive Council meetings and administrative reports, CO 131/4, Legislative Council minutes, 24 February 1858, pp. 454–5.

15 At the beginning of the trial of Captain Charles Pennington in October 1853 for the manslaughter of a black ship's cook, the juror Venancio Gutierres 'on being called objected to serve on so important a case, as he did not know English sufficiently – the objection was allowed'. Gutierres had, in a previous session, sat on a jury that had tried 12 Chinese defendants (seven on capital charges) and found eight of them guilty, *China Mail*, 29 July 1852, p. 123; Hong Kong Government, *Hongkong Register*, 11 October 1853, p. 163.

16 For a sympathetic assessment of late Qing justice see E. Alabaster, *Notes and Commentaries on Chinese Criminal Law*, London, Luzac & Co., 1899.

17 Sybille van der Sprenkel, *Legal Institutions in Manchu China: A Sociological Analysis*, London, University of London Press, 1962, chs 7 and 8.

18 Two defendants, in two separate and abandoned sodomy trials, cannot be identified.

19 Ordinance No. 10 of 1858; CO 129/68, Bowring to Stanley, 16 July 1858, pp. 123–4.

20 Davis believed that the comforts provided in the gaol tempted labourers 'to commit small crimes for the sake of being imprisoned', CO 129/23, Davis to Grey, 26 February 1848, p. 188.

21 Hulme strongly objected to the commutation of the death sentence against the nine pirates, arguing that it would send out the message 'that there was one law for avenging the murder of a Chinaman and another law for avenging the murder of an Englishman, whilst it is obviously of the first importance that the Chinese as well as other Foreigners should be fully impressed with the belief that Justice as administered under the Law of England is impartial and evenhanded', CO 129/41, Hulme to Grey, 8 July 1852, p. 211.

22 For a discussion of this theme in eighteenth-century English justice see Douglas Hay, 'Property, authority and the criminal law', in Douglas Hay *et al.*, *Albion's Fatal Tree: Crime and Society in Eighteenth-Century England*, Harmondsworth, Penguin Books, 1977.

23 CO 129/41, quoted by Hulme in Hulme to Grey, 8 July 1852, p. 206.

24 Hong Kong Government, *Hongkong Government Gazette*, 12 March 1859, p. 177; *China Mail*, 24 February 1859, p. 30.

25 *China Mail*, 2 October 1856, p. 158, 6 November 1856, p. 178.

26 *China Mail*, 5 November 1857, p. 179.

27 CO 129/66, Yorrick Jones Murrow to the Earl of Harrowby, 2 August 1857, p. 474.

28 *Hongkong Register*, 3 July 1855, p. 122.

29 *Hongkong Register*, 3 July 1855, p. 122; *China Mail*, 26 July 1855, p. 118.

30 *China Mail*, 1 February 1855, p. 19. Such practical difficulties rarely troubled Chief Justice Hulme.

31 The comment was made in *R. v. Lum-sing-yew*, Piracy, September 1855, *China Mail*, 11 October 1855, p. 162.

32 CO 129/58, Anstey to Mercer, 29 July 1856, p. 155.

33 *R. v. Chun-afook*, armed robbery, December 1848. *Hong Kong Register*, 19 December 1848, p. 202.

34 *China Mail*, 19 December 1850, p. 203.

35 Preamble to Ordinance No. 1 of 1851.

36 *Friend of China*, 5 March 1856, p. 75; *China Mail*, 6 March 1856, p. 39.

37 See note 36.

38 For examples, see especially *R. v. Wong-atung and Chun-assam*, December 1849; *R. v. Chung-tung-wang*, December 1850; *R. v. Lee Ah-seen and Wong Ah-see*, July 1856: *China Mail*, 20 December 1849, p. 203, 19 December 1850, p. 203, 7 March 1856, p. 127.

39 *Friend of China*, 2 January 1856, pp. 2–3; *China Mail*, 3 January 1856, p. 2.

40 *Friend of China*, 2 January 1856, p. 2.

41 *China Mail*, 6 March 1856, p. 39; CO 129/55, Bowring to Labouchere, enclosing Chief Justice Hulme's trial notes, 7 April 1856, pp. 73–101.

42 *China Mail*, 13 March 1856, p. 42.

43 CO 131/3, Executive Council minutes, 17, 22, 25 & 26 March 1856, pp. 58–9, 60–77; CO 129/55, Bowring to Labouchere, 24 April and 7 October 1856, pp. 180–3, CO 129/58, Bowring to Labouchere, pp. 258–9.

44 *R. v. Ow Aloong*, Abduction, April 1853, *Hongkong Register*, 26 April 1853, p. 66; *R. v. Tung Akow and 13 others*, Piracy, January 1855, *China Mail*, 1 February 1855, p. 19.

45 See, for example, the accounts of the Royal Navy's destruction of Shap-ng-tsai's fleet in October 1849, in which 1,700 pirates were estimated to have been killed. 'I fear,' wrote one eyewitness, 'that there were many women destroyed in the junks, unfortunate prisoners of the pirates, who had been plundering and burning the villages along the coast'. Such expeditions reaped thousands of pounds in head money for the naval personnel involved. Official communication by Commander John C. Dalrymple, 23 October 1849, *China Mail*, 1 November 1849, p. 174; Edward H. Cree, *The Cree Journals: The Voyages of Edward H. Cree, Surgeon R.N., as Related in His Private Journals, 1837–1856*, edited by Michael Levien, Exeter, Webb & Bower, 1981, p. 202.

46 CO 129/14, Cochrane to Davis, 27 January 1845, p. 124; CO 129/39, Wade's memorandum on petty piracy, 19 February 1852, p. 63.
47 CO 131/4, Petition of J.W. Johnson and R. Lechler, 7 February 1857; Executive Council Minutes, 9 February 1857, pp. 38–41.
48 CO 131/4, Statement of Wong Awah, 9 February 1857, pp. 41–4.
49 *China Mail*, 19 February 1857, p. 30.
50 The colony's three main newspapers differed considerably in their approach. Roughly speaking, the *Hongkong Register*, which was backed by Jardine, Matheson & Co., tended to be anti-Chinese and to advocate more summary forms of justice for the Chinese population. The *Friend of China* was edited by men who had well-founded grievances against the Hong Kong government and who seized on any item, especially abuses in the legal system, that might embarrass officials. The early *China Mail*, under the editorship of Andrew Shortrede, a patron of Chinese professionals such as Yung Wing and Wong Shing, condemned the judicial system for the injustices that it perpetrated and urged greater involvement by Chinese in deciding criminal cases.
51 *Hongkong Register*, 10 April 1849, p. 58.
52 For a summary of the very gradual extension of magistrates' powers in England see V.A.C. Gatrell and T.B. Hadden, 'Criminal statistics and their interpretation', in E.A. Wrigley (ed.) *Nineteenth-Century Society: Essays in the Use of Quantitative Methods for the Study of Social Data*, Cambridge, Cambridge University Press, 1972, p. 356.
53 *Friend of China*, 24 July 1847, p. 234.
54 These included Ordinances Nos 1 of 1850, 4 of 1852, 6 of 1856 and 7 of 1857.
55 Three convictions in February 1851, shortly after the enactment of the ordinance, depended on depositions (*R. v. Chung-wong-she*, False imprisonment; *R. v. Yee-aon*, Piracy; and *R. v. Yeong-assing*, Demanding money with menaces, *China Mail*, 6 March 1851, pp. 38–9). For some time after the controversy in the press, however, juries refused to convict in some prosecutions relying on depositions alone: see *R. v. Unnamed*, Piracy, *China Mail*, 15 May 1851, p. 79; *R. v. Cheong Apo*, Robbery, *Hongkong Register*, 21 October 1851, p. 166; *R. v. Joseph Schoentjes*, Aiding a soldier to desert, and *R. v. Richard Heycock and Henry W. Jackson*, Attempting to fire a ship, *Hongkong Register*, 20 April 1852, pp. 62–3.
56 Ordinance No. 4 of 1851.
57 Ordinance No. 3 of 1858.
58 For a wider discussion of the uniqueness of the Hong Kong jury see Peter Duff, Mark Findlay, Carla Howarth and Chan Tsang-fai, *Juries, a Hong Kong Perspective*, Hong Kong, Hong Kong University Press, 1992.
59 Ordinance No. 4 of 1852; Ordinance No. 4 of 1854, which reduced the jury panel from eighteen to ten. After the enactment of this ordinance, the same jury was often used to try all the cases in a single, rushed session.
60 *China Mail*, 18 December 1851, p. 202; *Friend of China*, 20 December 1851, pp. 414–15.
61 *Friend of China*, 20 December 1851, p. 415, 7 January 1852, p. 6.
62 Ordinance No. 15 of 1856.
63 Law Officers to Labouchere, 10 March 1857, CO 129/66, p. 22.
64 *Friend of China*, 22 December 1855, pp. 412–13.
65 Hong Kong, Public Record Office, HKRS 100, Correspondence received by the Chief Police Magistrate from the Colonial Secretary, 2 Feb. 1844 – 31 Dec. 1846, Shelley to Caine, 27 March 1846, p. 243.
66 CO 129/7, Davis to Aberdeen, 20 December 1844, pp. 302–3.
67 See, for example, *R. v. Long-sheihong*, Piracy, *China Mail*, 16 January 1851, p. 10.
68 Ordinance No. 2 of 1850.
69 *Hongkong Register*, 20 November 1849, pp. 186–7.

70 *Friend of China*, 25 February 1857, p. 62.
71 CO 129/62, Bowring to Labouchere, 29 January 1857, pp. 154–8; *Friend of China*, 28 January 1857, p. 31.
72 CO 129/62, Bowring to Labouchere, 28 February 1857, p. 62; *Friend of China*, 25 February 1857, p. 62.
73 CO 129/62, Labouchere to Bowring, 9 June 1857, p. 344; CO 129/63, Bowring to Labouchere, 22 July 1857, pp. 472–7.
74 CO 129/62, Bowring to Labouchere, 22 July 1857, p. 474.
75 CO 129/99, Robinson to Cardwell, 9 August 1864, pp. 332–42, CO 129/101, 27 December 1864, pp. 181–3; CO 129/109, Colonial Office to Mercer, 10 April 1865, pp. 58–63; Ordinance No. 13 of 1865; CO 129/136, MacDonnell to Granville, 20 February 1869, pp. 198–203.
76 For a survey of the legislation see, however, Peter Wesley-Smith, 'Anti-Chinese legislation in Hong Kong', in Ming K. Chan (ed.), *Precarious Balance: Hong Kong Between China and Britain, 1842–1992*, Armonk, NY, M.E. Sharpe, 1994, pp. 91–106.
77 Ordinances Nos 2 and 6 of 1857 and No. 8 of 1858.
78 Ordinances No. 15 of 1860 and No. 6 of 1863.
79 CO 129/125, MacDonnell to Buckingham, 29 October 1867, p. 104.
80 Votes and Proceedings of the Legislative Council, Hong Kong Government, *Hongkong Government Gazette*, 17 October 1868, p. 397.
81 CO 129/116, MacDonnell to Carnarvon, 23 November 1866, pp. 108–9.
82 Ordinance No. 7 of 1866.
83 Ordinance No. 6 of 1866.
84 Ordinances Nos 9 and 10 of 1867; Gambling Regulations of 1867 and 1868. Hong Kong, *Hongkong Government Gazette*, 9 February 1867, pp. 335–6, 19 September 1868, pp. 342–3.
85 CO 129/152, Report by T. Fitz Roy Rice on the state of the police, 5 October 1871, p. 298; CO 129/114, MacDonnell to Carnarvon, 27 August 1866, pp. 475–82; CO 129/114, Carnarvon to MacDonnell, 15 November 1866, pp. 490–4.
86 CO 129/115, MacDonnell's reply to an address on behalf of Chinese residents, October 1866, p. 221.
87 Ordinance No. 12 of 1865.
88 *Hongkong Daily Press*, 4 May 1866.
89 *Hongkong Daily Press*, 18 and 23 April 1866.
90 CO 129/116, MacDonnell to Carnarvon, 23 November 1866, pp. 113–14, CO 129/120, MacDonnell to Carnarvon, 14 January 1867, pp. 122–6; CO 131/5, Executive Council Minutes, 21 January 1867, pp. 289–90; Ordinance No. 4 of 1872.
91 CO 129/121, MacDonnell to Buckingham, 29 April 1867, pp. 389–90.
92 CO 129/149, May to Austin, 11 May 1870, pp. 146–50.
93 CO 129/144, MacDonnell to Granville, 12 April 1870, pp. 256–7.
94 CO 129/150, Austin to Whitfield, 6 June 1871, pp. 287–8.
95 Carnarvon to Hennessy, 3 January 1878, in *British Parliamentary Papers: China 25: Correspondence, Dispatches, Reports, Returns, Memorials and Other Papers Relating to the Affairs of Hong Kong 1862–81*, Shannon, Irish University Press, 1972, pp. 491–2. For an account of the state of justice in the late 1870s and of Hennessy's attempts at reform see Kate Lowe and Eugene McLaughlin, ' "An El Dorado of riches and a place of unpunished crime": the politics of penal reform in Hong Kong, 1877–1882', *Criminal Justice History*, 1993, vol. 14, pp. 57–89.
96 Endacott, *A History of Hong Kong*, pp. 124–5.
97 CO 131/5, Executive Council minutes, 8 September and 12 December 1866, pp. 238, 267.

98 Elizabeth Sinn, *Power and Charity: The Early History of the Tung Wah Hospital, Hong Kong*, Hong Kong, Oxford University Press, 1989; Jung-fang Tsai, *Hong Kong in Chinese History: Community and Social Unrest in the British Colony, 1842–1913*, New York, Columbia University Press, 1993.
99 CO 129/67, Bowring to Labouchere, 13 February 1858, p. 170.
100 George Wingrove Cooke, *China: Being the Times' Special Correspondence from China in the Years 1857–1858*, London, Routledge, 1858, p. 397.
101 Hong Kong Government, *Hongkong Hansard*, 14 March 1892, p. 110.
102 For a discussion of this question see Norman J. Miners, 'The use and abuse of emergency powers by the Hong Kong government', *Hong Kong Law Journal*, 1996, vol. 26, part 1, pp. 47–57.
103 For an examination of Hong Kong juries in a larger imperial perspective see Ellison Kahn, *Trial by Jury*, Hong Kong, University of Hong Kong Law Working Paper Series no. 6, 1992.
104 Endacott's description of the first two decades of colonial rule as an experiment in 'indirect rule' has become the standard interpretation of the relations between government and people in the early decades of colonial rule; Endacott, *A History of Hong Kong*, p. 124.
105 Carl T. Smith, *Chinese Christians: Elites, Middlemen, and the Church in Hong Kong*, Hong Kong, Oxford University Press, 1985; and *A Sense of History: Studies in the Social and Urban History of Hong Kong*, Hong Kong, Hong Kong Educational Publishing Co., 1995.

5

STATE BUILDING AND RURAL STABILITY

Stephen W.K. Chiu and Ho-fung Hung

Between 1899 and 1967, there appeared to be a dramatic change in the attitude towards the colonial government among rural residents in the New Territories. In 1899, the original inhabitants saw the British colonialists as barbarians, to be driven away from their native land in the New Territories.[1] By 1967, the colonial government seemed to have successfully accomplished a complete reversal in the way it was received in the New Territories, and emerged as an undisputed force of law and order and the legitimate government over all of Hong Kong.

The acceptance, and indeed active support, by the New Territories' villagers (or their prominent representatives) of British rule over Hong Kong is as puzzling as the remarkable stability which was achieved in the urban areas over the period of colonial rule when compared with other colonies. The imposition of political subjugation, in the form of imperialism and colonialism, is often sufficient cause for rebellion. Economic exploitation of the agrarian economy is also supposed to add fuel to agrarian unrest. Why did this not happen in Hong Kong?

In this Chapter, we shall take a fresh look at the 'paradox of stability' and examine the basis for the political stability in the rural areas of Hong Kong. By tackling this issue we also hope to contribute to the understanding of broader issues of colonial governance in Hong Kong and the relationship between state and society under British colonialism. We shall first review past attempts to answer the question of rural stability and pinpoint some of their shortcomings. Then we shall describe the development of colonial rule in the New Territories since the late nineteenth century. Our discussion will start with the state's evolving relationship with the original inhabitants, and move on to its relationship with the immigrant farmers since the Second World War. Then the changing contours of rural conflicts will be summarized, and a case of rural mobilization in the 1980s will be used to illustrate how changes in the political opportunities and organizational structures in the New Territories led to the intensification of rural protests.

The model of indirect rule

There is a sizeable literature addressing the paradox of stability in Hong Kong.[2] In particular, 'administrative absorption of politics' is a well-known notion explaining the phenomenon. According to King, the British rulers relied on the strategy of synarchy and methods of élite-mass integration to ensure the stability of the colony. Under the synarchical principle, members of the Chinese élite were co-opted into the administrative process of the government, either by recruiting them directly into the Executive Council, Legislative Council, Urban Council and other formal consultation channels, or by consulting them informally on specific issues. In this way, any emerging leaders in the Chinese community who were capable of mobilizing grass roots support and initiating political action against the state were co-opted to become partners of the government.[3] In a similar vein, Lau also describes the process of co-opting community leaders from the largely apolitical Chinese community as laying the foundation for Hong Kong's enduring stability.[4]

While King's and Lau's focus is on the urban area, the notion of the 'administrative absorption of politics' can easily be extended to the New Territories. Kuan and Lau found that, in the rapid urbanization of the New Territories, the government relied heavily on the traditional leaders in the rural communities to facilitate the process of compulsory purchase of land. The government offered the rural élite substantial material benefits in exchange for their co-operative attitudes towards rural development projects.[5] This co-optation of the rural élite by the colonial state found its institutional expression in the Heung Yee Kuk – rural deliberative office – and the Rural Committees, consisting of local village leaders from the villages. They were both important parts of the government's rural administration.[6]

Kuan and Lau argue that while the penetration of the colonial government was not extensive and intensive, it did create a coexistence between the formal political structure of the colonial state and the informal structure of village leadership. The informal and formal political structures were connected under a model of 'indirect rule'. The original rural leaders became the middlemen between the colonial administrative structure and the villagers. The government officials had to rely on the rural leaders to obtain information about the villages and to make sure their policies were enacted.

By the 1950s, however, with the tremendous expansion of urban population, the government began to urbanize the rural area. In doing this, the principle of indirect rule, the maintenance of the status quo in the New Territories, was violated. Hence a new kind of administrative strategy was required for rural Hong Kong, in order to 'smoothen the process of planned change'. The government's primary strategy was to support the more 'progressive' factions of the rural leadership. They called the process the 'resuscitation' of rural leadership. They felt that with the progress of modernization, rural leaders would have faded away without government intervention as communal solidarity declined. By giving some rural leaders an official status, and a role in colonial governance, their leadership role could be buttressed. In such a way, these rural leaders became a useful ally for the government in enacting its developmental policies in the New Territories. The new ruling strategy is termed 'neo-indirect rule'. On the one hand, the basic structure of indirect rule, i.e. the reliance on the rural leaders in ruling the New Territories, was not altered fundamentally; on the other hand, the ultimate goal of indirect rule had been changed, from maintaining the status quo in the New Territories to facilitating its 'modernization'.

As mentioned above, the strategy of neo-indirect rule was essentially one of 'incentive dispensation'. Between the colonial state and village leaders, the colonial state exerted influence over the village leaders by manipulating the distribution of the material benefits which flowed from the developmental process including information about the developmental plan not open to the public, and paying government compensation for compulsory land purchase. By distributing these benefits to co-operative village leaders, and restricting them for less compliant ones, the government succeeded in soliciting co-operation from most of the rural leaders towards the government's developmental plans.

Space does not allow us to develop a detailed critique of Kuan and Lau's thesis.[7] On the whole, while we recognize their contribution to our understanding of the social and political development of the New Territories, we feel there is a need to move beyond their models and postulates. In general, we find it useful to follow the leads of the recent approaches to social movements, which emphasize political opportunities and mobilizing structures.[8] We shall highlight the multifaceted penetration by the colonial state into the lives of the villagers, both before and after the Second World War. The complex relations and institutional interfaces between the state and the rural communities together constitute the distinctive structure of political opportunities that shape rural conflicts. We also think that the position of the immigrant farmers and their organizations in rural society need a deeper investigation than that done in Kuan and Lau's studies. In doing so we hope to shed new light on Kuan and Lau's assumptions of a smooth and 'frictionless' development of the New Territories under British colonialism, and the image of stagnant traditional rural villages.

The colonization of the New Territories

The so-called 'New Territories' leased to the British in 1898 constituted about three-fifths of Xin'an County under the Qing Dynasty. Like some other administrative regions in imperial China, the economy of pre-colonial Xin'an was agrarian and highly self-sufficient. It was dominated by a gentry class which based their power on control of land and markets, strong local military organizations, monopoly of land tax, as well as connections with the local government (or *ngamun*).[9] As the first group of settlers in the region, five lineage groups, the Tangs, the Haus, the Pangs, the Lius and the Mans, later became the so-called *punti* (indigenous) people, and were known as the 'five great clans'.[10]

Later, a large number of Hakka families from the north migrated into Xin'an and established their villages.

The power structure of the county was first reflected in the settlements of the different lineages. The great clans, especially the Tangs, owned most and the best of cultivated land. The Hakka people, who came after the five great clans, could only establish their villages on the hilly and infertile lands with poor water supply. The ownership of their farmland was mostly claimed by the Tangs, who appropriated a portion of their harvest as land rent. The share of land rent ranged from 40 per cent to 60 per cent, depending on the land's fertility, and was paid in kind.[11] The landlord-tenant relationship in Xin'an was characterized by a system of perpetual tenancy or the bottom-soil/top-soil system which was common in South China.[12] Under this system, landlords could only have bottom-soil rights or the rights to collect rent. They could neither expel their tenants nor increase the land rent (in terms of a proportion of the harvest). On the other hand, tenants owned top-soil rights or the right to cultivate. They had the right to stay on their farmlands perpetually or sell their rights to other villagers without notifying the landlords, as long as they paid their rent.

The southern Xin'an district was leased to the British as its 'New Territories' in 1898. Though it was only regarded as a buffer between Victoria City and China, the colonial authority was active in penetrating into this rural area. Despite the colonizers' guarantee of 'sympathy with native custom and prejudice', the construction of the colonial administration brought a 'great transformation'[13] to the agrarian communities, laying the foundation for future development in the post-war years.[14]

The first imperative of the construction of a colonial state is establishing a modicum of order/subordination to colonial power. It needs to pacify any resistance to colonization and establish 'effective occupation'. In the case of Hong Kong, the early phase of colonization was characterized by a wave of uprisings against British occupation. Under the powerful lineages and the landlords, a resistance was organized against the 'red barbarians'. The clans joined together to form local militias, and strong adults in Hakka villages were recruited by rumours and coercion.[15] The Tangs assumed the leadership of the movement, and a command centre was established in Ping Shan. The resistance force rose to a total of two thousand villagers, with canons and rifles. However, as they did not receive support from the Chinese government, their organizational and logistic problems soon gave the British regular army an overwhelming advantage.

After defeating the rebellion, the colonial authority raided their command centres in Ping Shan and Kam Tin and seized the remaining weapons. Some leaders were arrested while some fled to inland China. The first police station in the Territories was set on top of a hill overlooking the whole Ping Shan area. After they had military control of the New Territories, resistance from the landlord-gentry class prompted the British initially to adopt a ruling strategy aimed at reducing the landlord's power rather than seeking an alliance with them. It was duly reflected in the early institutionalization of colonial rule, characterized by the imposition of private landownership, and implementation of a 'rational' taxation system.

Between June 1900 and June 1903, an extensive land survey was carried out by the colonial administration. Villagers were obliged to submit their land deeds to the colonial officials and were issued with a Block Crown Lease in return. Any non-registered land would be converted into Crown Land. As mentioned before, all ownership of land in the New Territories was divided into top-soil rights and bottom-soil rights. To dismantle the great clans' power over the Hakkas, the British replaced this dual ownership of land by a unique ownership system, and granted the ownership to holders of top-soil rights exclusively. In this way, a 'land reform' was engineered by the colonizers, who deprived the great clans of most of their landholdings rented to the Hakkas.[16] After the 'reform', the tenant farmers were 'liberated' and became owner-cultivators tending their own lands. A decentralized system of landownership was instituted. We shall see later how it shaped the form of rural resistance during the period of planned development after 1950.

Nineteenth-century colonialism was, with few exceptions, largely premised upon the principle of financial self-sufficiency.[17] In the British case, it was pursued even more rigorously. In the urban area of Hong Kong, property tax and rates constituted a large portion of state revenue, since customs duties were limited, as a result of Hong Kong's free port status. In the New Territories, tax had to be imposed on land. More important, taxation had to be conducted in a more structural and predictable manner. Consequently, 'taxlordism' under the imperial state, i.e., the system by which the major clans were entrusted the task of collecting taxes on behalf of the government, was abolished, and a modern, direct taxation system was imposed after the land survey. Taxes were levied on each square of agricultural land and housing land (housing land was not taxed under imperial rule), and were collected directly from each owner of the property, rather than through the gentry. In doing this, the Tangs' privilege of extracting commission from state revenue was stripped away.[18] Unlike the imperial government, which collected taxes in kind, the colonizers collected taxes in cash. This caused the villagers to enter the cash economy and hence helped erode the self-sufficiency of agrarian communities in the New Territories.

Four District Offices were then founded in the New Territories. They performed such functions as arbitrating disputes between villagers, collecting information about the villagers' lives for the state, informing the villagers of government policies and collecting taxes.[19] When they had problems, New Territories' people, especially those from the Hakka villages, gradually got used to asking District Officers for help rather than the elders and gentry of the great clans.[20] The villagers gradually found that the District Officers were less biased towards the Tangs than the Qing magistrates.[21]

Repressed militarily, economically and politically, the great clans' efforts to resist colonial rule were thwarted.[22] The only thing they could do was to send humble petitions to the government expressing their opinions. They also tried to organize themselves into voluntary associations acceptable to the colonial state. In 1926, leaders from the great clans gathered to form the Heung Yee Kuk (HYK). New Territories people were allowed to join the Kuk, if they donated a certain sum of money to it. This made the Kuk an association of wealthy villagers which was dominated by the great clans, especially the Tangs, who still profited from their control of market towns. The Kuk adopted a constitution aimed at preventing the colonial government from misinterpreting it as a rebellious organization. This constitution confined its activities to (1) the initiation and support of local charitable work; (2) the promotion of local interests; (3) the rectification of undesirable customs and activities; and (4) the airing and redressing of local grievances.[23] From the beginning, the Kuk mainly represented the great clans' interests and actively called for reforms of the government's taxation and land policies. However, before the war, it was not a very powerful organization and its influence did not extend to the southern part of the New Territories. Lee noted that the Kuk was rarely mentioned by the District Officers in their reports.[24]

Thus, in the New Territories, the colonial state successfully replaced the pre-existing hegemony of the gentry–landlord class with its own hegemony. This laid the political and economic framework of colonial domination, leading to the post-war patterns of development and constrained resistance. In contrast to Kuan and Lau's formulation that indirect rule and minimal intervention into rural communities were maintained in the pre-war period, we argue that since the early period of colonial rule, the colonial state had in fact imposed substantial influence on rural communities and transformed their socio-economic configurations considerably.

The establishment of the consultative machinery in the New Territories

Before the Second World War, the New Territories was no more than a buffer of defence between the mainland and the city of Victoria. There were few construction works in the region, except the building of the Kowloon–Canton railway and roads for military and administrative purposes. While legal and administrative frameworks (the imposition of private landownership and the system of District Offices) for economic and political intervention by the colonial state had been laid before the War, the colonizers were not interested in utilizing these frameworks to develop the area. The *raison d'être* of the Crown Colony of Hong Kong was trade, not agrarian or primary extraction; the New Territories had no immediate economic significance to the colonial administration, although it was expected to supply some of the food for consumption in the urban area.

The situation changed in the 1950s, when the influx of immigrants and advent of industrialization in urban areas prompted the state to intervene more deeply and directly into the New Territories. First, land was appropriated extensively from the villagers for development purposes, such as building a reservoir for the urban population and providing space for new industrial or residential towns.[25] Second, agricultural production was increasingly placed under the regulation of the colonial state. While the government had not intervened and did not specifically support the industrial take-off directly owing to historical and institutional constraints, [26] it resorted to a variety of administrative means to lower the costs of labour reproduction in general.[27] One means by which they did this was by intensive intervention into both the production and trade (both domestic and international) in agricultural products to ensure a stable supply of essential foodstuffs at low prices.

The administrative apparatus was also reconstituted and new institutions were set up by the state to facilitate its increased involvement in New Territories affairs. Politically, this included the creation of Rural Committees and the forced 'reconstitution' of HYK, while economically there was the establishment of local co-operatives and a Vegetable Marketing Organization.

Though the Tangs and other great clans had declined since the nineteenth century and had been stripped of their political and economic privileges in the process of colonization, and most Hakka villages had been detached from their control, they were still wealthy and influential in rural Hong Kong. After the Second World War, a sign of their influence was their control of the HYK until the late 1950s. The conservatism of this once powerful gentry class, and its domination of the HYK, made it hostile to the colonial government and its development projects. It was only through high-handed manœuvres that the clans could be politically marginalized, and the HYK reconstituted into a compliant broker for the state.

During the Second World War, a village representative system was established under Japanese rule. The New Territories was divided into smaller sub-districts. Leaders were chosen (usually from village elders) in each sub-district to 'deal with the authorities and their own people, and to meet the potential threat to themselves arising from misdemeanours, crime and anti-Japanese activity'.[28] When the British returned after the Second World War, they inherited this Japanese system. The whole of the New Territories were divided into twenty-eight administrative areas and one Rural Committee was formed in each of them.[29] One or two village representatives were selected from each village to form the Committees.[30]

Rural Committees were the recognized mediators between agrarian communities and the government, and were also the recognized representatives of the New Territories people:

> The rural committees have as yet no statutory existence or powers, exercising only such functions as the district officer sees fit to delegate, in which some are more successful than others. Most of them, however, have already proved their usefulness not only as mouthpieces of public opinion, but also in the arbitration of local clan and family disputes, and generally as a bridge between the administration and the people.[31]

These village representatives, with their monopoly of information from the outside world, soon displaced the village elders and seized power in the lineages.[32] Naturally, the unofficial HYK's limited status of villagers-administration mediator was threatened by these committees. The Kuk quickly responded to this crisis by adopting a new constitution in April 1950, turning itself from an 'autonomous voluntary association' into a 'society of village representatives'.[33] The reformed HYK accepted as members only village representatives, serving directors and deputy executives in towns and villages. The new constitution also divided the whole New Territories into seven electoral districts, each returning a definite number of executive councillors to the Kuk. In this way, the HYK, led by the major clans, successfully increased its sphere of influence from the northern New Territories to the whole New Territories, and made itself essentially an assembly of Rural Committees. At this stage, the government could no longer afford to ignore the Kuk's opinion. The Kuk had become a more representative and stronger base of resistance against development plans and it was still under the control of the great clans.

The reconstruction of rural politics

The Tangs had had a tense relationship with the colonizers since the land and tax reforms at the turn of the century. Their hostility towards the government was not only the result of past resentment, but was fuelled by new contradictions arising from the post-war years. The expansion of the urban area brought development projects to relatively accessible areas in the New Territories, such as Tsuen Wan, Sha Tin, Tai Po and Tuen Mun, which had been at the periphery of the rural power structure. The leaders of Rural Committees in these areas enjoyed many benefits from these projects because of their cordial relationship with the colonial state.[34] They gradually emerged as a wealthy and powerful élite capable of challenging the political leadership of the great clans in the HYK. In contrast, grass roots villagers and tenants in the rapidly developing areas lost much and gained little. For them, development only meant undesirable resettlement and the destruction of their agriculturally based livelihoods. This polarized rural communities into either a pro-development (or pro-government) camp made up of Rural Committees leaders from urbanizing areas, or into an anti-development (anti-government) camp based on the alliance of the great clans and members from the rural grass roots. Due to their respective geographical distribution, they were known as the 'Tsuen Wan faction' (pro-development) and 'Yuen Long faction' (anti-development). The former was led by Ho Chuen-yiu, Chan Yat-san, and Cheung Yan-lung, while the latter was led by leaders of the Tang and Pang clans, and included Tang Tak-yuk and Tang Hoi-yip.[35] The struggle between the two camps, in addition to their alliance or conflict with the government, was the focus of the political dynamics in the HYK over the decades.

The early phase of government-led development in the 1950s met with strong resistance from the villagers. Any resumption of land or demolition of buildings easily triggered off local mobilizations. For example, when the colonial administration tried to demolish some temporary structures on a piece of Tangs' land in Yuen Long in June 1957, the clan reacted by mobilizing 2,000 villagers to demonstrate against the demolition. Violent confrontation was prevented only by a concession from the government allowing the building of permanent structures on the same spot.[36] Sometimes rural opposition was not confined to the local level. For example, construction of Tai Lam Chung Reservoir in the northwestern New Territories was the biggest project of the decade, involving the resettlement of a cluster of villages. The building of an extensive catchment system also affected the water supply for paddy fields in a large area in the vicinity. The villagers affected refused to be sacrificed under the plan; negotiations for cash compensation or land exchange broke down, and many villagers just refused to move. The construction project was delayed for years, and the issue rose to the political level when the HYK, dominated by the anti-development camp, stood decisively on the villagers' side against the project, even at a time when the faction was beginning to be challenged.[37]

Frequent protests against development projects eventually moved the colonial government to destroy the political influence of the traditional rural élite, and to reconstitute HYK into a complying institution. The opportunity to do this came in the late 1950s, when the internal struggle between the two camps intensified. From the mid-1950s onwards, the control of the HYK changed hands several times between the Yuen Long faction and the Tsuen Wan faction, due to manœuvres on both sides. Though the Yuen Long faction had always had control of the HYK, a new constitution was passed in 1955 that increased the representation of the Tsuen Wan faction. The power of the pro-development camp redoubled, and it was not surprising to find that Ho Chuen-yiu, Chairman of Tsuen Wan Rural Committee, was elected the chairman of the HYK. Power changes were often accompanied by a radically different approach to government developmental policies. For example, a general assembly on 18 May 1956 resolved that the grass roots villagers would petition the Governor if the Government refused to accept the Kuk's appeal to abandon the current land policies, restricting the private conversion of rural land use. Yet the petition was stalled by Ho, thereby nullifying a mobilization against the government.

The anti-development camp soon fought back. In an executive council meeting on 28 February 1957, the Yuen Long faction managed to revise the constitution again.[38] The new constitution would certainly have prevented the pro-development faction from holding leading positions after the election for the committee's thirteenth term of office, to be held in mid-1957. This rewriting of the constitution was regarded by observers as a '*coup d'état*'.[39] The Tsuen Wan faction reacted by secretly persuading the heads of the Rural Committees to boycott the election and gained the support of 21 out of 28 of them. The anti-development camp soon appealed directly to the rank-and-file village representatives, who formed the electoral college. Most village representatives overruled their Committee Chairmen and supported the election. This was the case, even in some of the Tsuen Wan faction's base such as Tai Po and Tuen Mun.

When the Kuk's internal struggles intensified, the District Commissioner, K.M.A. Barnett, seized the opportunity and started secret talks with the pro-development camp. A plan which was discussed was the founding of a new pro-government institution called the Council for Rural Administration so as to marginalize the anti-development camp. Then in June 1957, a letter was sent by the government to the HYK, telling it to register under the new Societies' Ordinance (Amendment) 1957 or else the Kuk would become illegal. An extraordinary meeting of the HYK's executive council was held in July to discuss the letter. The meeting was dominated by anti-government voices and decided, in a defiant mood, against registration. Available information does not allow us to ascertain whether the registration requirement was deliberately used by the colonial state against the Kuk, but it did provide the legal basis by which it could dissolve the Kuk at any time.

On the eve of the election in August, the government finally declared the Kuk illegal. According to the District Commissioner:

> The government was concerned about some recent activities under-taken by certain people in the name of the Heung Yee Kuk. In view of the development of events, the government has concluded that the Kuk has lost its value of representation and therefore should be disqualified from recognition.[40]

Chaos followed. The organization of the Council for Rural Administration was under way, demonstrations and lawsuits were initiated by the Yuen Long faction against the state under the auspices of a 'Kuk Protection Committee' headed by Cheung Tai-Wing and Tang Hoi-Yip, and lobbying by the government and the two opponent groups were frequent.[41] On 25 November, the government eventually introduced the Heung Yee Kuk Bill which was passed in the Legislative Council without discussion. Essentially the government had to be satisfied with the composition of the Kuk, before it could be recognized as the representative of rural opinion. Under the Bill, the essence of the 1955 Constitution was restored and pro-government elements were strengthened. The Justices of the Peace appointed by the Governor were assigned *ex-officio* status. The Tsuen Wan faction and their supporters registered HYK under this Ordinance on 11 December 1959, making it a statutory organization. Lying in front of the anti-government forces were two options: they could either boycott the reconstituted Kuk, and risk losing any influence over it, or join it to exert as much influence as possible. They chose the latter option. The election of councillors was held in 1960, and, not surprisingly, the pro-development faction won decisively.

From then on, the chairmanship of the Kuk has been held by leaders of the Tsuen Wan faction with few exceptions. Opposition to the government could still occasionally be heard, especially from members of the old Yuen Long faction. In particular, Tang Tak-yuk, who retained membership of the Kuk after the reorganization, and was described by the government as 'a troublemaker', formed an 'Anti New Territories Land Policy Sub-Committee' within the Kuk in 1960, to oppose the restrictions on the conversion of agricultural land to building purposes.[42] In 1962, the government also reported that there was a pro-Beijing faction within the Heung Yee Kuk, under the leadership of Kan Chung-hing (an ex-member of the pro-Beijing Society of Plantations dissolved by the government in 1959), which intended to develop friendly relations with other pro-Beijing organizations.[43] These isolated dissenting voices notwithstanding, the Kuk has been very co-operative with the state, and the District Commissioner in particular. The Kuk's councillors and the Commissioner held regular meetings exchanging views on development plans, land resumption, compensation schemes and land policies. Chan Yat-san, Chairman of HYK in the 1970s, and a member of the Tsuen Wan faction, summarized the Kuk's responsibility in a speech:

> It is the responsibility of the N.T. Heung Yee Kuk to protect the right of the N.T. people and their property. It is also its responsibility to ensure social harmony, political stability and economic prosperity in the N.T. Any councillor of the Kuk has the right to criticize the government on its mistakes and unfair measures but such criticism must be followed by constructive suggestions and a clear analysis of facts, and in the public interest.[44]

As Chun noted, after the 1950s voices of opposition to development projects were not heard in the Kuk any more. Instead, more time was now taken up by negotiations for material compensation.[45]

In this way, the colonizers successfully ruled out the danger of the HYK becoming a territory-wide base of resistance, and cleared the way for more intensive development in the New Territories. Opposition from villagers to land resumption for development was then confined to specific local areas and was prevented from spilling over into the political arena as the opposition to Tai Lam Chung reservoir had. The local élite in the Rural Committees were backed up by the colonial state and monopolized access to political power. In most cases, they became loyal supporters of the government, facilitating land resumption and preventing rural protests in exchange for 'selective interest dispensation' as described by Kuan and Lau. From the available historical evidence, however, we cannot agree with Kuan and Lau's characterization of the process, as the 'resuscitation', or 'revival', of a declining rural leadership and institution. The divisions between the two camps were not between a stubborn conservative group, waning in influence and legitimacy, and a rising modernizing group. Both groups represented concrete material interests and community bases. The government intervened steadfastly on the side of the pro-development group, which was by no means innocent 'resuscitation'. It was *realpolitik*, pure and simple.

State intervention in rural transformation

The prospects of the agrarian economy in the New Territories changed radically in the post-war years as a result of the surge in immigration. Many of the mainland Chinese refugees, who once crossed the border, chose to stay in the New Territories and rented land from Hakka or *punti* landlords to become tenant farmers. The lands which they rented were those left behind, through the outward migration of the original inhabitants.[46] These new arrivals were regarded as the 'immigrant farmers' of the New Territories and their significance was always overlooked.

If any development project posed a threat to rural livelihoods, the new immigrant farmers certainly suffered the most. They were excluded altogether from the hierarchy of rural administration and the representation system. Land resumption, for them, meant an end to their agricultural production and residence, and they usually received little or no compensation in the process. While protests from original inhabitant villagers were dealt with through the HYK–Rural Committees–village representative hierarchy, the limited instances of large-scale protest from these rural underdogs, the immigrants, was puzzling. This could perhaps be accounted for by examining state intervention into these immigrant communities through the regulation of vegetable production. State intervention not only affected the livelihood of the immigrant farmers, but also transformed the socio-economic structure of traditional villages, making the original inhabitants less reluctant to give up their land for development.

The government's post-war agricultural policy was to encourage a shift from rice to vegetable production. An Agriculture Department was founded soon after the Second World War, with the declared mission of raising the level of self-sufficiency in vegetable consumption in Hong Kong.[47] While this policy was largely economically motivated, its political background cannot be ignored.[48] Potter has listed three factors contributing to the shift to vegetable production. In addition to the influx of immigrant farmers, the colony was economically isolated from the mainland in the years after 1949, and this increased the need for the farmers of the New Territories to supply food for the expanding urban population. A third factor was the creation by the government of two marketing organizations (to be discussed later) that were designed to bring about the self-sufficiency of the colony in foodstuff production by encouraging vegetable production.[49] Of course, the colony, with scarce fertile farmland, could never achieve real self-sufficiency. The colonial state's concern was to minimize dependence on mainland China, especially in the turbulent post-war years and after the founding of the Chinese communist regime. In fact, since the early twentieth century, the rice consumed by the expanding urban population has been imported from Indo-China, Burma and Thailand.[50] However, vegetables and marine products were imported solely from China. The state's encouragement of local vegetable production was natural, if seen in this light. Eventually, the shifting of the cultivation pattern boosted the share of local vegetable production in relation to local consumption from a negligible amount in the early twentieth century to nearly 50 per cent in 1971.[51]

Government intervention into agriculture began with the establishment of a monopoly over the wholesale of vegetables. The Vegetable Marketing Organization (VMO) was formed in 1946. It was originally established under the Defence Ordinance, and later reconstituted under a VMO Ordinance in 1952. All vegetables produced in the New Territories, or imported into Hong Kong, were collected by the VMO at collecting points and then transported to the urban wholesale markets. The Ordinance gave exclusive rights to the VMO to transport vegetables in the colony.[52] The police were empowered to stop all lorries carrying vegetables without a permit issued by the VMO.

In the 1950s, an extensive network of local vegetable marketing co-operatives was also organized extensively under the supervision of the Agriculture Department. Members and non-members were allowed to submit their vegetables to these local organizations and a 10 per cent commission was charged to cover the operating costs. Low interest credit and cheap fertilizers (nightsoil) were the principal benefits of membership.[53] While the reception by the immigrant farmers of the co-operatives was by no means uniform, by 1962, over 76 per cent of locally grown vegetables were handled through the co-operatives in contrast with 35 per cent in 1952.[54] Gradually the co-operatives superseded the 'middlemen' involved in marketing and the marketing associations organized by the farmers themselves.[55] In addition, the VMO kept the imports from China at a low level so that a large demand for local products was created, thus inducing the expansion of vegetable production.

After the establishment of the marketing co-operatives, a variety of co-operatives and voluntary associations were organized one after the other under state sponsorship. They included Pig-Raising Societies, Irrigation Societies, Co-operative Building Societies, Fish Pond Societies and Credit and Consumers' Societies, etc. in each village. These societies performed a wide range of functions: sums of money were granted to farmers after a bad harvest; loans were given for the establishment of new vegetable farms or pig-raising enterprises; manpower was organized for small-scale public works from building footpaths to improving irrigation systems; experts were sent to the villages to introduce new technology in agricultural production and provide technical advice; production competitions were held to stimulate agricultural production; money was raised for collective entertainment within the immigrant communities.

Co-operatives supervised by the Agriculture and Fisheries Department became an important part of the immigrant farmers' lives, who were excluded from the village life of the original inhabitants.[56] After the Second World War, a network of state-sponsored secondary organizations permeated the rural communities. It is therefore incorrect to say that the New Territories had become devoid of social ties as a result of socio-economic modernization. Communal solidarity might have been weakened, but the important point is that the spate of state-sponsored modern associations had attempted to fill the gaps in village life.

The organizations played a certain role in the formation of group identities among the immigrant farmers. Based on fieldwork in So Kun Wat in the western New Territories, Chau and Lau observed that the election of the directors of the local co-operative was an important event in the lives of the farming community. Although the co-operative was not exclusive to immigrant farmers, it facilitated the emergence of immigrant leaders and the formation of a farming association representing immigrants' interests in the village. As most of the co-operative's functions depended on the resources from the Agriculture and Fisheries Department, the leaders usually maintained a good relationship with the government. Their legitimacy was more or less derived from this cordial relationship.

Vegetable growers, including immigrant farmers and Hakka villagers still engaged in agriculture, depended greatly on the co-operative for both financial support and technical assistance. The So Kun Wat co-operative expanded quickly and by the early 1960s, its membership had grown to 210, the majority of whom were immigrant tenants. Needless to say, the leadership was always controlled by the immigrants. The co-operative soon became a quasi-representative organization of the immigrant communities and facilitated the emergence of local leaders among them. In 1970, leaders of the tenant community formed a So Kun Wat Farming Association whose membership was restricted to immigrants. The heads of the Association had a good relationship with the officials of the Agriculture Department and District Offices.

The services offered by the Association included transportation of farmers' products to the vegetable market, operation of a clinic and a kindergarten, organization of tours to foreign cities, provision of relief to the families of deceased members, arrangement of funeral services, and assisting the Agriculture and Fisheries Department in the administration of government services. The Association was a spin-off of the co-operative, and its function was nearly identical to it. The only meaningful difference was that the Association was an exclusive organization for the immigrants and was therefore their legitimate representative in dealing with the Hakka original inhabitants as well as outsiders. It played an important role in enhancing the collective identity and solidarity among the immigrant tenant farmers.

In the mid-1970s, the government began to appropriate large amounts of land from So Kun Wat for the construction of a highway. Negotiations between the District Officers and the village representatives began. The immigrant farmers responded to the resumption by urging leaders of the Farming Association to hold similar negotiations with the government, as they had a good relationship with the officials. The Association did so and its status of representing immigrants' opinion was recognized by the District Office. Bargaining between the Association and District Office channelled the voices of tenant farmers along administrative channels acceptable to, and manageable by, the rulers. Its involvement had prevented an outbreak of resistance and confrontation among the powerless farmers.

Chau and Lau explained the peaceful resolution of the issue in terms of 'administrative absorption of conflicts' as the government kept the situation under control by granting official representative status to the would-be-confrontational leaders of the Association.[57] Nevertheless, what they failed to appreciate is that the government had not just extended the administrative absorption process to the immigrant communities by recognizing the immigrant leaders. It had in fact been actively and deliberately involved in the creation of these leaders and moulded the organizational structure among the immigrant communities over the decades by its agricultural policy and sponsorship of local organizations.

Counter-mobilization by left-wing organizations

Of course, government-sponsored societies were not the only, and always dominant, form of communal identity and solidarity. Migdal suggests that farming communities in contemporary Third World countries usually represent a contested terrain for different socio-political forces, such as the nation state, left-wing parties and local interest groups, both inside and outside the communities.[58] As mentioned above, even the HYK had pro-Beijing elements during the 1960s. Aijmer also finds that in Shatin the immigrant farmers did not form a homogeneous community.[59] Different logic of communal identity and solidarity criss-crossed each other. Farmers of the same geographic origins tended to cluster together and joined landsman associations whose membership was restricted to their place of origin. More important, Beijing-affiliated left-wing organizations and organizations with pro-Taiwan inclinations existed in the rural areas as well. Farmers were often divided in their political affiliations between either the Nationalists or the Communists. Aijmer discovered that it was common for immigrant farmers to hold a hostile attitude towards the colonial authority, which was thought to take too much from, but give too little to, the Chinese. Their perceived legitimacy of the colonial state was weak, making left-wing activists influential.[60] The latter were so dominant that the leadership of the local marketing co-operative studied by Aijmer was monopolized by the leftists. In 1967, farmers were also mobilized by the co-operative leaders to protest against the authority's act of suppressing urban demonstrations.

Though the existence of left-wing influence was not restricted to Shatin, it is wrong to exaggerate its influence.[61] Rural leftists were scattered amongst a few communities and were not much organized into a unified political force (except in 1967). They might be strong in some specific localities, but there were a negligible number of them in the New Territories as a whole. After the Second

World War, a Hong Kong and Kowloon Chinese Farming and Agriculture Association was founded under strong left-wing leadership which had intervened in local disputes between immigrant tenants and indigenous landowners. However, the organization was short-lived and dissolved by the colonial regime in the early 1950s because of the political dangers it posed.[62]

The overall weakness of left-wing forces, and the dominance of government influence in the rural immigrant communities were exposed in 1967, when a series of strikes and riots broke out in the urban area. To prevent urban unrest from spreading into the New Territories, People Security Units were formed by local residents in all twenty-eight administrative districts with the encouragement of the District Office. Local co-operatives and Rural Committees formed the backbone of these Units. The first principle of these Security Units was to 'support the government's effort in keeping local public order'.[63] They organized small teams to patrol each area. Suspected leftists were apprehended and taken to the police. The Units also conveyed the government's message and 'correct information' back to the grass roots communities through village representatives and co-operatives.

When the leftists called for a boycott of food markets and China briefly stopped sending agricultural products into the colony, the authority reacted by rallying direct support from vegetable and pig-raising co-operatives. The response of the co-operatives was gratifying from the government's point of view. Their leaders sent letters to the authority promising they would try their best to guarantee food supply.[64] The co-operatives redoubled their efforts in collecting agricultural products from their members. They seemed to have successfully forestalled the leftists' efforts to disrupt vegetable supplies in the New Territories. The head of the Agriculture Department summoned the co-operatives' heads again on 28 July 1967 to express his gratitude:

> Today I invite you all to express my special thanks. In the recent turbu-
> lent months, you have given great support to the government personally
> or on behalf of agricultural organizations. And you all have protected
> the peace and stability by concrete actions. It is a fact that Hong Kong
> is not capable of producing all the necessary foodstuffs. But it is also a
> fact that Hong Kong has to maintain a strong and reliable agricultural
> sector to cope with any challenges from incidents when importation of
> outside products is disrupted. I am very much confident in you, the ag-
> ricultural leaders, to continue shouldering this important responsibility
> in the coming days.[65]

It is beyond doubt that the agricultural co-operatives were important stabilizing forces among the tenants' communities in the eyes of the colonial state. It was only after 1967 that left-wing forces began to step up with their mobilizational efforts in the New Territories. By intervening actively in disputes arising from land resumption, they gradually built up a following in the villages. With a rapidly declining agricultural population, the membership of the left-wing Graziers Union nonetheless rose dramatically from 3,639 in 1971 to 22,655 in 1981.[66]

Strauch's study of Fung Yuen also reveals how government-sponsored organizations faced keen competition from the Graziers Union in forging a collective identity among the tenant farmers:

> The leftist union has a farmers' branch which actively recruits in Fung Yuen; membership in 1978 was growing, and included a few of the villagers who farm their own land. The union sponsored a 'six villages association', encompassing several neighboring villages as well as Fung Yuen, which organizes three communal banquets each year. Most of the informal leaders among the Fung Yuen tenant farmers are union members.[67]

As intensive development was coming to Tai Po, landlords in Fung Yuen in anticipation of a big increase in the value of their land were eager to get rid of the tenant farmers on it. The landlords' attempts were resisted by the tenants who were helped by the leftist union. In 1978, a land dispute between a landlord and a tenant triggered off a village-wide conflict between the original inhabitants and immigrant community. The Graziers Union duly stepped in on behalf of the immigrant tenant and confronted the landlord, who was supported by the other landlords cum original inhabitants.

Strauch noted that in spite of the land reform at the turn of the century which had legally terminated the perpetual tenancy system, the system persisted into the 1960s and 1970s in everyday tenant–landlord relations. Even the immigrant farmers would have expected the landowners to behave 'morally'. Expelling tenants from land for larger profits, and for reasons other than self-use, was regarded as immoral. It was also thought that the immigrant tenants had the right to transfer their land to another tenant without notifying the landlords, on condition that rents continued to be paid. This 'moral economy' restricted the Hakka villagers from selling the land to outsiders for non-agricultural use, and making big money. However, in the 1970s, the landlords' increasing desire to sell the land and the tenants' reluctance to move heightened tensions between the two parties. What the case of Fung Yuen illustrates is that after the 1960s, whenever conflicts broke out between immigrant farmers and the indigenous landlords, the leftist union was always on the side of the farmers.

Socio-economic changes and their significance

Meanwhile, the socio-economic structure of Hakka and *punti* villages was remoulded by a 'vegetable revolution'.[68] The 'land reform' in the early twentieth century had led to a decentralized landownership based on rice cultivation. Many Hakka villagers had benefited from the reform and were transformed from tenant farmers into owner–cultivators farming their own lands. Over 70 per cent of land was used for rice growing and the rest planted with sweet potatoes, groundnuts, sugar cane and different kinds of fruit.[69] Vegetable gardening was nearly non-existent. Rice cultivation buttressed the wealth of the Tang clans, as they occupied the best land for growing rice. This was especially so when international trade enabled the Yuen Long cultivators (the Tangs) to export their products to the United States, and import cheaper, low quality rice from Southeast Asia for their own consumption. The cash surplus generated by these transactions was considerable. In contrast, the cultivators (the Hakkas) of the marginal lands in the New Territories such as those in Tsuen Wan and Shatin, needed all the rice they could grow for their own self-subsistence. When cash became more and more important with the imposition of taxes payable in cash and expansion of the cash economy in general, the Hakka villagers could only make ends meet by sending their sons to work in the city or as seamen.

The situation changed abruptly after the immigrants began to rent land for vegetable gardening after the Second World War. With the strong technical, financial and organizational support from the colonial state, vegetable growing became a profitable business and attracted increasing numbers of immigrants and villagers alike.[70] According to Aijmer, the income of vegetable farmers was always higher than many waged labourers in the city.[71] It is consistent with his finding that in Hong Kong, many of the tenant vegetable farmers were originally urban workers (or even petty merchants), and in the early post-war period, economic difficulties in the urban area sometimes drove urban dwellers to settle in the New Territories.[72]

The wider the 'vegetable revolution' spread, the more the great clans lost the advantage gained from the fact that they occupied the best lands. Vegetable growing is intensive and requires a large amount of fertilizers. A small piece of land can produce a high yield and is manageable within a farming household. Also, soil fertility does not matter very much as the soil can easily be improved to suit the crops grown. The most important thing is that vegetable farms yielded five to eight crops a year in contrast to the one to two crops per year yielded by paddy fields.[73] This meant that the hilly, infertile lands of the Hakka villagers were equally capable of yielding good crops and generating quick returns. The spread of cash crops displaced any remnants of the New Territories' self-subsistence economy. The poor villagers in Shatin, Sheung Shui, Tsuen Wan etc. welcomed the immigrant farmers and rented land to them. The wealth of these villages quickly surpassed that of the great clans. Baker observed a paradoxical phenomenon in the New Territories that the poorer and weaker the village had been in pre-colonial times, the sooner the modern and beautiful village house made its appearance first.[74]

By the 1960s, land used for rice cultivation had decreased to a very small proportion of cultivable land. Census data in 1961 shows 66 per cent of vegetable farmers renting land from others.[75] The rest of them were mostly Hakka villagers, who converted their rice fields into vegetable gardens. But the adoption of vegetable growing was by no means popular among the original inhabitants. Traditionally, vegetable growers had had a very low status in relation to rice farmers who looked down upon the former.[76] So the New Territories' villagers, especially the *punti*, were reluctant to switch to vegetable farming. In fact, renting farmlands to immigrant tenants gave them a steady stream of income, sometimes exceeding what they received from rice cultivation themselves. It also enabled them to free themselves from the land and enter into other businesses.[77]

The percentage of tenant farmers increased after the census of 1961, as more original inhabitants left the agricultural economy and the ranks of owner-cultivators. According to Chun, 'land is a place for shelter' in the pre-colonial New Territories. Yet after the 'great transformation' and the intrusion of a market economy, the value of land was reduced to its exchange value and the perception became 'land is a commodity'. He argues that this transformation was mainly brought about by the establishment of private ownership of land in the early twentieth century.[78] In fact, the process lasted a much longer time, and continued into the 'vegetable revolution' in the 1950s and 1960s. In any case, a 'modern' land economy was constituted by the active intervention of the colonial state, and resumption of land no longer meant an end to the livelihood of the petty landlords, who had detached themselves from agricultural production after the drastic socio-economic change in the early post-war decades.

In a nutshell, post-war state intervention into agricultural production had two political consequences. First, by building pro-government organizations, it prevented the communities of immigrant tenants from becoming breeding grounds for opposition forces, such as left-wing organizations. The state successfully established an important role in the lives of immigrant communities through direct administrative action and establishment of voluntary associations. Second, the conversion of Hakka villagers from owner-cultivators into small landlords, as a result of the 'vegetable revolution', has made them less resistant to land resumption with compensation. Kuan and Lau's analysis misses the significance of both of these processes, as they consider the state to be largely alien to, and outside of, rural communities. In fact, the post-war development of the New Territories testifies to the enduring significance of the colonial state's actions in shaping the socio-economic modernization of the New Territories. The colonial state was at the core of the 'modernization' process, which was far from an autonomous and natural process, by actively preventing conflicts and resistance from getting out of hand.

Conclusion

Conflicts between development-inclined landlords and their farming tenants were not confined to Fung Yuen. Many students of rural communities in Hong Kong have documented such conflicts in various localities. For example, Aijmer tells us that though the Hakka landlords in Sha Tin tried to reconstitute the landlord–tenant relationship by introducing short-term contracts, the farmers still thought they had unlimited cultivation rights and refused to move when the villagers tried to force them to do so.[79] These disputes often ended in bloody fighting. Potter also found that when indigenous villagers tried to reclaim their land from the immigrants, they would face a request for compensation which was always so high that they had to abandon their plan to sell the land.[80]

Landlord–tenant conflicts in the New Territories might be violent, but they rarely spread beyond village borders to become large-scale mobilization. The disputes were always individualized and localized, and at most, extended to the village level (as the case of Fung Yuen illustrates). This helped to smooth the land resumption process by the colonial government, for many of the potentially rebellious immigrant tenants had already been expelled by their landlords before the authorities came to take over the land. As discussed above, after a long process of commercialization in the New Territories, and changes in the landownership system, the landlords, though probably not the tenants, were quite receptive to the idea of land as a commodity. They were quite ready to part with their land and reap the profits. In fact, there were numerous individual attempts to prepare for selling the land to the government, ranging from evicting tenants, replacing permanent with fixed-term tenancy, to leaving land fallow rather than renting it out. In other words, the contradiction between planned development and farmers' interests was diffused by the individual contradictions between landowners and tenant farmers. This was only possible because of the decentralized landownership system in the New Territories, which had evolved during the colonization process, and was facilitated by the socio-economic transformation in the post-war years.

The uneven pace of development and the process of land resumption in the New Territories also contributed to preventing the potentially rebellious immigrant communities from becoming a real territory-wide threat to colonial rule. The demolition of rural squatters' settlements built by immigrants and collective resumption of agricultural land occurred frequently in the New Territories, but land resumption always affected only a few villages at any one time. In the words of James Hayes, a former senior civil servant responsible for the New Territories affairs:

> The government's development programmes had proceeded in phases, and the old settlements were usually tackled one by one, making it harder to organize, and justify, any intervention.[81]

That is why at most times there were only sporadic protests in different localities, which rarely spilled over to cause instability in the colony as a whole, no matter how violent these local protests were.

When the structure of political opportunity began to change, however, the contours of rural conflict and stability also began to change. After the 1970s, the organizational and political structures of the New Territories were radically transformed, leading to an outbreak of large-scale, organized conflicts, in addition to the sporadic and small-scale ones already mentioned. One such example is the protest against the Waste Disposal Ordinance since the mid-1980s.[82] Farmers' organizations formed an alliance against the Ordinance when it was first drafted in 1985. The alliance took an uncompromising stand and threatened with violent action if it was passed. Over the years, rallies were organized and clashes with the police were common. When the bill went through its final reading in April 1994, farmers set free trucks of chicken and ducks onto the busy roads of Central to paralyze the traffic.

In the last analysis, rural stability was only relative in Hong Kong. The New Territories was far from conflict-free, and there were many instances of localized and transient conflicts. The content of such conflicts concerned mainly with concrete material interests rather than moral values. The rural élite were basically co-opted by the government. By co-operating with the state's developmental plans, they were rewarded with handsome benefits from either selling their land or receiving compensation for it. The HYK acted as their mouthpiece in soliciting more favourable terms of compensation. Nevertheless, we can observe the effects of a 'moral economy' on the side of the immigrant farmers. The moral expectation of the tenants that the landowners would protect their tenancy rights was always at odds with the latter's desire for compensation and profits from selling the land. But the tenant–landlord conflicts are mostly individualized and rarely spread into region-wide or colony-wide conflicts. The organizations among immigrant farmers were not sufficiently strong and co-ordinated to sustain large-scale opposition to the government's planned development. Left-wing organizations had always had an urban bias, and it was only after the setback in 1967 that organizational efforts began to be devoted to the rural area.

We agree with Kuan and Lau that a nexus of interest dispensation in which benefits exchanged for co-operation did exist between the government and the rural élite, but we think the latter's role, exemplified by the HYK, in the maintenance of rural stability has been misunderstood. On the one hand, the presence of the colonial state in the countryside was far from minimal before the planned development of the 1970s. It had, in fact, exerted a continuous influence on the society and economy of the rural communities. Such interactions between the villagers and the government had in fact 'normalized' and 'modernized' the relationship between them. First, the colonial state did not merely 'resuscitate' the rural leaders, it actually 'reconstituted' them into brokers acting in the interests of the colonial state, according to its own political designs. The 'coup' in the late 1950s purged the HYK of the anti-development group, and put it firmly under the control of the pro-development camp. Second, after the transformation, the colonial state no longer appeared to the villagers as an alien force threatening their traditional customs, but as the institutional complex that had been shaping their lives for decades. By enforcing law and order in the countryside, maintaining a modern landholding system, and regulating the agrarian economy, the state, to some extent, also acquired a sense of legitimacy in the minds of the villagers. When conflicts between the state and the indigenous villagers appeared, they were often not primordial ones with intense moral overtones, but a result of material conflicts which could be more or less pacified through negotiation and compensation. Third, within rural immigrant communities, the state pre-empted the growth of oppositional organizations among the tenant farmers by sponsoring the growth of a spate of voluntary associations and co-operatives in their communities, and maintaining cordial relationships with their leaders.

More important, rather than merely being bought off, and not causing any trouble themselves, the rural élite had a more active role to play than Kuan and Lau have acknowledged. The rural communities, even the immigrant ones, had some social and organizational bases for mobilization. We have documented the emergence of both spontaneous protests among villagers and protests supported by left-wing organizations. It was often through the manœuvres or repression of the co-opted élite that the resistance became dissipated.

As Skocpol's study of the great agrarian revolutions points out, the outbreak of social revolutions was only possible under a stringent set of conditions.[83] Unlike the modernization approach, she does not see traditional protests as a natural reaction to the modernization and commercialization of the countryside. If this is the case, the question that guides Kuan and Lau's study is somewhat misplaced. Instead of asking why there had been few conflicts during planned development and modernization, we really need to ask: 'during planned development and modernization, what were the possible sources, if any, of conflicts and in what forms did these conflicts manifest themselves?' This Chapter hopes to contribute, albeit in a preliminary way, to our understanding of this second question. For a more comprehensive and adequate answer, of course, we must await further historical and empirical studies of the New Territories.[84] Another area which requires further examination is how the overall political economy of development in Hong Kong shaped the development in the New Territories. As mentioned earlier, prior to the planned development of the 1970s, the rural areas do not figure significantly in the overall economic development of Hong Kong. Industrialization since the 1950s, for example, did not entail a large-scale transfer of labour and capital from the countryside to the urban area. Because of space constraints there are bound to be gaps in our analysis, and this short Chapter only aims at stimulating further research in the area. In any case, our essay suggests that state actions and its institutionalized presence, together with the relationship and shifting alliances between the state and the rural élite, and the social differentiation within the villages, must be taken as the core of such inquiries.

NOTES

1 R.G. Groves, 'Militia, market and lineage: Chinese resistance to the occupation of Hong Kong's New Territories in 1899', *Journal of Hong Kong Branch of Royal Asiatic Society*, 1969, vol. 9, pp. 31–64.

2 For an example, see Lau Siu-kai, *Society and Politics in Hong Kong*, Hong Kong, Chinese University Press, 1982.

3 Ambrose Y.C. King, 'Administrative absorption of politics in Hong Kong: emphasis on the grass roots level', in Ambrose Y.C. King and Rance P.L. Lee (eds), *Social Life and Development in Hong Kong*, Hong Kong, Chinese University Press, 1981, pp. 127–46.

4 See Lau, *Society and Politics*.

5 Kuan Hsin-chi and Lau Siu-kai, 'Development and the resuscitation of rural leadership in Hong Kong: the case of neo-indirect rule', CUHK Social Research Centre occasional paper no. 81, Hong Kong, Chinese University of Hong Kong, 1979; and 'Planned development and political adaptability in rural areas', in King and Lee, *Social Life and Development*, pp. 169–93.

6 Norman J. Miners, *The Government and Politics of Hong Kong*, Hong Kong, Oxford University Press, 1975.

7 See Stephen W.K. Chiu and Ho-fung Hung, 'Engineering rural stability: the New Territories in Hong Kong's colonial history', paper presented at the International Workshop on 'Hong Kong: Society, Polity and Economy under Colonial Rule', Sinological Institute, Leiden University, the Netherlands, 22–24 August 1996.

8 See Craig J. Jenkins and Bert Klandermans (eds), *The Politics of Social Protest*, London, UCL Press, 1995.

9 There is controversy over what the power base of the Chinese gentry class was. Some argue that there were basically office holders of the imperial administration who used their status to buy land and increased their wealth (e.g. Chung-li Chang, *The Chinese Gentry: Studies on Their Role in Nineteenth Century Chinese Society*, Seattle, WA, University of Washington Press, 1955). Some think the gentry class were at first wealthy landlords, and that their holding of office was the result of their wealth (e.g. Philip A. Kuhn, *Rebellion and Its Enemies in Late Imperial China: Militarization and Social Structure, 1796–1864*, Cambridge, MA, Harvard University Press, 1970). Nevertheless, we are more inclined towards Skocpol's view that the Chinese gentry class, in fact based their power both on their wealth, control of lands and political/military backup from the Imperial state; Theda Skocpol, *States and Social Revolutions: A Comparative Analysis of France, Russia, and China*, New York, Cambridge University Press, 1979, pp. 71–2.

10 By 'lineage' and 'clan', we adopt Baker's definition. Lineage means a group of people having a kinship relationship and living together to form a village, while clan is a cluster of lineages. See Hugh D.R. Baker, 'The five great clans of the New Territories', *Journal of Hong Kong Branch of Royal Asiatic Society*, 1966, vol. 11, pp. 25–47.

11 Majorie Topley, 'Capital, saving and credit among indigenous rice farmers and immigrant vegetable farmers in Hong Kong's New Territories', in Raymond Firth and B.S. Yamey (eds), *Capital, Saving and Credit in Peasant Societies*, London, George Allen & Unwin Ltd, 1964, p. 163; Hong Kong Government, *Hong Kong Annual Report 1947*, p. 47.

12 For an excellent discussion of the bottom–top soil land system, see Michael Palmer, 'The surface-subsoil form of divided ownership in late imperial China: some examples from the New Territories of Hong Kong', *Modern Asian Studies*, 1987, vol. 21, pp. 1–119.

13 In the sense used by Karl Polanyi, *The Great Transformation*, Boston, MA, Beacon Press, 1957.

14 J.H.S. Lockhart, *Extracts From Papers Relating to the Extension of the Colony of Hong Kong*, Hong Kong, Hong Kong Government, 1899, p. 178; Allen J. Chun, 'The land

revolution in twentieth century rural Hong Kong', *Bulletin of the Institute of Ethnology Academia Sinica*, 1987, no. 61, pp. 1–40.

15 Groves notes that a rumour saying that all lands would be confiscated by the colonizers was spread before the British takeover, making many villagers feel that it was necessary to join the resistance. Notices were also sent by the Tangs to villages to call for support. One of them said:

> The English barbarians are about to enter our territory, and ruin will come upon our villages and hamlets. All we villagers must enthusiastically come forward to offer armed resistance and act in unison. When the drum sounds to the fight, we must all respond to the call for assistance. Should anyone hesitate to take part or hinder or obstruct our military plans he will most certainly be severely punished and no leniency will be shown. This is issued as a forewarning.
>
> (Quoted in Groves, 'Militia, market and lineage', pp. 42–3, 51ff.)

16 Chun, 'The land revolution', pp. 1–40.
17 Crawford Young, *The Colonial State in Comparative Perspective*, New Haven, CT, Yale University Press, 1994.
18 An important point to note is though the colonizers intended to ensure their revenue through land tax in the early twentieth century, they decided to freeze the land tax for nearly 70 years as a result of the strong opposition from the villagers. The state's revenue was guaranteed by a land policy restricting private conversion of agricultural land into housing land. Under that policy, the government could take over agricultural land from the villagers at a low price, convert it into housing land, and then sell it on as housing land at a high price. In this way, the state could earn a lot from the development of the rural areas which started in the 1920s.
19 For a description of the work of District Officers, see James Hayes, *Friends and Teachers: Hong Kong and Its People 1953–87*, Hong Kong, Hong Kong University Press, 1996.
20 Maurice Freedman, 'Shifts of power in the Hong Kong New Territories', *Journal of Asian and African Studies*, 1966, no. 1, pp. 3–12.
21 Lockhart, *Extracts From Papers Relating to the Extension of the Colony of Hong Kong*, p. 57.
22 The colonial authority passed a law forbidding the possession of arms, which made it impossible for the Tangs to organize armed resistance again.
23 Lee Ming-kwan, 'The evolution of the Heung Yee Kuk as a political institution', in David Faure *et al.* (eds), *From Village to City: Studies in the Traditional Roots of Hong Kong Society*, Hong Kong, Center of Asian Studies, 1984, p. 166.
24 As in note 23, p. 167.
25 M.R. Bristow, *Land Use Planning in Hong Kong*, Hong Kong, Oxford University Press, 1984.
26 Stephen W.K. Chiu, 'Unravelling Hong Kong's exceptionalism: the politics of laissez-faire in the industrial takeoff', *Political Power and Social Theory*, 1996, vol. 10, pp. 229–56.
27 Jonathan R. Schiffer, 'State policy and economic growth: a note on the Hong Kong model', *International Journal of Urban and Regional Research*, 1991, vol. 15, no. 2, pp. 180–96.
28 James Hayes, 'The nature of village life', in David Faure *et al.*, *From Village to City*, pp. 55–72.
29 The first Rural Committee was formed in 1947. By 1958, all twenty-eight Committees had been founded.
30 Sometimes there was violence when the rural committee leaderships were elected. Two examples were the bloody warfare between different local powers competing to

control such a committee in Cheung Chau (Changchou) and Sap Pat Heung (Sibaxian). See Hong Kong Government, District Commissioner, New Territories, *Annual Department Report 1955*, & *1961*, cited hereafter as District Commissioner.

31 District Commissioner, 1956, p. 13.

32 Sometimes the village representative and village elder were the same person, but most of the time they were not. The representative was usually a young and wealthy member of the lineage who was able to 'buy' the support of his villagers.

33 See Lee, 'The evolution of the Heung Yee Kuk', p. 171.

34 According to Kuan and Lau, the government offered a lot of resources in exchange for the rural leaders' co-operation. These resources included money, 'land exchange entitlement' in compensation for land surrendered, advance information on development plans, rights to private development, etc. Kuan and Lau, 'Development and the resuscitation of rural leadership', p. 33.

35 Great Britain, Public Record Office, *Colonial Office Records*, CO 1030, Original Correspondence, CO 1030/1333, Governor to the Secretary of State for the Colonies on 3 March 1960 on the Heung Yee Kuk.

36 See Kuan and Lau, 'Development and the resuscitation of rural leadership', p. 21.

37 District Commissioner, 1959, p. 10.

38 Now the number of councillors from each election district was proportional to the number of village representatives there instead of its population size. The *ex-officio* status of Rural Committees chairmen was also cancelled. Furthermore, the electoral college electing the councillors was no longer formed by the all twenty-eight Rural Committees chairmen, but by all of the 900 village representatives.

39 See Lee, 'The evolution of the Heung Yee Kuk', p. 173.

40 See Kuan and Lau, 'Development and the resuscitation of rural leadership', p. 24.

41 See the correspondence in CO 1030/1333, Governor to the Secretary of State for the Colonies on 3 March 1960 on the Heung Yee Kuk.

42 CO 1030/1333, extracts from Hong Kong Police Special Branch Report, pp. 18, 22.

43 CO 1030/1333, extracts from Monthly Intelligence Report, p. 31.

44 Chan Yat-san, 'The British government should keep up with the times in the administration over the New Territories', speech delivered on 17 February 1981, mimeograph.

45 See Chun, 'The land revolution in twentieth century rural Hong Kong'.

46 Góran Aijmer, 'Migrants into Hong Kong's New Territories: on the background of outsider vegetable farmers', *Ethnos*, 1973, vol. 38, pp. 57–70; and 'An enquiry into Chinese settlement patterns: the rural squatters of Hong Kong', *Man*, 1975, vol. 10, pp. 559–70; Judith Strauch, 'Middle peasants and market gardeners, the social context of the "Vegetable Revolution" in small agricultural community in New Territories, Hong Kong', in David Faure *et al.* (eds), *From Village to City*.

47 Hong Kong Government, *Hong Kong Annual Report 1947*, p. 49. The Department was later reorganized as the Agricultural, Fisheries and Forestry Department in 1953.

48 Of course, it is difficult to distinguish 'economic' reasons from 'political' reasons, as the two are always intertwined. Hence we are using the term 'economic' in a very rough sense here.

49 Jack M. Potter, *Capitalism and the Chinese Peasant: Social and Economic Change in a Hong Kong Village*, Berkeley and Los Angeles, CA, University of California Press, 1968, p. 59.

50 Hong Kong Government, *Hong Kong Annual Report 1949*.

51 The share of fisheries production was increased to 85 per cent; Schiffer, 'State policy and economic growth', pp. 180–96.

52 Hong Kong Government, *Hong Kong Annual Report 1956*, p. 124.

53 Loans were made from the VMO Loan Fund, which provides credit, usually for periods of less than a year, at interest rates of 0.25 per cent a month (compared with

10 per cent from other sources). The co-operatives also handled other governmental or non-governmental loan funds for the farmers, such as Kadoorie Agricultural Loan Fund and the Joseph Trust Fund; Topley, 'Capital, saving and credit', p. 182.

54 Hong Kong Government, *Hong Kong Annual Report 1963*, p. 118; Hong Kong Government, *Hong Kong Annual Report 1952*, p. 68.

55 Topley, 'Capital, saving and credit', pp. 180–1.

56 After examining the immigrant farming communities in Shatin, Aijmer finds that the Hakka villagers and the immigrant farmers were avoiding contact with each other. The farmers rarely resided in the village. Instead, they lived in huts built on their farmlands; see Aijmer, 'An enquiry into Chinese settlement patterns'.

57 Unfortunately, there is no description of the outcome of the bargaining in Chau Lam-yan and Lau Siu-kai, 'Development, colonial rule, and intergroup conflict in a Chinese village in Hong Kong', *Human Organization*, 1982, vol. 41, no. 2, pp. 139–46.

58 Joel S. Migdal, *Peasants, Politics, and Revolution: Pressures toward Political and Social Change in the Third World*, New Jersey, Princeton University Press, 1974.

59 Göran Aijmer, *Economic Man in Sha Tin: Vegetable Gardeners in a Hong Kong Valley*, London, Curzon Press, 1980; and *Atomistic Society in Sha Tin: Immigrants in a Hong Kong Valley*, Gothoburgensis, Acta Universitatis Gothoburgensis, 1986.

60 Aijmer was impressed by the 'red-hot' political atmosphere in the area during the turbulent period 1967–8. He saw a vegetable lorry painted with the slogan 'Down with Soviet Imperialism!'. He was also surprised to find that the farmland rang with the sound of revolutionary songs, as the immigrant farmers listened to the Canton radio station when they were working in the fields. See note 59.

61 Strauch notes a competition for local influence over immigrant farmers in a village in Tai Po between a leftist union and the co-operative; Strauch, 'Middle peasants and market gardeners'.

62 See Aijmer, *Atomistic Society in Sha Tin*, pp. 244–5; District Commissioner, 1951. After 1967, some urban leftists went into the immigrant communities to rebuild their 'second front' organizations. In the 1970s, leftist unions and farmers' associations based on rural membership developed considerably. The Nung-muk chik-kung-ooi (The Graziers' Union) mentioned by Strauch was one such example.

63 *Wah Kiu Yat Po*, 25 June 1967.

64 *Wah Kiu Yat Po*, 30 June 1967.

65 *Wah Kiu Yat Po*, 29 July 1967, our translation. The stoppage of rice importation from China did not cause a serious problem, as the problem was easily remedied by increasing the import of rice from Southeast Asia, the United States and Australia (*Wah Kiu Yat Po*, 4 July 1967).

66 Registrar of Trade Unions, *Annual Departmental Report*, Hong Kong, Government Printer, 1972, 1982.

67 Strauch, 'Middle peasants and market gardeners', p. 198.

68 It is a term coined by Strauch to describe the drastic shift from rice cultivation to vegetable gardening over the 1950s (see note 67).

69 Hong Kong Government, *Hong Kong Annual Report 1938*, p. 51.

70 The importance of the government's support can be seen in the late 1970s and early 1980s when the foodstuff supply from mainland China became more stable owing to the open-door policy. Subsequently, government support of local production was withdrawn, and resulted in a drastic decline in the New Territories' vegetable production.

71 See Aijmer, *Economic Man in Sha Tin*, p. 61; and 'An enquiry into Chinese settlement patterns', p. 564.

72 Aijmer, 'Migrants into Hong Kong's New Territories'.

73 Charles J. Grant, *The Soils and Agriculture of Hong Kong*, Hong Kong, Government Printer, 1962.

74 Baker, 'The five great clans of the New Territories', pp. 25–47.
75 Hong Kong Government, Census Commissioner, *Report of the Census 1961*, table 408.
76 See Topley, 'Capital, saving and credit', p. 171.
77 As in note 76, p. 167.
78 Allen J. Chun, 'Land is to live: a study of the concept of Tsu in a Hakka Chinese village, New Territories, Hong Kong', unpublished Ph.D. dissertation, Chicago University, Illinois, 1985.
79 Aijmer, *Atomistic Society in Sha Tin*, pp. 219–35.
80 Potter, *Capitalism and the Chinese Peasant*, pp. 117–22.
81 Hayes, *Friends and Teachers*, p. 95.
82 For a discussion of the protest movement, see Chiu and Hung, 'Engineering rural stability'.
83 Skocpol, *States and Social Revolutions*.
84 For a fuller explanation of the paradoxical 'rural stability', together with the changes in the 1980s, see Ho-fung Hung, 'The colonial state and rural protest in Hong Kong: a historical and sociological analysis', M.Phil. thesis, Chinese University of Hong Kong, Hong Kong, 1998.

6

SOCIAL MOVEMENTS AND PUBLIC DISCOURSE ON POLITICS

Tai-lok Lui and Stephen W.K. Chiu

Many researchers in the field of Hong Kong politics, regardless of the differences in their approach to the study of political development, have made the observation that:

> The persistence of the colonial constitutional order has been accompanied by remarkable political stability. Hong Kong has never experienced any large-scale revolt or revolution. On the contrary, it is reputed for its lack of serious disputes.[1]

King sees this as a question of political integration in a colonial city under rapid urbanization and suggests that the 'administrative absorption of politics' is 'the way Hong Kong's political system has coped with the problem of stability'.[2] In his seminal work on society and politics in Hong Kong, Lau calls 'the existence of political stability under highly destabilising conditions' in Hong Kong a 'miracle' of the twentieth century.[3] In a recent review of the study of social conflict and collective actions in Hong Kong, Leung notes that

> Although a rapidly modernizing society under colonial rule, Hong Kong has been exceptional in having been spared the frequent turmoil and instability that have plagued other countries of a similar socio-economic and political status. Since they have not been a particular salient feature of the society, social conflict and social movements have rarely been the subject of inquiry in studies of Hong Kong.[4]

Of course, few observers of Hong Kong politics would deny the existence of social conflict and social movements in contemporary Hong Kong. Rather, they argue that 'conflicts will be confined in scale because, under normal conditions, it is extremely difficult to mobilize the Chinese people in Hong Kong to embark upon a sustained, high-cost political movement'.[5] Given that most local collective actions have not been able to present a forceful challenge to the colonial state

101

and thus do not constitute a serious threat to the stability of the existing political order, social conflict and social movements are relegated to a position of secondary importance, if not of total insignificance, in the analysis of Hong Kong politics.

However, this so-called politically quiescent society has, since the 1970s, witnessed wave after wave of collective actions – from student activism, urban protests, to organized actions of civil service unions – indicating a change in the parameters of the political arena under colonial rule. While these collective actions have not shaken the social basis of political stability in Hong Kong, their significance, as pointed out by a number of authors,[6] has gone far beyond the issues and domains of social life which gave rise to them and they have had repercussions for Hong Kong politics as a whole.

This Chapter explores the development of social movements in contemporary Hong Kong in the context of historical changes in Hong Kong society. In particular, we highlight the effects of the changing political opportunity structure, state–society relations, how changes in the framing of collective action have shaped social movements in Hong Kong and how the latter, in turn, have restructured the institutional environment of Hong Kong politics.[7] We argue that popular mobilization and collective action constitute important components of social life in Hong Kong. They are constituted and constitutive of the changing political parameters, state–society relations, and public discourse on politics.

Chinese politics on Hong Kong soil

The 1966 Kowloon disturbances and the 1967 riots were a watershed in the configuration of Hong Kong politics.[8] They best sum up the changing contours of Hong Kong politics before and after the mid-1960s. Before coming to a discussion of the two events in the mid-1960s, we would like to give a brief note on social conflicts in the late 1940s and the 1950s. Actually, the early post-war years were not short of social conflict. A series of strikes concerned with wage issues started in 1946. Indeed, the years between 1946 and 1949 marked a period of high intensity of industrial conflict in post-war Hong Kong. Economic hardship as a result of the war with Japan partly explained the sources of grievances among workers in this period. What was equally significant was the intervention of political forces. It was a period of internal war in mainland China, with the Nationalists and the Communists contending for political power. Their impacts on Hong Kong were evident in the formation and consolidation of two politically oriented trade unions councils, namely the pro-communist Federation of Trade Unions (established in 1947) and the pro-Nationalist Trade Union Council (established in 1948). The last major confrontation symbolizing the end of this phase of industrial actions was the Hong Kong Tramway workers' strike:

The confrontation came to a climax when in the evening of 30 January 1950 a violent clash occurred when the police attempted to break up a meeting of the strikers and the supporters, numbering over 1,000, outside the premises of the Tramways Union....[S]ome 100 workers were injured, and around a dozen arrested, during the clash. Several leaders of the Tramways Union, including the Chairman [sic], were subsequently deported for breaches of peace and order.[9]

Mainland politics continued to have its impact on Hong Kong in the 1950s. Disturbances broke out in Kowloon in March 1952 as a result of the Hong Kong government's decision not to allow a relief group on their way by train from China to visit and to comfort the fire victims of Tung Tau Village. A worker was shot dead during the confrontation and twelve people under arrest were later deported.[10] Another incident was the so-called 'Double Tenth Riots' of 1956. The outbreak of disorder was triggered by the alleged destruction of the Nationalist flags in resettlement estates and workers' quarters in Kowloon and Tsuen Wan. This led to a large-scale attack on pro-communist communities. In the report on the *Riots in Kowloon and Tsuen Wan, October 10th to 12th, 1956*, it was suggested that those responsible were:

...people of Nationalist persuasion egged on by criminals bent on personal gain and power. In Tsuen Wan, although there is no evidence of any planning prior to the outbreak of disorder in Kowloon, it would appear that people of Nationalist persuasion joined in collaboration with triad gangs to redress old scores and to attempt to win a dominant position in the labour world.[11]

Political actions prior to the 1966 Kowloon disturbances were largely extensions of confrontation between the pro-Nationalist and pro-Communist groups. Or, in Lee's description, 'Chinese politics on Hong Kong soil'.[12] Political concerns expressed in these social conflicts were mainly ideological differences based upon larger political contentions between the two regimes in mainland China and Taiwan. While these confrontations took place in Hong Kong, the issues at stake lay elsewhere.

Given such a background, the 1966 Kowloon disturbances symbolized a turning point in the history of social conflicts in Hong Kong. The disturbances were a series of demonstrations, marches, riots, and street violence triggered by a hunger strike in opposition to a fare increase by the Star Ferry, lasting from 4 April to 9 April 1966.[13] As pointed out by the Commission of Inquiry of the 1966 Kowloon disturbances, the direct causes seem to lie in the escalation of events from the much publicized opposition and petitions concerning the Star Ferry fare increase (September 1965 – 4 April 1966), to the 'hunger strike' by one man (4 April), to his defiance of authority (5 April), to the organized march ending in more serious defiance and clashes with authority (5–6 April), to the further demonstrations merging into riots (6–7 April).[14]

The significance of the 1966 Kowloon disturbances lies in the fact that they symbolized the arrival of a new generation ready to express their hopes and frustrations. As noted in the official report, *Kowloon Disturbances 1966: Report of Commission of Inquiry*, '[t]here is evidence of a growing interest in Hong Kong on the part of youth and a tendency to protest at a situation which their parents might tacitly accept'.[15] The actions were 'spontaneous and unco-ordinated and that there appeared to be no central organization or control'.[16] More importantly, 'there was no indication of any political or triad control or exploitation of the situation'.[17] It was the suggestion of the Commission of Inquiry that the underlying cause of the disturbances was 'failure of communication' between the public and the government. Whether the analysis presented by the Commission of Inquiry is convincing or otherwise is not our concern here. The important point is that the sudden outbursts of anger by the young people have caught the colonial administration totally unprepared. The Commission of Inquiry had to recognize that 'with a new generation growing up who have never had experience outside Hong Kong it is important to develop avenues for participation in the life of the community and to give expression to young peoples' zeal for service'.[18] The disturbances represent the first major, spontaneous attempt by the post-war baby boomers to express their discontent openly. Although their demands were diffuse and not well articulated, their sense of uneasiness was clear.

In May 1967, while the colonial administration was still working on new programmes to address issues brought up in the 1966 Kowloon riots, twenty-one men were arrested at a plastic flower factory in San Po Kong. This incident was soon followed by further clashes between communist supporters and the police, and riots broke out. Confrontations soon gave way to other forms of collective action, from work stoppages, strikes and boycotts to terrorist attacks (for example bomb attacks). The 1967 riots had clear and specific political objectives: their origins 'lay in the Cultural Revolution in China',[19] and local communist supporters used them to challenge the colonial rule. However, the participants in the confrontational actions organized in the early stage of the riots were by no means confined to local supporters of communist China.[20] The subsequent development of these anti-colonial actions into terrorism in fact brought about a difference of opinion on this political matter among the local population. Indeed, as Scott remarked:

[t]here can be little doubt that by December 1967 the communists had lost whatever public sympathy the labour disputes had initially generated....Ironically, in the light of communist objectives, the end-result of the disturbances was to increase the support for, and the legitimacy of, the existing order. Faced with a choice between communism of the

Cultural Revolution variety and the, as yet, unreformed colonial capitalist state, most people chose to side with the devil they knew.[21]

Of course, one has to be cautious in interpreting the change of popular mood in
the mid-1960s. There had not been a sudden swing of support from one political
and ideological camp to another. As noted by many observers, at that time, Hong
Kong was considered by many local Chinese as a 'lifeboat' in a sea of political
turmoil. On the one hand, their emigration to the colony was essentially an
attempt to stay away from the flux and change of China's politics. On the other,
there is little evidence to show that the Hong Kong Chinese accepted colonial
rule as a legitimate political order.[22] Until the start of the negotiations over Hong
Kong's future in 1982, the 1967 riots can be seen as a temporary end to the
discourse on 'Chinese politics' in Hong Kong which had prevailed in the post-
war decades. This discourse viewed Hong Kong politics as an extension of the
Communist–Nationalist struggle, and was based on a fear that China would
intervene in Hong Kong.[23] The 1966 disturbances and the 1967 riots marked the
end of an era and the beginning of a new one – (a temporary) farewell to politics
phrased within the framework of 'Chinese politics' and the start of a phase
where political demands were perceived as spontaneous, issue-driven and non-
ideological. Politics had now been localized.[24]

The disturbances and riots in the mid-1960s led to the drawing up of a new
political agenda, especially for the new generation. Lo Wai Luen, a local expert
on the development of literature in Hong Kong, recalls that most of her friends
in the 1950s and 1960s had a rather negative evaluation of life in the colony and
few identified with either Hong Kong or China.[25] But the shocks coming from
the bank runs in 1965, the 1966 disturbances, and the 1967 riots had given rise
to a series of new questions. Young people began to rethink their relations with
Hong Kong – What was this place? What should be done? How did they see
themselves as Chinese growing up in a colony?[26] The effect of the events in the
mid-1960s on the ideological and political minds of the post-war baby boomers
is a question awaiting more serious research and documentation. Existing data
related to this issue is so scarce that it would be premature to draw any definitive
conclusion.

Our conjecture is that the 1966 and 1967 riots did have a significant impact
on Hong Kong society in terms of (1) loosening the existing institutional
structure of the colonial administrative state and (2) re-framing issues for public
debate. The former can best be observed in the government's moves towards
strengthening the communication channels between the bureaucracy and the
grass roots, notably the establishment of the City District Officer Scheme. This
type of administrative reforms did not, however, open new channels for political
participation, as its main purpose was to strengthen communication between the
bureaucracy and the non-élite public.

Nevertheless, such moves together with other reforms in response to social
problems exposed during the riots, for example labour conditions, contributed to

the creation of a new political and social climate, which promoted public discussion about improving the current state of affairs and 'of the problems which were still to be overcome',[27] and helped bring popular frustrations and discontent to the public domain. An atmosphere was created which facilitated a confluence of the young generation's quest for a Hong Kong identity and the redressing of grass roots' grievances. For example, the status of the Chinese language and the suggestion to institute an ombudsman system were among the issues brought to the public domain at that time. This turn towards more emphasis on social concern and criticism was also evident in various activities organized by young intellectuals and students.[28]

Identity politics and challenge against the colonial order

The late 1960s was a period of reaction to the issues brought up by the disturbances and riots in 1966 and 1967. While the colonial government tried hard to find official means to deal with issues highlighted by the disturbances and riots, ranging from government-sponsored dance parties for young people and the establishment of the City District Officer Scheme to the launching of the Hong Kong Festival, the new generation had already taken the initiative of identifying social problems which were previously hidden behind the façade of growing affluence. College students' involvement in public affairs began with conflicts over campus issues (the university reform campaign in the University of Hong Kong and the protest actions against the dismissal of Chu Hai College students) and later developed into 'getting out of the ivory tower' and more active intervention in various community issues. But the spur to the student movement was the territorial dispute concerning the status of Diaoyutai Islands.[29]

Although the 'Defend Diaoyutai Movement' was an 'imported' movement, inspired by student actions abroad, it very quickly became one of the most widely mobilized campaigns in the history of Hong Kong's student movement. While inspired by Chinese nationalism, it was not a repetition of earlier Communist–Nationalist contentious politics. While the two governments did try to intervene and articulate (or de-articulate) the issues to suit their own political agenda, the movement was more about the expression of student nationalistic sentiments than about the political projects of individual governments.

The movement had different layers of meaning. First, it showed that colonialism failed to provide the new generation a framework for their quest for identity after the disturbances and riots in the 1960s. Nationalism, mainly in cultural terms, could constitute the source of identity. The fads of Chinese nationalism on college campuses generated by the movement were a good indication of the appeal of nationalism to the new generation. Second, at that historical conjuncture, nationalism (being well suited to the political vision of communist China after the 'Defend Diaoyutai Movement') served both as a source of identity formation and as an ideology for the critique of colonial administration. Young people of different political persuasions, ranging from cultural nationalism to radicalism criticizing colonialism and capitalism, could work together under the same nationalist umbrella.

Only at a later stage did this multi-layered nationalism reveal its own internal contradictions, leading to an internal political and ideological struggle within the student movement. The struggle between the two lines of nationalism and social activism could be seen as an outcome of the tension within the project of identity formation in a colonial setting. While nationalism promised to transcend colonialism and lead its supporters to a grander national project, it was also very remote from the daily life under colonialism. This was especially true in the context of Hong Kong in the 1970s: Communist China had no plans to intervene into local affairs after the 1967 riots, and was more concerned with maintaining the *status quo* while promoting nationalism within the colony. The social activist camp, very much inspired by New Left radical ideology, attempted to address local issues with the objective of exposing and publicly voicing the hidden pain and discontent of people living under the colonial regime. The ideological struggle between these student camps became evident during the 'Anti-corruption, Arrest Godber Movement' (a protest movement against severe corruption in the colonial administration) and the gap between them subsequently continued to widen until the fall of the 'Gang of Four' in Communist China.

The change in Party line after the death of Mao in China was a blow to the pro-China nationalist camp within the student movement. As a result, ideological struggle was replaced by a more locally oriented approach to social intervention. While the ideological critique of colonialism and capitalism was still important as a guiding principle, by the late 1970s, the student movement was merely one among many factions participating in the emerging pressure group politics. Student bodies were active members of the leadership of two important movements – the 'Yaumati Boat People Action' (a series of protest actions against the government's resettlement policy and the arrest of protesters) and the 'Golden Jubilee Secondary School Incident' (a series of actions triggered by alleged corruption in school management and against the subsequent action taken by the government to close down the secondary school). But the ideological and organizational leadership was primarily in the hands of the emerging pressure group leaders.

We can look at the twists and turns in the development of the student movement from different angles. From one angle, it was a question of the rise and fall of a social movement in terms of mobilization. But it can also be seen as a failure to make use of the new social and political climate created by events in the mid-1960s and establish a framework of nationalism. In view of space limitations we shall not dwell upon these questions. What interests us here is the framing of political demands by various social movements in the 1970s. In this regard, the student movement can be seen as the vanguard of social movements of the 1970s in the sense that of all the social movement organizations and political groups (with the possible exception of the Trotskyite Revolutionary Marxist Alliance), it was the student movement that articulated a radical ideological framework to challenge the colonial social order. Implicit in most of the students' organized actions, ranging from social actions to protest government policy to the cultural critique of everyday life, there was an underlying agenda of criticizing the colonial government and the capitalist economy.[30] While the criticisms of colonialism and capitalism had never taken the form of a political programme, they did constitute a kind of tacit understanding among social movement organizers. In the context of colonial Hong Kong in the 1970s, this tacit understanding among social movement organizations and protest groups much facilitated joint and collaborative action.

Collective action against political exclusion

Before elaborating on the above, we shall first look briefly at the growth of contentious actions in the 1970s. The early part of the decade witnessed several waves of collective action. While the student movement addressed broader ideological and political issues of that period, urban protests and industrial actions in the public sector were driven by community-based and work-related interests. When we look at the social movements in the 1970s, two characteristics can be noted. First, most of the collective actions were protest actions.[31] This partly reflected the limited resources of the movement organizations – the main strategy was to rally the support of the third parties for the purpose of exerting pressure on the government, which showed that their resources for mass mobilization were limited and that they had a relatively weak bargaining position vis-á-vis the colonial state. Second, it was an outcome of the political configuration of political action under the so-called 'consultative democracy' arrangement. Prior to the reform of local administration (i.e. the establishment of district boards and the related elections) in the early 1980s, the channels for open political participation were confined (through election) to the Urban Council. More importantly, within this 'consultative democracy' framework, the administrative state was politically insulated from society, and depoliticization was the ruling strategy of the colonial administration.[32] While the élitist interest groups could gain access to the government through the appointment of representatives or related persons to consultative bodies and exert political influence on the bureaucrats, political demands made by the general public were channelled to the non-institutional arena. Simply put, the structure of the colonial state and the system of representing political interests forced those who wanted to voice popular claims and demands to organize protest actions.[33]

By the end of the 1970s, something like a 'social movement industry' was taking shape. The proliferation of different types of collective action had greatly broadened the scope of contentious politics. A variety of interests and latent groups had been mobilized and their claims and demands were recognized.

Protest groups and pressure groups were formed to sustain mobilization.[34] In a way, the early activism of the student movement in organizing collective action, and the subsequent decline in importance of students in leading popular mobilization, revealed the growth of social movement organizations and the formation of the 'social movement industry'. The increased importance of pressure groups such as the Hong Kong Professional Teachers' Union and the Society for Community Organisation, and the formation of *ad hoc* alliances for joint action under the leadership of these pressure groups, illustrated a change towards a consolidation of social protest through pressure group politics.

The rise of pressure group politics in the late 1970s and early 1980s can be understood in terms of the institutional configuration of social protest. In essence, pressure group politics was more a continuation of than a break with protest actions in the early 1970s.[35] Despite the fact that some of them were co-opted into the colonial administrative system through appointment to advisory committees (mainly on individual and not on a group basis), most pressure groups were active outside formal institutional politics.[36] Indeed, the fact that most activist groups were 'outsiders' helped create some kind of tacit under-standing among them. In the joint actions organized in the late 1970s and early 1980s, they could easily get together to form *ad hoc* organizations for a common cause. Though ideological differences among different groups still played a role, on the whole they had little difficulty in making common claims and staging jointly organized protest actions.

The affinity among these groups was largely a consequence of the restricted opportunity for political participation in that period. The closed political system created a common understanding among the activists because they shared the experience of being rejected and sometimes repressed by the colonial state. Restricted entry into the formal channels of the polity gave rise to an opposi-tional force active in the non-institutional political arena. Some of these groups (for example, the student activists), were critical of colonialism and/or capitalism. Others, such as residents' organizations, did not have elaborate ideological programmes but were equally critical of the colonial administration which was not responsive to their demands. By the early 1980s and on the eve of the Sino-British negotiations over Hong Kong's future, there was a loosely knitted network of pressure groups, social movement organizations, and grass roots protest groups constituting an oppositional force resisting the colonial adminis-trative state.

The restructuring of colonial hegemony

Paradoxically, while various social movements brought up different types of claims and demands, the capability of the colonial state in meeting these challenges facilitated the restructuring of colonial hegemony in terms of governmental responsiveness and administrative efficiency. The accommodation of popular demands within the political parameters of the growing administrative state was of paramount importance in re-structuring Hong Kong's state–society relations of that period.[37] As noted earlier, the colonial administration in the 1970s maintained its insulation from society by rejecting the idea of political reform and of re-structuring the channels of political participation.[38] To accommodate the growing demands for political reform in the aftermath of the disturbances and riots in the mid-1960s and in the context of emergent demands for social and political reforms, the colonial administration recruited the emerging young professionals and executives into the major decision-making bodies to replace some of the old élites.[39] Furthermore, it strengthened its position by increasing the state's responsiveness to local demands, fighting corruption, broadening the scope of social services, and improving administrative efficiency.

On the one hand, the colonial state was able to change its image gradually through its re-organization of the civil service, strengthening its reach to the local communities through the 'Fight Crime' and 'Clean Hong Kong' campaigns, and the establishments of the mutual aid committees, assuming a high profile in combating corruption by establishing the Independent Commission Against Corruption, and new initiatives in providing public housing, developing new towns, education, welfare and medical services.[40] In the face of more vocal expressions of discontent since the mid-1960s, the colonial administration had taken the initiative 'to stir up a sense of citizenship among residents' and to change its style of governance and public image 'from benevolent authoritarianism to wider consultation and a concern with achieving "consensus government"'.[41] However, given the absence of political reform in opening channels for more active political participation, such initiatives were more of 'citizenship from above' than really including ordinary people into the political community. On the other, the articulation of grass roots' demands for access to social services provided by the government propelled anti-colonial activists to assume, unintendedly though, a political position of asking the colonial administration to be more responsive to popular grievances (framed as political demands for a more open and accountable government), rather than that of an outright rejection of British colonialism.

In the 1970s, then, a paradoxical development took place where the attempts to challenge the colonial authority and the capitalist order were gradually replaced by a demand for rights and entitlements (an attitude which was very different from the earlier conception of 'Hong Kong as a lifeboat'), giving the colonial state an opportunity to restructure its hegemony through its response to these demands. It was paradoxical because this was the period in which we find the rise of various kinds of social movements, with some of them (such as the student movement) openly voicing ideological criticisms to the colonial administration. However, as we argue here, it was also the period in which the colonial government had been successful in meeting these challenges and at the same time through its own reform initiatives had been able to convince the public that it was an efficient government capable of bringing them prosperity and stability. The colonial state was subsequently perceived as an efficient administration which could meet the needs of the population and provide them with an institutional framework enabling the Hong Kong Chinese to improve their livelihood through entrepreneurship and/or credentialism.[42] Indeed, the performance of the colonial administration was evaluated on the basis of its policy outputs – the outcomes (prosperity and stability) justified its existence.[43] The basis of this hegemony was the belief that as long as the administrative state was able to uphold law and order and the legal framework, and to attend to the basic needs of the local population (for instance, mass housing), they were best off being left alone and free to pursue their own goals and careers.[44]

Thus, the social movements in the 1970s had made an interesting turn. In the beginning, the quest for identity was paramount, in response to issues brought up during the events of 1966 and 1967, and subsequently re-framed by the student movement into a quest for cultural nationalism. Thereafter, identity politics gradually faded into the background and was replaced by a series of collective actions centring on the allocation of resources.[45] The attempts to embarrass the colonial authority with demands and actions and anti-colonial rhetoric paradoxically ended up confirming the role of the colonial state as the major agency for resource-allocation in order to cope with rapid economic and social development. The problems were now framed in issue-specific and functional terms. While the social movements certainly contributed to the liberalization of Hong Kong's civil society and the bringing of popular demands to the public arena, their scope was much confined. This was in accordance with the broader context of de-politicization in the 1970s, when contentious politics was replaced with a concern for specific policies and concrete administrative issues. The colonial nature of the administrative state was left unscathed.

Decolonization and the new political order

The Sino-British negotiations over Hong Kong's future and the subsequent agreement between the two governments on returning the colony to China on 1 July 1997 brought drastic changes in both the political agenda and the parameters of Hong Kong politics. The agreement signalled the beginning of the decolonization process. Although initially, the pressure groups, social movement organizations and grass roots protest groups had their doubts about participating in formal institutional politics,[46] they were quickly drawn into electoral politics, first at the level of election to the district boards and Urban and Regional Councils, and later in direct and indirect elections to the Legislature. The new question was: how can a new political order be instituted within the parameters of 'decolonization without independence' and the diplomatic politics between Britain and China? People prepared to formulate politics for the transitional period. In the realm of *realpolitik*, the 1980s was a period of political contention through electoral politics.

Studies of social conflicts in 1975–91 have shown that from 1984 onwards, there was a drastic increase of conflicts related to political issues (i.e. those

111

concerning constitutional matters and issues about political and civil rights).[47] Prior to 1984, constitutional matters rarely appeared in the agenda of local social movements. This was not due to political indifference but to the fact that prior to political reforms in the 1980s, the question of democratization was regarded by most activists as being remote from the political reality, since it was unlikely to have any practical meaning in the face of a closed colonial administration. The growing importance of political issues after 1984 was a result of the rise of political opportunities brought about by decolonization, and of the increased attention for political participation in formal institutional politics on the part of pressure groups, social movement organizations and grass roots protest groups. The struggle for democracy became the major concern of the activists in the 1980s and 1990s.[48] The aims were to deepen political reform before 1997 and democratize the political structure of the future Special Administrative Region government.

The new political opportunities had a double-edged effect on the development of social movements in Hong Kong. On the one hand, there were new opportunities for political intervention in the sphere of electoral politics and in the process of designing the future political structure of Hong Kong. Overcoming their initial reservations, activists from pressure groups, social movement organizations and grass roots protest groups quickly came to form new political groups for the purposes of preparing for elections at different levels and voicing their opinions to the Chinese government in regard to the blueprints for the transition and the post-1997 administration.[49] The proliferation of political groups in the 1980s was largely a response to the emerging political order triggered by the process of decolonization. Many of these political groups actively participated in the democracy movement for the purpose of securing the establishment of a more democratic political structure before 1997. Former pressure groups, social movement organizations, and newly formed political groups formed a loosely defined group of democrats on the basis of previous collaborative experience and some tacit understanding of the need to fight for the democratic cause. In the early 1980s, many activists saw the 1997 question as an opportunity for societal mobilization – to place topics which had previously been suppressed on the political agenda (e.g. democratization) for public discussion.[50] The move towards the establishment of a representative government in 1985 and 1988 meant that for the first time in colonial history, the Hong Kong populace elected representatives to the Legislature, albeit only indirectly, through functional constituencies and electoral colleges. This brought about the further politicization of pressure groups and social movement organizations. Political parties were subsequently formed for consolidating the existing networks of activists and concerned groups.

On the other hand, participation in formal political institutional politics also gave rise to divisions among the groups involved. The twists and turns during the Sino-British talks about political reforms, the political structure of the future Special Administrative Region government, and the emphasis on convergence towards a social and political system which China would find acceptable, posed new questions to the political groups and social movement organizations. Division ensued in regard to the choice between pragmatism (i.e. accepting the parameters prescribed by China) and continuing to play the role of an oppositional force (especially after the military crackdown of the democratic movement during the June 4th Incident in 1989). The loosely formulated consensus among activist groups in the 1970s lost its relevance and the solidarity among the so-called democrats was weakened. Previous informal political networking was replaced by formal party participation and inter-organizational linkages.

A gradual separation took place, between mobilization and community action on the one hand, and party politics on the other.[51] After a short period of active participation in local elections, some pressure groups and grass roots protest groups changed their strategy, assuming a low profile in the 1991 and 1995 elections to the Legislative Council.[52] The position of the democrats' leaders became more problematic as a result of the separation. Most of them had started their political careers in organizing protest actions and social movements in the 1970s and 1980s. Their close connections with social movement organizations created expectations from the grass roots that they would continue to play the role of leading popular mobilization against government policies. While they assumed a double role in Hong Kong politics – they were both the leaders of protest actions and politicians assuming an oppositional position in the elected bodies at different levels – it was also becoming clear that grass roots mobilization is different from that of electoral politics. The rapid development of electoral politics and the increased concern for parliamentary struggle had led to a 'hollowing out' of political organization at the grass roots level. This problem was also found among local unions.[53]

The mass actions which took place before and after the June 4th Incident did not really change the picture. While more than one million people joined the street rallies and marches in protest against the suppression of the student movement in Beijing, the pro-Chinese democracy movement quickly 'fell from the peak' after the crackdown.[54] Nor did the controversies over the political reform programme put forward by the Governor, Chris Patten, trigger another round of pro-democracy popular mobilization. As Hong Kong approached 1997, it was increasingly difficult to mobilize the public and to stage open confrontational action against China.

All in all, the changes since the Sino-British negotiations had not really brought social movements into institutional politics. To be sure, the 1980s and 1990s witnessed the participation of pressure groups, social movement organizations, and protest groups' leaders in electoral politics, but this did not necessarily imply the political transformation of social movements. While it is true that popular demands were brought to public discussion in the electoral bodies through collective action, they were mediated by party and electoral politics.

The odd situation in Hong Kong is that, on the one hand, there was a kind of party politics operating in a political institutional setting that did not allow parties to assume decision-making power. This setting made party and electoral politics a kind of oppositional politics, in close connection with grass roots social movements. On the other hand, the agenda and room for manœuvre of this kind of oppositional politics were significantly restricted by the peculiar decolonization process. The very fact that the future of Hong Kong politics had to be accommodated within the broader framework of Chinese politics, and the crafting of the future blueprints of governance was restricted to diplomatic talks between the Chinese and British governments, made it very difficult for the opposition to convince the masses of the viability of a form of alternative politics which could go beyond the restrictions imposed by the existing framework of decolonization.

At the same time, the approaching issues brought about by the 1997 question drove almost all active political participants to concentrate on political matters, especially those concerning China–Hong Kong relations. Issues which were most relevant to grass roots mobilization were not successfully articulated in the 1997 political agenda, reinforcing the separation of party and electoral politics from social movements and popular mobilization.

Moreover, the social movements in Hong Kong were unable to consolidate popular solidarity by focusing on major social contradictions (e.g. ethnic conflicts in some developing countries) or institutions (e.g. religion). Despite growing tensions among political groups, pressure groups and social movement organizations, the latter still maintained loose and often informal connections with various political groups, especially those which were broadly categorized as the democratic camp.[55]

The overall picture is that social movements played a rather limited role in the transition to 1997. Under the shadow of 'decolonization without independence' and the dominant position of China on Hong Kong matters, the collective identity of being 'locally Hong Kong' and the belief in a liberal and open socio-political order, which were partly an outcome of the rise of collective actions in the 1970s, did not become the basis for popular mobilization and political action. In a sense, the agenda once articulated by social movements and collective actions in the 1960s and 1970s was abandoned precisely in a political context where such issues were extremely pertinent.

Concluding remarks

In contrast to the claim that Hong Kong has been politically stable thanks to the colonial social and political order, we have seen that social movements constitute an important part of Hong Kong's social and political life. We argue for the need of a closer look at the interactions among the changing political opportunity structure, state–society relations, and the public discourse on politics in our understanding of the development of social movements in Hong Kong. Social movements in Hong Kong are both constituted and constitutive of the political environment. On the one hand, they are socially constructed. The emergence of various kinds of social movements since the mid-1960s and the subsequent proliferation of pressure group politics and party politics were outcomes of rising demands for social rights and political participation, the changing political representation system, and the reactions of the state to challenges from below. The form taken by most social movements, primarily in terms of protest actions and the role of political opposition outside the political system, was shaped by the changing state–society relations. On the other hand, they are constitutive of Hong Kong politics in that they restructure public political discourse and open political opportunity. Indeed, it would not be an overstatement to say that one can hardly grapple with the configuration of the colonial state and the changing state–society relations (including the political transition in the 1980s and 1990s) without an understanding of social movements in Hong Kong. The emergence of social movements in Hong Kong since the mid-1960s represents the gradual change of political activity from the orientation of 'Chinese politics on Hong Kong soil' to that with a local social and political agenda. It shows the participation of activists as well as ordinary people in shaping the development of contemporary Hong Kong society. Social movements are by no means marginal in the constitution of political life in Hong Kong.

NOTES

1 Hsin-chi Kuan, 'Political stability and change in Hong Kong', in Tzong-biau Lin *et al.* (eds), *Hong Kong: Economics, Social and Political Studies in Development*, New York, M.E. Sharpe, 1979, p. 146.

2 Ambrose Y.C. King, 'Administrative absorption of politics in Hong Kong: emphasis on the grass roots level', in Ambrose Y.C. King and Rance P.L. Lee (eds), *Social Life and Development in Hong Kong*, Hong Kong, Chinese University Press, 1981, p. 129.

3 Lau Siu-kai, *Society and Politics in Hong Kong*, Hong Kong, Chinese University Press, 1982, p. 1.

4 Benjamin K.P. Leung, *Perspectives on Hong Kong Society*, Hong Kong, Oxford University Press, 1996, p. 159.

5 Lau, *Society and Politics*, p. 20.

6 See, for example, Anthony B.L. Cheung, 'Xin zhongchan jieji de maoqi yu zhengzhi yingxiang' (The new middle class: its emergence and political influence), *Mingbao yuekan* (Ming Pao Monthly), 1987, no. 253, pp. 10–15; Tai-lok Lui, 'Mishi yu jiju zhuanbian zhengzhi huanjing de Xianggang minzhong yundong' (The Path of Development of Hong Kong's popular movements), *Xianggang shehui kexue xuebao* (Hong Kong Journal of Social Sciences), 1994, no. 4, pp. 67–78.

7 On relevant theoretical literature, see for example, Doug McAdam, John McCarthy and Mayer Zald (eds), *Comparative Perspectives on Social Movements*, Cambridge, Cambridge University Press, 1996.

8 For a summary of the two incidents, see Ian Scott, *Political Change and the Crisis of Legitimacy in Hong Kong*, Hong Kong, Oxford University Press, 1989, ch. 3.

9 Benjamin K.P. Leung and Stephen W.K. Chiu, 'A social history of industrial strikes and the labour movement in Hong Kong, 1946–1989', Social Sciences Research Centre occasional paper no. 3, Hong Kong, University of Hong Kong, 1991, pp. 23–4.

10 Grantham, the Governor of Hong Kong then, commented on the incident:

> Their [the communists'] press made bitter attacks on the government, but a
> more dangerous tactic was the intention they expressed of sending from Can-
> ton a 'comfort mission', the outcome of which was not difficult to foresee. The
> mission would have come to Hong Kong; fiery speeches would have been
> made against the 'imperialists', aid would have been promised from 'Mother
> China'; all this be it noted, on Hong Kong soil.

Quoted from Lee Ming-kwan, 'Hong Kong identity – past and present', in S.L. Wong
and T. Maruya (eds), *Hong Kong Economy and Society: Challenges in the New Era*, Tokyo,
Institute of Developing Economies, 1998, pp. 158–9.

11 Quoted from Steve Tsang (ed.), *Government and Politics: A Documentary History of Hong
Kong*, Hong Kong, Hong Kong University Press, 1995, p. 289.

12 Lee, 'Hong Kong identity', p. 158.

13 For the details of the 1966 Kowloon disturbances, see Commission of Inquiry,
Kowloon Disturbances 1966: Report of Commission of Inquiry, Hong Kong, Government
Printer, 1967; cited hereafter as Commission of Inquiry.

14 Commission of Inquiry, p. 118.

15 Commission of Inquiry, p. 129.

16 Commission of Inquiry, p. 112.

17 Commission of Inquiry, p. 112.

18 Commission of Inquiry, p. 126.

19 Scott, *Political Change*, p. 96.

20 There are no publicly available documentary records of the participants of the 1967
riots. In a recent interview, Mr. Tsang Yuk Sing [Zeng Yucheng], a leader of the pro-
China political group, Democratic Alliance for the Betterment of Hong Kong, gave
an account of the 1967 riots and the imprisonment of his siblings: 'My brother was a
Form 6 student at St. Paul's, and was a timid boy....I was obviously leftist by then...I
had no idea what my brother was doing...He printed some leaflets at home calling
for the reform of the school curriculum, denouncing the British for the Opium War,
and so on. He got a pile of those leaflets and handed them out during lunchtime at
school....[W]hen classes resumed, the riot police were there....My brother was
arrested straight away, tried, and sentenced to two years.... A couple of months later,
my fifteen-year-old sister was also arrested. She was a Form 3 girl at Belilios Public
School. She was in the playground with thirteen other girls, and when the school bell
rang they refused to go back to the classroom....[The headmistress] called the police,
and all fourteen were tried, and found guilty of breaching the emergency legislation
in force during 1967, and sent to the women's prison in Lai Chi Kok [Li Zhi Jiao] for
one month.' See Sally Blyth and Ian Wotherspoon, *Hong Kong Remembers*, Hong Kong,
Oxford University Press, 1996, pp. 96–7. St. Paul's and Belilios Public School are
prestigious secondary schools in Hong Kong. Both this fact and Mr. Tsang's account
of the two incidents indicate that non-Communist students were also mobilized in
1967.

21 Scott, *Political Change*, p. 104.

22 It could be argued that, at least in that period of time, legitimacy was not a real
political issue for the Hong Kong Chinese making a living under colonial rule. In his
seminal work on Hong Kong politics, Lau noted that '[t]he colonized Chinese people
came to Hong Kong to subject themselves voluntarily under the rule of an alien
colonial administration'. See Lau, *Society and Politics*, p. 7. He then moved on to look at
the characteristics of Hong Kong society as a minimally integrated socio-political
system, bypassing the question of legitimacy. When most of the Hong Kong Chinese
saw themselves as migrants or refugees, legitimacy of political rule was simply

irrelevant. Hughes also made a note of this Hong Kong mood: it is 'one of masterly expedience and crisis-to-crisis adjustment and recovery. It is partly a gambler's mentality, partly fatalism. As in Shanghai, no foreigner came to Hong Kong to make a home there; he came to make a living and get out. Nor does any Chinese live in Hong Kong against his will.' See Richard Hughes, *Borrowed Place Borrowed Time: Hong Kong and Its Many Faces*, 2nd rev. edn, London, André Deutsch, 1976, p. 126. This gradually changed in the 1970s when more and more demands were put to the colonial administration and a new state–society relation took shape.

23 One way to look at this question is to compare and contrast the interpretation of the relevance of Chinese politics to the riots in 1956 and 1966. About the approach of 'firmness without provocation' in handling Chinese politics in Hong Kong by the colonial administration, see Tsang, *Government and Politics*, pp. 290–4.

24 The emergence of a form of localized politics was recognized, though not explicitly, in the official report on the 1966 Kowloon disturbances. See Commission of Inquiry.

25 Wai Luen Lo, *Xianggang gushi* (Hong Kong Story), Hong Kong, Oxford University Press, 1996. For a review of related research on the changing perception of life in Hong Kong, see Thomas Wong, 'Discourses and dilemmas: 25 years of subjective indicators studies in Hong Kong', in Lau Siu-kai *et al.* (eds), *Indicators of Social Development: Hong Kong 1990*, Hong Kong, Hong Kong Institute of Asia-Pacific Studies, 1992, pp. 239–68.

26 Lo, *Xianggang gushi*, p. 62.

27 See Hong Kong Government, *Hong Kong Annual Report 1968*. The title of the leading article in this report is 'Progress'.

28 On the gradual change of orientation of *Zhongguo xuesheng zhoubao* (The Chinese Student Weekly), see Lo, *Xianggang gushi*, pp. 54–73.

29 On the development of the student movement, see Yuandong shiwu pinglun she (Observers of Far Eastern Affairs) (ed.), *Xueyun chunqiu* (The Student Movement), Hong Kong, Yuandong shiwu pinglun she, 1982; and Hong Kong Federation of Students, *Xianggang xuesheng yuandong huigu* (A Review of the Hong Kong Student Movement), Hong Kong, Wide Angle Publications, 1983.

30 Yuandong shiwu pinglun she, *Xueyun chunqiu*.

31 Tai-lok Lui and James K.S. Kung, *Chengsi zongheng* (City Unlimited: Community Movement and Urban Politics in Hong Kong), Hong Kong, Wide Angle Publications, 1985.

32 Lau, *Society and Politics*; Peter Harris, *Hong Kong: A Study in Bureaucratic Politics*, Hong Kong, Heinemann Asia, 1978.

33 Craig J. Jenkins and Bert Klandermans (eds), *The Politics of Social Protest*, London, UCL Press, 1995; Lui and Kung, *Chengsi zongheng*.

34 On the formation of protest groups and pressure groups concerning community politics, see Hong Kong Council of Social Service, *Community Development Resource Book*, various years.

35 Tai-lok Lui, 'Yali tuanti zhengzhi yu zhengzhi canyu' (Pressure group politics and political participation), in Joseph Cheng (ed.), *Guoduqi de Xianggang* (Hong Kong in the Transitional Period), Hong Kong, Joint Publications, 1989, pp. 1–18.

36 The best example of the attitude of the colonial administration towards local pressure groups is the comment made in the 1979 report of the Standing Committee on Pressure Groups. See Lee Ming-kwan, 'Yali tuanti yu zhengdang zhengzhi (Pressure groups and party politics)', in Lee Ming-kwan, *Bianqian zhong de Xianggang zhengzhi he shehui* (Hong Kong Politics and Society in Transition), Hong Kong, Commercial Press, 1987.

37 Also see Lee, 'Hong Kong identity', p. 168 for a similar observation.

38 See Hong Kong Government, *White Paper: The Urban Council*, 1971.

39 Stephen Tang, 'The power structure in a colonial society: a sociological study of the Legislative Council in Hong Kong', unpublished senior B.Soc.Sci. thesis, Sociology Department, Chinese University of Hong Kong, Hong Kong, 1973.

40 The strengthening of the administrative state in the 1970s and the reforms initiated in the 'MacLehose era' are best summarized and discussed in Scott, *Political Change*, ch. 4. Also see *South China Morning Post*, 'The MacLehose years 1971–1982', *South China Morning Post Supplement*, April 1982.

41 James Hayes, *Friends and Teachers: Hong Kong and Its People 1953–87*, Hong Kong, Hong Kong University Press, 1996, pp. 279 and 281, respectively.

42 This is the hegemonic ruling strategy of the colonial administrative state. For an interesting (and symbolic) account of this strategy, see Patten's address at the opening of the Legislative Council session in 1996, Christopher Patten, *Hong Kong: Transition – The 1996 Policy Address*, Hong Kong, Government Printer, 1996.

43 Cf. Ambrose Y.C. King, 'The political culture of Kwun Tong', in King and Lee (eds), *Social Life and Development*, pp. 147–68.

44 Harris, *Hong Kong*, p. 12.

45 We thank Tak-Wing Ngo for alerting us to this change in the direction which social movements underwent in the 1970s.

46 Lui, 'Yali tuanti zhengzhi'; Lui and Kung, *Chengshi zongheng*.

47 Anthony B.L. Cheung and K.S. Louie, 'Social conflicts in Hong Kong, 1975–1986', Hong Kong Institute of Asia-Pacific Studies occasional paper no. 3, Chinese University of Hong Kong, 1991; Ernest Chui and On Kwok Lai, 'Patterns of social conflicts in Hong Kong in the period 1981 to 1991', mimeograph, 1994.

48 Ming Sing, 'Mobilisation for political change: the pro-democracy movement in Hong Kong (1980s–1994)', in Stephen W.K. Chiu and Tai-lok Lui (eds), *The Dynamics of Social Movement in Hong Kong*, Hong Kong, Hong Kong University Press, forthcoming.

49 On the formation of political groups in the early 1980s, see Joseph Cheng (ed.), *Hong Kong: In Search of a Future*, Hong Kong, Oxford University Press, 1984.

50 For an impression of the activists' mood in the early 1980s, see Shu-ki Tsang *et al.*, *Wuxingqi xia de Xianggang* (Hong Kong Under the Red Flag), Hong Kong, Twilight Books, 1982.

51 See Tai-lok Lui, 'Fanpu guizhen' (Back to basics: rethinking the roles of residents' organizations), in Hong Kong Council of Social Service, *Community Development Resource Book 1989 & 1990*, pp. 12–14; C.B. Leung, 'Community participation: the decline of residents' organizations', in Joseph Cheng (ed.), *Hong Kong in Transition*, Hong Kong, Oxford University Press, 1986, pp. 354–71.

52 Tai-lok Lui, 'Two logics of community politics', in Lau Siu-kai and K.S. Louie (eds), *Hong Kong Tried Democracy*, Hong Kong, Hong Kong Institute of Asia-Pacific Studies, 1993, pp. 331–44.

53 See Stephen W.K. Chiu and David Levin, 'Contestatory unionism', in Chiu and Lui *The Dynamics of Social Movements in Hong Kong*.

54 P.W. Wong, 'The pro-Chinese democracy movement in Hong Kong, 1976–95', in Chiu and Lui, *The Dynamics of Social Movement in Hong Kong*.

55 Lui, 'Two logics of community politics'.

7

INDUSTRIAL HISTORY AND THE ARTIFICE OF *LAISSEZ-FAIRE* COLONIALISM

Tak-Wing Ngo

British colonialism in Hong Kong is commonly seen as having been a transforming agent which brought prosperity and modernity to a previously inhospitable, barren territory. The rapid economic development, effected on 'borrowed place, borrowed time'[1], is often seen as proof of the benevolent nature of colonial rule in Hong Kong. This stands in sharp contrast to many other colonies where economic development was thwarted by colonial rule. In most of the British colonies, the colonial authorities were hostile to the emergence of indigenous capitalism, being either unable or unwilling to facilitate industrialization because of their inertia and/or deference to British commercial interests.[2]

This Chapter argues that the supposedly 'transforming role' of colonial rule is largely the product of a one-sided account of Hong Kong's development trajectory given by the dominant historiography. Colonial rule in Hong Kong, at least before the Second World War, was not much different from that in other British colonies in its attitude to, and its role in, economic development. The incentive of the British colonial authorities to develop their annexed territories into modern metropolises was no greater for Hong Kong than that for other colonies. The difference lies in the one-sided historical narrative about Hong Kong's development. This narrative records only those activities sanctioned by the ruling authorities; justifies policy bias by denying the existence of alternative policy choices; and ascribes economic successes to the 'good policies' of the colonial authorities by *post hoc* rationalization.

It is neither the intention here to question the development of the Hong Kong economy in the past century and a half, nor will there be any attempt to identify the factors contributing to Hong Kong's economic success. What this Chapter tries to examine is the 'constructed belief' of what determined that development. The construction of such a belief, as will be argued, is based on political domination. It is a construction which defines, and is defined by, power relations.[3]

The barren-rock-turned-capitalist-paradise legend

According to the account of the dominant historiography, Hong Kong's development under British colonialism has an almost legendary ring to it: a barren rock was turned into a capitalist paradise by benevolent rule.[4] The account consists of a number of characteristic, recurring elements. First and foremost is the instrumental role British colonial rule played in giving Hong Kong a history. As Sayer writes, 'when this island passed into English hands it was a barren and sparsely inhabited spot; and had been so for a century and more'.[5] In Endacott's words, 'the history of Hong Kong really begins with the coming of the British in 1841'.[6] Hong Kong had no history until the British government 'applied all its empire-building experience to transforming the "inhospitable, pestilence-ridden" island into a salubrious haven of trade and enterprise'.[7]

Thereafter, the account continues, Hong Kong emerged to become a Far Eastern entrepôt. The entire pre-war period is presented as the history of a trading post, in which the vast majority of inhabitants, Chinese and foreign alike, were not settlers, but merely temporary residents – traders or artisans. 'Entrepôt trade was the source of Hong Kong's growth over the first one hundred years of the Colony's existence', until the outbreak of the Second World War.[8] The growth of the entrepôt trade is attributed to benevolent colonial rule and good policy. The main cause of growth, it is said, was the colonial government's application of its nineteenth-century belief in the free market, free trade and minimal government – encapsulated in the doctrine of *laissez-faire*. In Eitel's words, colonial rule in Hong Kong was a 'praiseworthy example of free trade principles and humane government'.[9] Endacott holds that '[b]oth Europeans and Chinese were content to be governed provided there was a minimum of government consistent with security of life and property and opportunity for commercial enterprise'. 'Benthamite *laissez-faire*', he said, 'suited the Chinese as well as the free-trade western merchants'.[10]

The account then continues to narrate how, in the next phase of Hong Kong's development, the colony was industrialized by refugee capital. When the entrepôt trade was halted by the Communist takeover in China and the outbreak of the Korean War, it is said, Hong Kong was forced to transform from an entrepôt into an industrial economy. Industrialization took place with the arrival of capital, skill and entrepreneurs from mainland China, particularly Shanghai. Many of these capitalists sought refuge in Hong Kong 'because of its accessibility, stability, and relative absence of government regulation in economic life'.[11] Thereafter, the industrial economy took off and Hong Kong became one of the Four Little Dragons in the 'East Asian Miracle', widely endorsed as a development model.[12] The government's policies of economic *laissez-faire* and political non-intervention are widely regarded as the major factors contributing to this miracle. In Hong Kong, unlike other colonies, colonial rule and economic development are seen as going hand in hand.

Recovering the untold stories

The one-sidedness of this dominant account can be shown by uncovering those aspects of Hong Kong history that it leaves untold. The account sees the economy of pre-war Hong Kong as having been exclusively based on entrepôt trade, and makes little mention of the development of the manufacturing industry.

Conventionally, shipbuilding is regarded as having been Hong Kong's only significant industry before the Second World War.[13] Other industries mentioned in early twentieth-century official records include sugar refining and rope making.[14] In the 1930 *Hong Kong Administrative Report*, manufacturing industry was grouped under the category 'production', which also included forestry, agriculture and botany; fisheries; mining; and shipbuilding. Within the category 'manufactures', only four entries appeared: sugar refining, hosiery, preserved ginger and rope making.[15] The growth of the manufacturing industries reached its pre-war peak during the 1930s, when the following sectors were recorded in the 1935 *Administrative Report*: shipbuilding, sugar refining, cement, preserved ginger, knitted goods, flashlight torches, rubber shoes and lard. The report, however, remarked that '[t]he Colony itself produces comparatively little, though the shipbuilding, cement, rope, tin and sugar refining, rubber shoe and cotton knitting industries are not unimportant'.[16]

A high-powered government economic commission set up in 1934 admitted that there was 'considerable industrial activity apart from shipping', which had become 'a not unimportant activity in the Colony'. The commission, however, emphasized that the growth of the manufacturing industry was 'somewhat haphazard', and that 'the real basis of the Colony's commercial existence is, and must continue to be, the handling of the trade of China'. The reason given was that '[a]s far as its commercial existence is concerned Hong Kong's *raison d'être* is the entrepôt trade of South China'.[17]

Official records in the post-war period reiterated the unimportance of the manufacturing sector. When Sir Alexander Grantham gave his Governor's address to the colony's legislature in 1949, he said: 'Trade is the life blood of this Colony ... I am proud of being Governor of a Colony of shopkeepers.'[18] In an internal dispatch to the Secretary of State for the Colonies, Grantham described the factories set up in the 1930s as 'relatively inefficient small-scale consumer goods industries'.[19] In a 1958 review of Hong Kong's industrial development in the *Hong Kong Annual Report*, the economy during the period 1841–1941 was described as 'an entrepôt, a mart and storehouse for goods in transit to Asia and the West'.[20] The government paid so little attention to industry that one critical observer stated that until the 1960s, 'forestry was given almost as much space as manufacturing' in the *Hong Kong Annual Reports*.[21] With hardly any forestry to speak of, one can imagine the significance of manufacturing in the government's eyes.

The official account has become the standard interpretation of the pre-war economic history of Hong Kong. Szczepanik, one of the earliest to make a study of Hong Kong's industrialization, suggests that the colony's first hundred years may be described as 'a century of the growth of an entrepôt economy'.[22] Others describe pre-war Hong Kong as a 'pre-industrial society'.[23] The lonely voice that challenges this account comes from Leeming's study of the number of Chinese factories in the pre-war period. Based on the entries in the *Hong Kong and Macao Business Classified Directory*, Leeming found 3,000 factories and workshops in 1927 and about 7,500 in 1940, while official records only registered 1,523 and 1,142 factories in those same years. Leeming argues that Chinese industry in Hong Kong in 1940 was much larger in total, and 'much more advanced in style' than what has been suggested by the conventional account.[24]

However, Chinese publications come up with different figures. In a guide published by the Chinese Manufacturers' Union, the number of factories in 1931 was estimated to be around 600 to 700, employing some 100,000 workers.[25] This matched the figures in a later publication, which reported the number to be around 800 by 1930.[26] In one survey, the number of factories in the years 1938–40 was reported to be around 1,000, employing 100,000 workers[27], while another estimated the number of factories to be more than 2,000.[28] In all these Chinese publications, shipyards, rope-making factories, cement and sugar-refining factories were excluded in the figures, because these factories were owned by the British.

We can see that the estimations and records differ substantially, thus preventing us from drawing any definitive conclusions. One of the reasons for this variation, besides the lack of comprehensive surveys and registrations of factories, is the tremendous ups and downs experienced by the economy during the first half of the twentieth century. The number of factories had grown steadily since the early 1900s, and peaked during the early 1930s. Thereafter, the manufacturing industry was severely affected by the Great Depression. One report recorded that only 300–400 factories survived in the mid-1930s.[29] Towards the end of the 1930s, industrial development picked up again and the number of factories reached a record high of more than 2,000. However, the number dropped again during the Japanese occupation, and did not fully recover until the end of the 1940s. Because of all these rapid fluctuations, a reliable estimation is difficult. For this reason, the number of factories cannot be used, as Leeming has done, as a basis for challenging the official claim that manufacturing was unimportant. Instead, the following discussion argues that it is not the number of factories, but the mode of operation of manufacturing establishments that provides evidence about the importance of industry in the pre-war Hong Kong economy. The fact that this evidence was excluded from the official records shows that the dominant account is biased and selective.

A number of indicators suggest that the beginning of Hong Kong's modern industries can be traced back to at least the turn of the twentieth century rather than to a sudden spurt after the Korean War as commonly assumed.[30] In the first

Table 7.1 The working population in Hong Kong according to the 1931 census

Total population	849,751
Working population	470,794
Number engaged in manufacturing	111,156
Number engaged in commerce and finance	97,026
Number engaged in transport and communications	71,264
Number engaged in fishing and agriculture	64,420

Source: 1931 Census Report quoted in 'Report of the commission appointed by His Excellency the Governor of Hong Kong to enquire into the causes and effects of the present trade depression in Hong Kong and make recommendations for the amelioration of the existing position and for the improvement of the trade of the colony', *Hong Kong Legislative Council Sessional Papers 1935–36*, p. 80.

place, employment figures confirm the importance of industrial activity. Indeed, there was some surprise when the 1931 census reported that the number of people engaged in manufacturing was 111,156 (see Table 7.1). This was one-quarter of the working population and one-seventh of the total population. The breakdown of the working population, as shown in the table, indicates that the manufacturing industry had already absorbed a large proportion of labour. This stands contrary to the established assumption that the vast majority of the workforce were employed in trading, shipping and other services directly related with the shipping trade, such as dockyards, warehouses, banking and insurance, but not manufacturing.

The official data on employment figures match the estimations from records published in Chinese. One survey of Chinese factories in 1931 estimated that over 100,000 workers were employed.[31] Another survey reported that more than 100,000 people worked in Chinese factories during the late 1930s.[32] Still another estimated that there were no less than 100,000 workers in the manufacturing industry after the outbreak of the Sino-Japanese War in 1937.[33]

Such was the growth of employment in manufacturing that it prompted the passing of factory legislation. The first bill, passed in 1922, forbade child labour. Another bill was passed in 1927 to empower the government to introduce regulations on factory safety. Two years later, a bill was drafted to regulate the employment of women and young persons.[34]

In the second place, the importance of industrial activity in Hong Kong is evidenced by the fact that some producers became successful competitors in both the domestic and the overseas markets. In particular, rubber shoes were one of the most successful exports. Britain was a major export market especially after

Table 7.2 Selected examples of factories established before the Second World War

Name of Factory	Year of Establishment	Number of Workers[a]	Size of Premises (ft²)
Nanyang Brother Tobacco Co. Ltd.	1904	1,000	24,000
Li Man Hing Kwok Weaving/Manufacturing Co. Ltd	1908	340	27,000
Castle Peak Celemic Co. Ltd.	1911	340	2,000,000
Kwong Cheung Hing Co. Ltd. (machine-tools)	1913	300	12,000
Ngai Hing Machine Manufacturers	1913	125	12,000
Kwong Man Lung Fire Cracker	1913	120	85,000
Tai Hing Knitting Factory	1914	450	11,000
China Brothers Hat Manufacturers Co.	1916	400	13,000
Chung Fat Co. (preserved food)	1917	100	5,000
Kwong Sang Engineering Co.	1918	160	10,350
Koon Chuen Kow Knitting Factory	1920	500	8,000
Blood Protection Co. Ltd. (mosquito incense)	1920	200	70,000
Wei San Knitting Co.	1920	220	20,000
Wing Fat Printing Co. Ltd.	1920	400	30,000
Tai Hang Rubber Factory	1922	500	100,000
Min Ngai Knitting Co.	1922	580	10,000
Continental Commercial Canery Co. (can-making)	1924	100	9,000
Yau Tack Shing Dragery Factory (dyeing)	1924	180	50,000
Fung Keong Rubber Factory	1925	2,000	10,000
Yuen Hing E. & M. Weaving & Dyeing	1927	100	10,000
Man Yuen Weaving Mill	1927	600	30,000
Chow Ngai Hing Knitting Factor	1927	130	5,000
Lee Kung Man Knitting Factory	1928	130	6,000
Nam Jam Factory (flashlights)	1928	1,000	50,000
Sam Hsing Weaving Factory	1929	2,600	88,000
Chung Nam Flashlight Factory	1929	210	1,600
Ling Nam Hardware Manufacturing Co. (flashlights)	1929	400	30,000
Merry Battery Factory	1930	300	19,000
Amoy Canning Corp.	1930	200	360,000
Sunbeam Manuf. Co. (flashlights)	1930	170	8,000
Num King Flashlight Factory	1930	190	4,000
Sing Chow Electric Factory (flashlights)	1930	230	12,000
Sincere Co. Perfumery Manufacturers	1930	130	30,000
Hop Hing Oil Factory	1931	150	40,000
Nam Shing Flashlight Manufacturer	1931	140	5,000

124

Name of Factory	Year of Establishment	Number of Workers[a]	Size of Premises (ft²)
Ming Wah Metal Works (flashlights)	1931	210	7,000
China Can Co. Hong Kong Branch	1931	500	50,000
Cheung Yuen E.M.W. Dyeing Factory	1933	100	10,000
The World Light Factory (flashlights)	1933	700	30,000
Cheong On Metal Works (flashlights)	1934	100	6,000
United Flashlight Factory	1934	200	3,000
The China Can Co. Ltd., Hong Kong Branch	1935	700	40,000
Ah Hing Cheung Dyeing & Weaving Factory	1936	130	8,000
Cheung Hing Wo Manufacturer of Tin Cans	1937	130	10,000
Chun Ah Metal Works Factory	1937	450	20,000
Chung Wah Weaving & Dyeing Factory Ltd.	1937	110	10,000

Source: Compiled from Hong Kong Chinese Manufacturers' Union (ed.), *Xianggang Zhonghua changshang chupin zhinan* (A Guide to the Products of Chinese Factories in Hong Kong), Hong Kong, Hong Kong Chinese Manufacturers' Union, 1936; and Wang Chuying (ed.), *Xianggang gongchang diaocha* (Survey of Hong Kong Factories), Hong Kong, Nanqiao News Enterprise, 1947.

Note: The figures include permanent and long-term casual laborers. It was very common for factories in this period to employ male permanent workers, and female workers paid on the basis of a daily rate or piece-rate.

the signing of the 1932 Ottawa Agreement on Imperial Preference which allowed free trade in the British and Commonwealth markets. An inter-departmental committee set up in Britain in 1934 complained about the 'invasion of the United Kingdom market' by colonies such as Hong Kong.[35] Specifically, the Committee pinpointed Hong Kong's export of cheap rubber shoes produced under 'Oriental conditions' as an 'evil'.[36] Other industries also performed well. Locally produced leatherwear and cosmetics, for example, had totally displaced imports in the domestic market by the 1920s and the 1930s.[37] By the 1930s, the torch industry had captured the entire Southeast Asian market, which used to be monopolized by British and Japanese producers.[38]

There are no comprehensive statistics on the export value of locally manufac-tured goods. It is estimated that the annual average value of manufactured exports exceeded $90 million between 1938 and 1940.[39] This constituted more than one-sixth of the value of Hong Kong's total export and re-export trade ($512 million) in 1938. The value of textile exports alone amounted to $55.8 million in 1938, representing one-tenth of the total export and re-export value.[40]

A further indication of the growth of Hong Kong's industrial exports is that it led to the imposition of export quotas and the raising of customs tariffs. On two occasions in the 1930s, both the Canadian and the British governments attempted to impose quotas on the import of footwear from Hong Kong. However, no action was taken in the end because Canadian and British producers could not reach an agreement among themselves.[41] At about the same time, mainland China increased the customs tariffs on foreign goods, including Hong Kong's locally manufactured products. The measure was a severe blow to Hong Kong, which had already suffered from the world recession. When Hong Kong manufacturers petitioned the Chinese authorities to lower tariffs on Hong Kong products, the Chamber of Commerce in Canton objected to the request, because manufacturers in Canton feared that the import of Hong Kong products would 'tremendously affect mainland commerce and industry'.[42]

In the third place, while the conventional view claims that inefficient small-scale handicraft workshops dominated Hong Kong manufacturing, the size of factories was in fact quite large, and operation considerably modernized. Most factories had already mechanized by the 1930s, and '[h]andicraft industry soon became history'.[43] Moreover, the range of industrial products was far more extensive than that recorded in official publications, with more than 3,000 different kinds of products being made each year. Within each sector, there were a substantial number of well-established factories, with some employing up to 1,000 workers in factory premises of over 50,000 square feet. Table 7.2 shows some of the well-established factories recorded in factory surveys.

All signs point to the fact that the manufacturing industry had become a significant economic activity by the 1930s. In fact, if we compare the manufacturing sector with that in mainland China, the significance of Hong Kong's industrial development becomes even more obvious. According to official statistics of the Republican government, there were 3,935 registered factories in mainland China in 1937.[44] During the same period, the number of industrial establishments in Hong Kong, according to the most conservative estimates, was around 1,000, a quarter of that in the whole of mainland China. If we further compare the provincial distribution of factories, we find that Hong Kong came only second to Shanghai (see Table 7.3).

It should be stressed that while the above discussion is indicative of the extent of industrial activity in Hong Kong, it is far from a definitive assessment of the situation. Unfortunately, it is impossible to determine the precise proportion of industrial production in the national account. The main reason is the lack of economic statistics. Official estimates of GDP only date back to 1961, and no industrial statistics were collected before the 1970s. Trade statistics before 1959 did not separate domestic exports from re-exports, although the figures for the

Table 7.3 Distribution of factories in Mainland China by province in *1937*

Province	Number of factories	Number of workers
Shanghai	1235	145,226
Zhejiang	781	39,795
Jiangsu	318	105,223
Shandong	228	18,818
Hubei	206	30,072
Fujian	170	2,597
Qingdao	148	10,458
Sichuan	115	13,019
Nanjing	102	4,462
Guangdong	101	10,814
Beiping	101	4,565
Henan	100	13,330
Shanxi	82	12,699
Hunan	55	7,546
Tianjin	52	10,976
Weihaiwei	43	4,149
Yunnan	42	6,353
Hebei	19	7,662
Shaanxi	10	4,635
Gansu	9	1,152
Jiangxi	7	2,397
Chahaer	3	486
Guizhou	3	229
Guangxi	3	174
Anhui	2	136

Source: Republican Government Economic Ministry, *Statistics of Registered Factories in Republican Year 21–26*, quoted in Liu Guoliang, *Zhongguo gongyeshi (jindaijuan)* (Chinese Industrial History Modern Period), Jiangsu, Jiangsu Science and Technology Publisher, 1992, p.270.

value of exports of locally manufactured goods can be traced back to the early 1950s from the annual report of the Department of Commerce and Industry. The annual report of the Hong Kong General Chamber of Commerce contains data on 'local exports' from as early as the 1920s, but these are expressed in quantities (such as tons, bales, rolls, etc.), not in value. The absence of comprehensive statistics reflects, in part, the government's lack of concern about industry, and illustrates the difficulty of recovering information that was not included in colonial documents.[45]

In sum, although it is undeniable that trading was extremely important to the pre-war economy, it has also been shown that it was not the only significant economic activity in pre-war Hong Kong as suggested by established historiography, since other economic activities, notably industrial manufacturing, had also become important at the turn of the twentieth century. Further research into the extent of industrialization is needed, but, as the foregoing discussion has also shown, such research is impeded by the fact that pre-war industry in Hong Kong is a non-existent area as far as the official records are concerned.

Why the story was untold

An immediate question raised by the foregoing discussion is why the story has remained untold; and in whose interests this was so. The answer to this question is power politics. Struggles over power are intimately connected to struggles over interpretation. Actors with unequal access to power and knowledge struggle to tell their stories and construct their own versions of history. Some stories and interpretations triumph over others because those who promote them hold stronger power positions. In our case, industrial history was excluded from official accounts because the British colonizers were only interested in Hong Kong's entrepôt trade. The manufacturing industry was entirely left to the Chinese, who were politically too weak to make their voice heard.

From the very outset, Britain defined the status of Hong Kong as being exclusively an entrepôt for China's trade. British policy in Hong Kong was clearly spelt out by Lord Stanley, the Secretary of State for War and the Colonies, in 1843. Hong Kong was 'occupied not with a view to Colonization but for diplomatic, commercial and military purposes'.[46] The aim of the colony was neither settlement nor the acquisition of natural resources, but to serve as a foothold for British trade in the Far East, especially China. This viewpoint was to predetermine the economic history of pre-war Hong Kong.

The entire colonial administration was designed and set up to facilitate trade: administering the colony and administering the China trade were seen as two sides of the same coin. The government was to serve the interests of the merchants: it was to encourage, but not to interfere with, the conduct of trading and related businesses. This ensured that the British merchant houses had little difficulty in dominating the entrepôt trade. Many of them had been engaging in the China trade, including the trade in opium, long before Hong Kong became a British colony. Among the first to settle in Hong Kong were Lindsay & Co., Jardine, Matheson & Co., and Dent & Co. Then came Butterfield & Swire, Dodwell & Co., and later John D. Hutchison.[47] They acquired large plots of land on which they built their empires: offices, warehouses, residential quarters, junior and senior messes, and stables. Some operated their own fleet of clippers, trading in opium and tea. These merchant houses became so pre-eminent that they came to be known as the princely *hongs* (merchant houses), while the merchant princes were known as *taipans* (great managers).

To advance their interests, the *hongs* built up an extensive social and political network. They formed a Hong Kong General Chamber of Commerce as early as 1861, with Alexander Perceval of Jardine, Matheson & Co. as its first chairman. Ever since its inception, the Chamber of Commerce was firmly controlled by the big British *hongs*. During half of its first hundred years of existence, it was under the chairmanship of four merchant houses: Jardine, Matheson & Co. (19 years);

P&O Steam Navigation Co. (12 years); Butterfield & Swire (10 years); and Turner & Co. (10 years).[48] The Chamber claimed to represent the entire business community in Hong Kong, stating that it 'embodies in its membership all the leading business houses in the Colony'.[49]

In addition, although the *hongs* had bitter conflicts with the colonial bureaucracy over its policies in regard to taxation, land rent and public expenditure, they were the main power interlocutors of the colonial administration.[50] Represented in the Legislative and Executive Councils – the highest law-making and policy-making bodies – since 1850 and 1896, they were the ones, together with the imperial and colonial authorities, who helped construct the official version of Hong Kong's economic history.

The reason why entrepôt trade continued to be defined as the *raison d'être* of Hong Kong, even though the manufacturing industry had gradually become the largest employment sector, was that the latter developed totally outside the imperial plan and the *hongs'* activities. In the first place, the British government believed that any economic investment other than in trade was politically risky, given the turbulent situation in mainland China. Hong Kong was deemed unsuitable for developing long-term projects, especially industrial investment. Thus most economic activities in the colony, such as banking, shipping and insurance, were seen as related exclusively to trading. A British Cabinet paper of 1949 clearly stated:

> ...the demand for the return of Hong Kong to China is always latent and often vocal....Thus long-term planning for the Colony cannot look beyond the next 50 years....Development in the usual sense has a comparatively minor part to play in Hong Kong's future...Hong Kong is a trading centre almost exclusively, and one whose only 'lung' may be cut away in 50 years' time, in which event it is far from certain that Hong Kong itself could survive the operation. Only minor investment for productive purposes is therefore required, and development needs are those which will facilitate trading activities.[51]

Echoing this policy, the *hongs*, throughout the pre-war period, viewed trade as their prime concern. The entrepôt trade was so successful that there was little incentive to manufacture. The profits the *hongs* amassed were used to expand trade, not to engage in industrial production. There were some isolated ventures into industry, most of which were related to the sea trade. Examples included Hongkong and Whampoa Dock Co., Taikoo Dockyard (owned by Butterfield & Swire), Hongkong Rope Manufacturing Co. (Shewan, Tomes & Co.), Green Island Cement Co. (Shewan, Tomes & Co.), Hongkong Ice and Cold Storage Co. (Jardine, Matheson & Co.), China Sugar Refinery Co. (Jardine, Matheson & Co.) and Taikoo Sugar Refinery Co. (Butterfield & Swire).

The lone voice in support of local industry during the period came from Sir William Robinson, who was the Governor from 1891 to 1898. In his first speech to the Legislative Council, Robinson argued that the colony should be less dependent on trade and should develop its own industries.[52] In response to Robinson's encouragement, one of the few *hong* ventures into the manufacturing sector was Jardine, Matheson & Co.'s attempt in 1895 to go into spinning and weaving, which, however, ended in failure. This reinforced the *hongs'* belief that manufacturing had no prospects in Hong Kong.

A survey of all non-Chinese establishments in Hong Kong conducted in 1911 gives a good picture of the situation. The survey recorded over 7,000 entries of European firms engaged in import, export and manufacturing. The actual number of companies in operation was fewer than this because the survey counted the entries by products, and there were companies which engaged in the handling of more than one product. Among these 7,000, only 100 entries were recorded as manufacturers. They represented 40 companies, 28 of which were British. The larger ones, besides those owned by the big *hongs*, included Fenwick, Geo & Co. (machinery and metal); David Storer & Sons (dyes and paints); Wilkinson, Heywood & Clark (dyes and paints); and Watson A.S. & Co. (mineral water and pills).[53]

The British merchants' lack of interest in industrial development left the entire manufacturing sector to the Chinese. It was the Chinese manufacturers from Southern China who started to develop light industry in Hong Kong. Publications and archival sources in Chinese indicate that with the exception of public utilities and a few heavy industries (such as dockyards and cement production), all manufacturing establishments were financed by Chinese capital.[54] These manufacturers started organizing themselves in 1934 when they established the Chinese Manufacturers' Union, which became the main organization of local Chinese manufacturers. From 1938 onwards, it organized annual exhibitions of products manufactured by Chinese factories in Hong Kong, with the aim of promoting industrial production and establishing its own export networks. Its influence, however, was in no way comparable to that of the General Chamber of Commerce. Unlike the few Chinese merchants who were co-opted into the colonial administration as the representatives of the Chinese population, Chinese manufacturers in general did not possess sufficient wealth and social status to warrant political co-optation, hence remaining marginal in the political arena.[55] It is therefore no accident that even those studies that attempt to write 'history from below' stop short at mentioning the manufacturers (as a subordinate group) in pre-war Hong Kong society.[56] The role of manufacturers in Hong Kong's pre-war economic history has remained obscured.

Historical representation and political domination

The dominant historical narrative goes further than marginalizing the presence of subordinate actors in the historical scene: it also justifies a particular mode of intervention and rules out alternative possibilities of action. This is especially prominent in its uncritical support for the pre-war government economic policy of promoting trade at the expense of industry. Under the consensus that trade represented the only genuine source of growth for Hong Kong, any tariff or market protection measures which could have assisted industrial growth were rejected in pursuance of free trade. This policy was also implemented in other British colonies.

In Hong Kong, such a policy was institutionalized in the 1930s, based on a policy review conducted in response to the Great Depression. The outcome represented the views and the interests of the *hongs*. It occurred when the Governor, Sir William Peel, appointed a Commission in 1934 to study the causes and effects of the Depression in Hong Kong and to make recommendations for trade improvement. The Commission was chaired by the Postmaster-General, and included representatives from the major British *hongs*: Stanley Dodwell (managing director of Dodwell & Co.), Vandeleur Grayburn (chief manager of the Hongkong and Shanghai Banking Corporation), William Keswick (head of Jardine Matheson & Co.), William Thomas (manager of the Chartered Bank), and Charles Mackie (partner of Mackinnon, Mackenzie & Co.).[57]

The report was the most comprehensive economic review ever produced in Hong Kong before the Second World War. It presented a very thorough review of the domestic economy and formed the basis of subsequent government policy towards trade and industry. Discussing the relative importance of trade development *vis-á-vis* industrial development, the report argued that the colonial government should adhere to a policy of free trade and abstain from industrial promotion – at a time when the manufacturing industry was already the largest labour-absorbing sector.

The Commission took great pains to convey the message that it was sympathetic to industrial development, although, as mentioned earlier, it considered industrial growth as 'somewhat haphazard', and insisted that 'Hong Kong's *raison d'être* was the entrepôt trade of South China'. It recommended that the government should carefully investigate the conditions of each industry established in the colony, and 'where investigation shows that some measure of assistance in present times of difficulty may result in the survival of a factory on a sound basis, such assistance should be afforded'.[58] How this assistance should be afforded was not mentioned, although the report did set down what should not be done. Direct subsidy to industries was out of the question, because the Commission members 'do not believe that uneconomic industries should be subsidised', and 'there is every reason to believe that once a subsidy was granted to an industry in Hong Kong it would have to be continued'.[59] The fear was that subsidies of this kind would lead to an increase in taxation, something which the merchants consistently resisted.

Tariff protection of domestic industries, a central debate in many other colonies at that time,[60] was also rejected, because, the Commission insisted, 'Hong Kong's prosperity is still largely due to its free trade status'.[61] Like the commercial interests in other colonies, the *hongs* maintained that there was not a single article manufactured in Hong Kong that deserved protection.

In the end, the only concrete recommendations to assist industry were that a Special Committee should be set up to review the economic welfare of the colony; that Hong Kong should come to an understanding with China to enable its industrial products to have free or preferential entry into China; and that the government should avoid the introduction of stringent enforcement of legislation on working conditions. The Commission concluded that there was 'little scope in a Colony like Hong Kong, having no natural raw products and but a small domestic consumption, for the ambitious schemes of economic reconstruction or national planning which have become the modern fashion'.[62]

The British government was also against the establishment of protective tariffs in the colonies to assist infant industries, in order to prevent colonial industrialization that would compete with British industries. The Colonial Office opposed not only the demands for tariff protection but also any assistance to colonial industry, including training facilities, developing industrial estates, selective subsidies, and improvements in the credit and banking system.[63] In the case of Hong Kong, the Colonial Office even asked the colonial government to limit the export of manufactured goods from Hong Kong to Britain. However, disagreement over the size of the proposed quota resulted in a deadlock in the negotiations, and in the end no quota was imposed.[64]

The resulting policy decision thus not only endorsed the dominant view about the unimportance of Hong Kong industry, but also ruled out other possibilities of action. The Commission's policy recommendations were adopted without any alternative view on industrial promotion measures being voiced. Since, in sharp contrast to the *hongs*, the Chinese manufacturers were barely organized and did not articulate a view of their own, their interests were not considered. The British merchants, being the *de facto* spokesmen of the business community, entirely dictated both the agenda and the content of the policy discussions. Under such circumstances, the possibility of adopting any alternative policy was ruled out before it was even voiced or considered. This is a perfect example of the 'non-decision making' described by Bachrach and Baratz, in which domination is achieved by preventing alternative goals from making their way to the political agenda.[65]

To be fair, the *hongs* might not even have been consciously aware of their 'non-decision' to exclude alternative considerations. They were in fact less hostile to industry than the merchants in other colonies, such as Malaya or Singapore. In those cases, industrial expansion was frowned upon because domestic industrial production competed directly with goods imported and marketed by the merchant houses. Industries sprouted in Malaya during the Depression, when the domination of commerce was temporarily weakened, but their development halted after trade recovered.[66] In Singapore, the wisdom of heavy dependence on trade was called into question in the 1920s, but proposals to protect infant industries were rejected by British merchants.[67]

The merchant houses in Hong Kong, on the other hand, were mainly involved in entrepôt trade between China and Western Europe. Domestic industrial production, which was targeted at local consumption or export to China, Southeast Asia and only some parts of Europe, did not affect their market share. They could thus easily take a 'leave-it-alone' attitude towards industry, although they were ready to fight any policy which might increase their tax burden or affect their trading interests. Other than that, they simply left industry to either float or sink.

The artifice of 'good policy'

We have seen how the powerholders in Hong Kong, on the basis of their political domination, were able to present their own view of things as historical 'facts'; and how these 'facts' in turn justified a particular mode of intervention that reinforced their political domination. What is more, this mode of intervention was rationalized *post hoc* as being a 'good policy' which has contributed to growth and prosperity. The colonial government was presented as having always been committed to rational doctrines of macroeconomic management.

The government's 'good policy' is commonly described as being based on the principle of *laissez-faire*, which included such practices as a balanced budget, low taxation, free enterprise and free trade, ostensibly pursued in accordance with the nineteenth-century Smithian ideas of the free market and market rationality. However, as the foregoing discussions suggest, it was not a simple reflection of Smithian or Benthamite principles about how an economy should be managed. Previous studies have found that a balanced budget was pursued in order to avoid laying a financial burden on the imperial government, and that a policy of low taxation was adopted under the pressure exercised by the British merchants. Furthermore, the practice of free enterprise was highly selective, as shown by John Carroll in Chapter 2 of this volume, when the production and sales of lucrative commodities such as opium, salt, liquor and tobacco were regulated by a system of monopolies, thus offering huge rewards to a privileged few. To these we can add that the free trade policy was maintained to safeguard the traders' interests and to avoid colonial industrialization that might have competed with the home industry in Britain. In other words, the policy of free trade in Hong Kong was merely the result of the imperial policy to protect its own market: it was not based on any commitment to a specific macroeconomic doctrine.

The exclusion of industrial history from Hong Kong's historiography conceals the self-interest and short-sightedness of imperial and colonial policies in refusing to develop the colony. By denying the significance of industrial activity, the economic policy pursued to serve imperial and colonial interests has been rationalized, *post hoc*, as a 'good policy' that contributed to the prosperity of the entrepôt trade. In the words of one well-known work, '[t]he once bare rock progressed peacefully and profitably, and with a certain smugness, from the Victorian to the Edwardian period, pinning its faith in free trade, individualism and hard work'.[68]

In this way, the 'good policy of *laissez-faire*' became a legitimation factor for colonial rule, not only in the pre-war period, but also in the post-war era when the entrepôt trade diminished drastically. This established consensus has not been challenged until very recently.[69] The commonly accepted account portrays Hong Kong's industrial transformation as taking place in the early 1950s, as a result of China's civil war, the Communist takeover, and the outbreak of the Korean War. 'What is surprising', says one economist, 'is the speed, extent and success of the transformation of the economy from an entrepôt to an industrial city within the short span of less than a generation'.[70] This 'rapid transformation' is again attributed to the 'good policy of *laissez-faire*'. Szczepanik argues that *laissez-faire* capitalism was an 'institutional datum of the utmost importance for understanding the recent growth of Hong Kong's economy'.[71] Government officials stated complacently that 'it is partly because businessmen enjoy this freedom [of government non-intervention under the policy of *laissez-faire*] in Hong Kong that our manufacturing industries have been so successful'.[72] Thus, ironically, the pre-war policy of not supporting industrial development was claimed to be responsible for the post-war industrial success.

In this celebration of the correctness of colonial policies, the weak dissenting voice of the Chinese manufacturers could hardly be heard. In one of the monthly bulletins published in 1948 by the Chinese Manufacturers' Union, the discontent of the Chinese manufacturers was summarized in bitter words:

> Hong Kong's industries feel that their current status is a homeless or-
> phan…[b]ecause they are not on the land under Chinese jurisdiction,
> but in Hong Kong or Kowloon under British rule.…On the one hand it
> was not protected or assisted by the home government, at the same time
> it was not given attention by the sovereign state. Such status greatly hin-
> dered the development of the Hong Kong Chinese industry.[73]

It is hardly surprising to see that such grievances were simply ignored when industry was considered non-existent in the politically constructed narrative. In response to the policy bias against industry, manufacturers could only rely on their own networks and resources, by developing a kind of guerrilla strategy of flexible manufacturing, as discussed by Lee in Chapter 9 in this volume.

The historical narrative had important political implications for Hong Kong's subsequent development. By selective interpretation and *post hoc* rationalization, it became part of the popular legend of the barren-rock-turned-capitalist paradise, achieved by good policy under capable rule. The post-war government has repeatedly attributed the economic success of the colony to the way it was governed. One Governor, Sir Robert Black, stated that the determinants of the 'mainspring of growth' were the quality of the people – their thrift, industrious-ness and quickness to react to economic stimuli – which had been 'given full scope' by the government policy of 'a stable currency, low direct taxation, freedom of enterprise, and absence of governmental control or interference with the free interplay of the forces of the market'.[74] 'What are our prospects?' the Governor asked, and he answered, 'There seems no reason why we should not go on to even greater prosperity, provided we remain true to our liberal policies.'[75]

It is worth noting that the construction of this artifice of good policy is as much the work of the prominent members of the business community as of the colonial government. For instance, Lydia Dunn, a high-level Swire executive and once Senior Member of the Legislative and Executive Councils, in her reflection after serving some twenty years in public functions, repeated in 1996 essentially what Sir Robert Black had said in 1964:

> I think there is a straightforward reason for our success...in Hong Kong, government provides the framework for a free-enterprise system to operate efficiently, while the entrepreneurial flair and hard work of a highly motivated immigrant population enable them to take full advantage of its opportunities.[76]

Ironically, this view has also been taken over by the Special Administrative Region government under Chinese sovereignty. In his ceremonial speech at the establishment of the new government on 1 July 1997, the shipping magnate turned Chief Executive Tung Chee Hwa reiterated the same cliché when he declared that

> Free enterprise and free trade; prudent financial management and low taxation; the rule of law, an executive-led government and an efficient civil service have been a part of our tradition....It is the responsibility of the Special Administrative Region Government to create a good business environment, plan for and train the necessary manpower, and uphold the principles of free trade, fair competition and non-interference in the market.[77]

This view has indeed become an officially sanctioned historiographic position maintained by mainland Chinese officials and historians. The policy of *laissez-faire* is hailed as one of the major factors contributing to Hong Kong's economic prosperity.[78] The pervasiveness of such a historical representation lies, perhaps, as one critical observer remarks, in the fact that either the myth of *laissez-faire* capitalism as projected by the colonial regime has appeared so real that mainland Chinese officials and historians have accepted its characterization; or that the hypocrisy of *laissez-faire* colonialism with its record of unfair and discriminatory practices allows the in-coming power interlocutors to claim special privileges under the new regime as the British *hongs* had done under colonial rule.[79]

Conclusion

British colonialism imposed similar constraints on Hong Kong's industrial development as it did in other colonies during the same period. The fact that these constraints have seldom been mentioned, and that colonial rule in Hong Kong has been seen as playing nothing but a positive role, highlights the political nature of selective historical representation. Our reappraisal of the commonly accepted economic history of pre-war Hong Kong shows that this history is not a neutral record of activities and events, but that it shapes, and is shaped by, political domination under colonial rule. It has not only served political rule in the past, but continues to do so in the present, by compelling us to see the present from the same biased viewpoint which colonial historiography has used to construct the past.

It is this politically sustained selective interpretation of history that this and other contributions in this volume seek to redress. The various contributions in this volume – on the unfair and coercive criminal justice system targeted at the Chinese population, the manipulation of rural politics by the government, the unwillingness of the colonial state to help industrial upgrading, and so on – reveal aspects of British rule in Hong Kong which were hitherto neglected or suppressed in the established historiography.

We should, however, avoid jumping to the conclusion that colonial rule in Hong Kong rested solely upon deceit and hypocrisy, or what Balandier called 'pseudo-justifications and rationalizations'.[80] To do so would mean substituting one selective interpretation by another. Indeed, domination and subordination can be found in all kinds of political rule. The tendency to record one's own version of events and marginalize others is universal. Hence, criticism of the history and politics in a colony should not, as Cooper reminds us, be reduced to anti-colonial history and politics.[81]

Hong Kong's economic achievement under British rule, especially after the Second World War, is undeniable. This Chapter, in its effort to redress the 'romanticized' view of the British role in Hong Kong's modernization process, admittedly tends to highlight the constraining role of colonial rule at the expense of its positive contributions. To arrive at a more balanced understanding, more research will be needed.

One thing which urgently needs to be done, in this context, is to examine the activities of subordinate actors whose voices have been marginalized in the established account. This Chapter does not contribute directly to this need, as it still covers an élite theme: the analysis of the operation of dominance as it subordinated and excluded certain forms of activities and their histories. The analysis only aims at providing a setting in which the voices of the excluded can be restored and debated. Having lifted a small part of the curtain covering the importance of industrial activity in pre-war Hong Kong, it points to the need of studying the actual activities, i.e. of restoring the agency, of those subordinate actors. To a certain extent, this has been taken up by Lee in Chapter 9, when he examines the guerrilla strategy of manufacturers as a response to the subordination of industry in a colonial economy. For a fuller exposition, we have to examine how the subordinate actors interacted with the colonial government and the ruling élite in multiple ways; how they formulated their own strategies of action; and how these strategies helped define and refine élite options. This kind of research will make visible what established historiography has left obscured, and increase our understanding of the complexity of coloniality in the shaping of British Hong Kong.

NOTES

1 Richard Hughes, *Borrowed Place Borrowed Time: Hong Kong and Its Many Faces*, 2nd rev. edn, London, André Deutsch, 1976.
2 Michael Havinden and David Meredith, *Colonialism and Development: Britain and Its Tropical Colonies, 1850–1960*, London, Routledge, 1993, pp. 310–18.
3 Florencia E. Mallon, 'The promise and dilemma of subaltern studies: perspectives from Latin American history', *American Historical Review*, 1994, vol. 99, no. 5, December, p. 1507.
4 The term 'capitalist paradise' is rhetorically used by Jon Woronoff, *Hong Kong: Capitalist Paradise*, Hong Kong, Heinemann Asia, 1980.
5 Geoffrey Robley Sayer, *Hong Kong: Birth, Adolescence, and Coming of Age*, London, Oxford University Press, 1937. p. 5.
6 First published in 1958, Endacott's work has become the standard text for Hong Kong history. It was already in its eighth impression by 1985, the edition from which this statement was taken; G.B. Endacott, *A History of Hong Kong*, rev. edn, Hong Kong, Oxford University Press, 1973, p. 4.
7 Solomon Bard, *Traders of Hong Kong: Some Foreign Merchant Houses, 1841–1899*, Hong Kong, Urban Council, 1993, p. 40.
8 James Riedel, *The Industrialisation of Hong Kong*, Tübingen, J.C.B. Mohr (Paul Siebeck), 1974, p. 5.
9 E.J. Eitel, *Europe in China: The History of Hong Kong from the Beginning to the Year 1882*, London, Luzac & Co., 1895, p. 57.
10 Endacott, *A History of Hong Kong*, p. 121.
11 Wong Siu-lun, *Emigrant Entrepreneurs: Shanghai Industrialists in Hong Kong*, Hong Kong, Oxford University Press, 1988.
12 World Bank, *The East Asian Miracle: Economic Growth and Public Policy*, New York, Oxford University Press, 1993.
13 Shipbuilding is described as Hong Kong's 'premier industry' in *Commercial and Industrial Hong Kong: A Record of 94 Years Progress of the Colony in Commerce, Trade, Industry, and Shipping (1841–1935)*, Hong Kong, Bedikton Co., 1935, p. 43.
14 These were the only two entries recorded under the section 'industry' in the Hong Kong Government, *Hong Kong Administrative Report 1925*.
15 Hong Kong Government, *Hong Kong Administrative Report 1930*, pp. 6–7.
16 Hong Kong Government, *Hong Kong Administrative Report 1935*, p. 15.
17 'Report of the commission appointed by His Excellency the Governor of Hong Kong to enquire into the causes and effects of the present trade depression in Hong Kong and make recommendations for the amelioration of the existing position and for the improvement of the trade of the colony', *Hong Kong Legislative Council Sessional Papers 1935–36*, pp. 72, 73, 76, 80, and 89; cited hereafter as 'Report of the Trade Depression'.
18 Hong Kong Government, *Hong Kong Hansard 1949*, p. 59.

19 Great Britain, Public Record Office, *Colonial Office Records*, CO 1030, Original Correspondence, CO 1030/292, Grantham to Alan Lennox-Boyd, M.P. Secretary of State for the Colonies, 2 July 1955.

20 Hong Kong Government, *Hong Kong Annual Report 1958*, p. 3.

21 Frank Leeming, 'The earlier industrialisation of Hong Kong', *Modern Asian Studies*, 1975, vol. 9, no. 3, p. 338.

22 Edward Szczepanik, *The Economic Growth of Hong Kong*, London, Oxford University Press, 1958, p. 3.

23 A.J. Youngson, *Hong Kong Economic Growth and Policy*, Hong Kong, Oxford University Press, 1982, p. 2.

24 Leeming, 'The earlier industrialisation of Hong Kong', p. 338.

25 Liang Qianwu, 'Xianggang huaqiao gongye zhi niaokan' (A bird's eye view of Chinese industry in Hong Kong), in Hong Kong Chinese Manufacturers' Union (ed.), *Xianggang Zhonghua changshang chupin zhinan* (A Guide to the Products of Chinese Factories in Hong Kong), Hong Kong, Hong Kong Chinese Manufacturers' Union, 1936, p. A23.

26 Chan Tai Tung and Chan Man Yuen (eds), *Bainian shangye* (A Century of Commerce), Hong Kong, Guangming wenhua shiye gongsi, 1941.

27 Jingji ziliaoshe (Economic Information Agency) (ed.), *Xianggang gongshang shouce* (Hong Kong Industry and Commerce Directory), Hong Kong, Jingji ziliaoshe, 1946, p. 11.

28 Chan and Chan, *Bainian shangye*.

29 Liang, 'Xianggang huaqiao gongye', p. A23.

30 This view of post-war industrialization as a continuation of pre-war development is mentioned in passing by Y.C. Jao, 'Financing Hong Kong's early postwar industrialisation: the role of the Hongkong and Shanghai Banking Corporation', in Frank H.H. King (ed.), *Eastern Banking: Essays in the History of the Hongkong and Shanghai Banking Corporation*, London, Athlone Press, 1983, p. 549.

31 Liang, 'Xianggang huaqiao', p. A23.

32 Jingji ziliaoshe, *Xianggang gongshang shouce*, p. 11.

33 Chan and Chan, *Bainian shangye*.

34 Norman J. Miners, *Hong Kong Under Imperial Rule, 1912–1941*, Hong Kong, Oxford University Press, 1987, p.21.

35 CO 885/HO XC/A29033, Report of the Inter-Departmental Committee on the Industrial Development of the Colonial Empire, March 1934, p. 5.

36 See note 35.

37 Zhang Xiaohui, 'Jindai Xianggang de huazi gongye' (Chinese industry in modern Hong Kong), *Jindaishi yanjiu* (Studies in Modern History), 1996, vol. 91, no. 1, p. 163.

38 Liang, 'Xianggang huaqiao gongye', pp. A23–4.

39 Zhang, 'Jindai Xianggang', p. 142. All values given here and hereafter are in local currency at current prices.

40 Zhang, 'Jindai Xianggang', p. 155.

41 Havinden and Meredith, *Colonialism and Development*, p. 170.

42 Quoted in Zhang, 'Jindai Xianggang', p. 158.

43 Zhang, 'Jindai Xianggang', p. 145.

44 Quoted in Liu Guoliang, *Zhongguo gongyeshi (jindaijuan)* (Chinese Industrial History (Modern Period)), Jiangsu, Jiangsu Science and Technology Publishers, 1992, p. 270.

45 A thoughtful reflection on this problem can be found in Ranajit Guha, 'The prose of counter-insurgency', in Ranajit Guha (ed.), *Selected Subaltern Studies*, New York, Oxford University Press, 1988, pp. 45–84.

46 Extract from 'A Dispatch from Lord Stanley, Secretary of State for War and the Colonies, to Sir Henry Pottinger, the Governor of Hong Kong, no. 8, 3 June 1843, on the Functions and Purpose of Hong Kong and the Problems of its Administration',

in G.B. Endacott (ed.), *An Eastern Entrepôt: A Collection of Documents Illustrating the History of Hong Kong*, London, Her Majesty's Stationery Office, 1964, p. 255.

47 For a more comprehensive list of the early traders, see Bard, *Traders of Hong Kong*.

48 Compiled from 'Officers of the Hong Kong General Chamber of Commerce', in Hong Kong General Chamber of Commerce, *Hong Kong General Chamber of Commerce Report*, various years.

49 Hong Kong General Chamber of Commerce, *Hong Kong General Chamber of Commerce Report 1948*, p. 10.

50 Conflicts between the British merchants and the colonial bureaucrats are documented in G.B. Endacott, *Government and People in Hong Kong 1841–1962: A Constitutional History*, Hong Kong, Hong Kong University Press, 1964.

51 CO 537, Supplementary, CO 537/4844, Far Eastern (Official) Committee, Final Report by Working Party on Far Eastern Economic Survey, 31 August 1949.

52 Endacott, *A History of Hong Kong*, p. 259.

53 CO 129, Dispatches from the Governor of Hong Kong, CO 129/379, Schedule of Hong Kong Importers, Exporters and Manufacturers other than Chinese, prepared by the Hong Kong General Chamber of Commerce to W.D. Barnes, Colonial Secretary, 4 July 1911.

54 See the various issues of *Changshang yuekan* (Manufacturers' Monthly Bulletin); and Hong Kong Chinese Manufacturers' Union, *Xianggang Zhongguo huopin zhanlanhui* (Pictorial Record of the Exhibition of Hong Kong Chinese Products), Hong Kong, Hong Kong Chinese Manufacturers' Union. See also K.C. Wong, *Zhonghua shangye zhinan* (China Commercial Directory), Hong Kong, 1933; Gongshang ribao bianjibu, *Xianggang huazi gongchang diaochalu* (A Survey of Chinese-Capital Factories), Hong Kong, Gongshang ribao yingyebu, 1934; Hong Kong Chinese Manufacturers' Union, *Xianggang Zhonghua changshang chupin zhinan*; Chan and Chan, *Bainian shangye*; Jingji ziliaoshe, *Xianggang gongshang shouce*; and Wang Chuying (ed.), *Xianggang gongchang diaocha* (Survey of Hong Kong Factories), Hong Kong, Nanqiao News Enterprise, 1947. Cf. English publications such as *Commercial and Industrial Hong Kong*.

55 The earliest study to notice this commerce-industry separation and the dominance of commercial interests was Chung-Tong Wu, 'Societal guidance and development: a case study of Hong Kong', Ph.D. dissertation, University of California, Los Angeles, 1973.

56 See, for example, Jung-fang Tsai, *Hong Kong in Chinese History: Community and Social Unrest in the British Colony, 1842–1913*, New York, Columbia University Press, 1993; Chan Wai Kwan, *The Making of Hong Kong Society: Three Studies of Class Formation in Early Hong Kong*, Oxford, Clarendon Press, 1991.

57 A full membership list of the Commission can be found in the 'Report of the Trade Depression', p. 67.

58 'Report of the Trade Depression', p. 89.

59 'Report of the Trade Depression', p. 90.

60 See, for example, Wong Lin Ken, 'Singapore: its growth as an entrepôt port, 1819–1941', *Journal of Southeast Asian Studies*, 1978, vol. 4, no. 1, pp. 75–6.

61 'Report of the Trade Depression', p. 79.

62 'Report of the Trade Depression', p. 113.

63 David Meredith, 'The British government and colonial economic policy, 1919–39', *Economic History Review*, 1973, vol. 28, no. 3, pp. 484–99.

64 Miners, *Hong Kong*, p. 23.

65 Peter Bachrach and Morton S. Baratz, 'Two faces of power', *American Political Science Review*, 1962, vol. 56, no. 4, December, pp. 947–52.

66 Jomo Kwame Sundaram, *A Question of Class: Capital, the State, and Uneven Development in Malaysia*, Singapore, Oxford University Press, 1986, chs 5 and 9.

67 Garry Rodan, *The Political Economy of Singapore's Industrialization: National State and International Capital*, Kuala Lumpur, Forum, 1989, ch. 2.

68 Hughes, *Borrowed Place*, p. 126.

69 Chiu argues that the post-war policy of *laissez-faire* was adopted under the continued domination of merchant interests. This view is echoed by Alex Choi in this volume. Stephen Chiu, 'The politics of laissez-faire: Hong Kong's strategy of industrialisation in historical perspective', Hong Kong Institute of Asia-Pacific Studies occasional paper no. 4, Hong Kong, Chinese University of Hong Kong, 1994.

70 Ho Yin-ping, *Trade, Industrial Restructuring and Development in Hong Kong*, London, Macmillan, 1992, p. 5.

71 Szczepanik, *The Economic Growth of Hong Kong*, p. 7.

72 Hong Kong Government, *Hong Kong Hansard 1987/88*, p. 1334.

73 Ai Ming, 'Lun Xianggang huaqiao gongye zhi diwei' (On the status of Chinese industry in Hong Kong), *Changshang yuekan* (Manufacturers' Monthly Bulletin), 1948, March, pp. 9–10. The quotation is my own translation from the Chinese text.

74 Hong Kong Government, *Hong Kong Hansard 1964*, pp. 35–6.

75 Hong Kong Government, *Hong Kong Hansard 1964*, p. 38.

76 Lydia Dunn, 'The way we are', in Hong Kong Government, *Hong Kong Annual Report 1996*, p. 1.

77 Tung Chee Hwa, 'A future of excellence and prosperity for all', speech by the Chief Executive the Honourable Tung Chee Hwa at the ceremony to celebrate the establishment of the Hong Kong Special Administrative Region of the People's Republic of China, 1 July 1997, pp. 12 and 14.

78 See, for example, Liu Shuyong, 'Hong Kong: a survey of its political and economic development over the past 150 years', *China Quarterly*, 1997, no. 151, September, p. 591; Wu Tianqing, *Xianggang jingji yu jingji zhengce* (The Hong Kong Economy and Economic Policy), Hong Kong, Zhonghua shuju, 1990, ch. 1; and Zheng Deliang, *Xianggang jingji wenti chutan* (A Preliminary Review of Hong Kong's Economic Problems), Guangdong, Zhongshan daxue chubanshe, 1984, ch. 1.

79 Ming K. Chan, 'The legacy of the British administration of Hong Kong: a view from Hong Kong', *China Quarterly*, 1997, no. 151, September, pp. 576–7.

80 G. Balandier, 'The colonial situation: a theoretical approach', in Immanuel Wallerstein (ed.), *Social Change: The Colonial Situation*, New York, John Wiley & Sons, 1966, p. 50.

81 Frederick Cooper, 'Conflict and connection: rethinking colonial African history', *American Historical Review*, 1994, vol. 99, no. 5, December, p. 1519.

8

STATE–BUSINESS RELATIONS AND INDUSTRIAL RESTRUCTURING

Alex H. Choi

The studies of Hong Kong's industrialization have been dominated by neo-classical economic theory. This theory maintains that Hong Kong was able to industrialize rapidly because of its open economic structure. This openness allows its industries to specialize in areas in which they have comparative advantage.[1] Utilizing the abundant and cheap labour resources, the manufacturing sector achieved amazing growth by exporting to the international market. Export-Oriented Industrialization (EOI) wrought miracles for the Hong Kong economy. This view was not challenged until the late 1980s and early 1990s when many statist writers advanced theories concerning the 'politicalization' of the free market theory. They show that neoclassical interpretations neglected institutional aspects of economic policy-making. Embarking on a course of free market growth requires a strong state to insulate the decision-making process from rent-seeking and market-irrational social demands. It is essential to elucidate the political dynamics that make possible the pursuit of a free market growth strategy.

From this statist perspective, non-interventionism prevailed in Hong Kong because the Financial Secretaries, all of them committed free marketeers, were extremely powerful within the colonial structure. Directly appointed from London to head the colonial economic bureaucracy, they owed little to local political circles, and were able to create the political frameworks within which markets could thrive. According to the statists, this institutional structure is the foundation of Hong Kong's free market economy and industrial prosperity.[2]

Despite statism's not insignificant contribution in transcending the free market debate on Hong Kong, it has not gone further than identifying the commitment and the authority of the Financial Secretaries as the main underlying factor in the Hong Kong miracle. One can even say that it risks further romanticizing the benevolent colonial rule paradigm. The implication of such an argument is that colonial rule enabled the bureaucratic authorities to be insulated from popular political pressure. This allowed the authorities to carry out policies objectively in accordance with rational market principles.

This Chapter argues that the ideology and power of the Financial Secretary cannot be viewed in isolation from the broad parameters of conflict in the Cold War era, the colonial crisis, and the dynamics between the industrial and commercial interests.

After a decade of rapid industrialization in the 1960s, Hong Kong's export manufacturers had encountered various difficulties including protectionism, rising labour costs and foreign competition. The economically powerful industrial bourgeoisie demanded government assistance to restructure industry from labour-intensive to high-tech production. These demands were met with lukewarm response from the colonial government. Focusing on state–business relations in the historical context of the 1960s, this Chapter shows that the colonial state's apathetic response to the demands of the industrial bourgeoisie were not only due to the opposition of the Financial Secretary, but also to various structural obstacles and intra-élite conflicts that worked against the allocation of state resources to industrial restructuring. The subsequent development trajectory of Hong Kong – far from being an outcome of free entreprises' response to free market conditions under indirect rule – constitutes a failed industrial restructuring effort shaped by the institutional dictum of colonial power structures.

The pressure for industrial restructuring

Nicholas Owen's widely read article, 'Economic Policy in Hong Kong', is renowned for its critique of the functioning of the self-regulating market in the colony.[3] A less noted aspect, however, is the inconsistency he has unconsciously committed in the discussion of the relation between industrial upgrading and labour-intensive EOI. Typical of his generation of writers, Owen was optimistic about export manufacturing. His optimism was founded on the argument that this form of industrialization provided 'the opportunity of "manufacturing up", that is moving into the better quality end of a product range through experience, better design and improved quality control'.[4] But in a later section of the same article, he contradicted his own expectation by providing a list of figures showing that industrial deepening had not taken place in Hong Kong after more than one and a half decades of rapid industrialization. He concluded that,

> we would *expect* industry to become more capital-intensive as the economy develops...the surprising result...is that there is no evidence of any capital deepening in the seven-year period 1960–7.[5]

Although Owen did not explain why there was no capital deepening, it should be pointed out that his expectation of a more mature industrial structure for Hong Kong was largely justifiable and widely shared.[6] By the time of his writing, Hong Kong had gone through two full decades of rapid industrialization, and signals for the need for industrial upgrading, such as labour shortage, protectionism and foreign competition, had been flashing for almost ten years since the end of the 1950s.

The problem began with Britain's imposition of restrictions on Hong Kong's exports under the 1959 Lancashire Pact. Since then, protectionism became a serious menace to export-oriented industries. Britain's attempt to enter the European Community in 1961 created another serious threat to Hong Kong's industries. In order to become a member of the Community, Britain had to terminate the Imperial Preference system under which Hong Kong's exports were given tariff concessions when entering the British market. Such concessions were considered crucial to exclude Japan, Hong Kong's most significant competitor, from the British market.[7]

Other additional factors exacerbated the problem. Land rent and wages increased sharply during the 1960s, raising the costs of industrial production.[8] Moreover, since the mid-1960s, Taiwan, South Korea and Singapore had one by one jumped on the export manufacturing bandwagon and presented Hong Kong with formidable competition.[9] Despite the fact that Hong Kong had had an early start in EOI, its manufacturing industry remained in the labour-intensive stage, while its competitors were already on their way to capital-intensive production. Symptomatic of its weakness was that Hong Kong industrialists preferred to engage in so-called 'cutthroat competition', i.e., the scramble to produce low-priced goods at the expense of quality and durability.[10] Since short-run cost-cutting was the primary concern, there was little incentive to invest in design, mechanization and labour training to raise productivity. Even the most advanced and well-capitalized textile sector only maintained its share of the British market, not by high productivity and efficiency, but by relying on the Imperial Preference tariff concession, and, most importantly, by 'using its spindles and looms twice as intensively as in Europe', through operating the machinery in three eight-hour shifts.[11]

In spite of all these problems, the Hong Kong government was determined not to pursue industrial restructuring. This was clearly expressed by Governor Robert Black in his 1964 remark that Hong Kong could never hope to catch up with the developed countries, 'because our only competitive advantage is clearly lower labour costs', and, he continued, 'I do not see how we can compete on the basis of capital intensive industries'.[12] Governor Black's lack of confidence on developing capital-intensive industry closely paralleled that of his predecessor, Alexander Grantham, who declared in 1949, a time when fundamental socio-economic changes were already well under way, that he was proud to be the 'Governor of a Colony of shopkeepers', and found the prospect of Hong Kong's industrialization 'obscure'.[13]

While these remarks could be used to show that the colonial administrators were uninnovative and complacent, one should not lose sight of the fact that in adhering to the entrepôt principle and refusing to allocate resources for industrial upgrading, the government acted in the interest of the commercial and financial bourgeoisie. It will be argued that these interests were mediated by factors including the crisis of colonialism; the ambivalent relation between the trading and industrial élites; and the internal division of the industrial class.

By demonstrating the centrality of the interests of commercial and financial bourgeoisie in shaping the post-war economic policy, it is hoped that the pitfall of what Irfan Habib has called 'studying a colonial economy without perceiving colonialism' can be avoided.[14] Looking at Hong Kong's economic policy through the prism of colonialism, we can see that the colonial state's agenda and its resource distribution policy were strongly influenced by the interests of the metropole country and the British commercial and financial interests. By showing that these interests were intimately tied up with the *laissez-faire*[15] doctrine, this study challenges the gentle and benevolent picture deceptively painted by the hegemonic colonial discourse, appropriately named the 'Barren-Rock-Turned-Capitalist-Paradise Legend' by Tak-Wing Ngo in his contribution to this volume.

One of the pillars supporting the benevolent image of colonialism is the free trade policy, which is portrayed as the engine generating economic prosperity for the entire population. In the colonial discourse, free trade has been credited with numerous positive contributions, such as laying the foundation for Hong Kong's industrialization and rapid economic growth. However, upon closer examination, it turns out that the free trade policy was neither the driving force behind Hong Kong's industrial transformation in the 1950s, nor amenable to the upgrading of the industrial sector in the 1960s.[16] The real reason why the state steadfastly adhered to this policy was that it economically benefited the British commercial and financial élite. The colonial state has been averse to the redistribution of resources to the Chinese industrial élite since this was incompatible with its class nature. To analyse this constraint on the restructuring of Hong Kong's industries, three factors need further elaboration: the insecurity of Hong Kong's colonial structure; the crisis of British imperialism; and the dominance of the financial and commercial elite in the colonial state.

The insecurity of colonialism

Political insecurity was the hallmark of colonialism in post-war Hong Kong. Discussion on the political future of Hong Kong is not new: in at least two critical periods after the Second World War the security of the colonial system was in doubt, first after the Communist victory in China in 1949, and then around the time of the Vietnam War and the Cultural Revolution in the second half of the 1960s. These incidents showed that Hong Kong's political status did not depend solely on the expiration of the New Territories lease – although no one doubted that, if Hong Kong's colonial regime could last for so long, 1997 would be a year of reckoning between China and Britain – but also on the rise and fall of the great powers and Cold War politics. The good old days of British hegemony were over, and China, which underwent Communist transformation, emerged as a strong regime reluctant to tolerate foreign intrusion. In this situation of Britain's decline and China's ascendancy, Hong Kong's continued existence as a British colony came to rely largely on the goodwill of China.

To a certain extent, the sense of insecurity in the colony was ameliorated by the fact that China derived considerable economic benefits from the status quo: the colony became China's major source of exchange earnings.[17] To avoid excessive reliance on the Soviet Union, China wanted to maintain trade with the West, but was conscious of the importance of preventing the re-emergence of foreign control of its economy. As a result, it centralized international trade in the hands of state trading agencies and confined business contacts with the West in Hong Kong. According to David Clayton, China reverted to the Canton system of trade, i.e., state-controlled trade in designated areas, of the eighteenth century.[18] Periodically, pro-China sources in Hong Kong conveyed messages from the mainland expressing China's intention of not altering the colony's political status in the near future.[19] Despite these reassurances, the Hong Kong people, living in the shadow of the Cold War, knew that at any time, strategic needs could outweigh economic considerations. Especially since the Sino-Soviet dispute broke into the open in the early 1960s, the Soviet Union constantly accused China of collaborating with capitalism and colonialism by tolerating the existence of the colonial enclave.[20] Insecurity was also exacerbated by the Vietnam War, at least in its early stage. It generated a great deal of anxiety in Hong Kong because the war might escalate into a major conflict between the US and China, potentially affecting the status of the colony.[21]

In this situation, Hong Kong's capitalist class was caught in a huge dilemma. They were totally powerless to protect the private property system which was fundamental to their survival. While an editorial in the *Far Eastern Economic Review* claimed that they calmly handled the threat as 'an accepted fact of local life',[22] they did become a factor in the uncertainty in their investment decisions. Since the long-term future was insecure, industrialists did not invest in projects with long maturation dates, and bankers did not extend loans for such purposes. Joe England and John Rear commented that this 'fast buck' mentality (i.e., quick profit, short vision) dominated the Hong Kong entrepreneur, who 'is committed to making money, not to making goods for sale'.[23] This has resulted in what Kim-Ming Lee called a 'guerrilla strategy' of manufacturing in his contribution to this volume. What is more, the colonial state itself, as the investor of collective resources, was affected by the same logic engendered by this political environment. Investing social resources in industrial restructuring projects carried great risks, since by the time such projects would mature, Hong Kong might no longer be under British control. At the same time, the colonial government had to take care of the immediate interests of Britain and the resident financial and banking class, who were not in complete agreement with the idea of an industrial Hong Kong.

The crisis of British imperialism

The decline of Britain's industrial economy and the concomitant rise of Hong Kong as a world exporter created, in the words of Susan Strange, a 'bizarre' situation whereby foreign exchanges earned by tiny Hong Kong had become a major pillar supporting the ailing sterling empire.[24] This meant that Hong Kong's surplus was not made available for re-investment in Hong Kong. Britain was apparently not interested in using the surplus to upgrade Hong Kong's industrial structure since it needed the funds for its own use, and given Hong Kong's uncertain future, making such investment decisions did not seem politically sound.

The debate on Hong Kong's surplus underlies the bigger issue of the level of London's control over Hong Kong's affairs. The colonial administration in Hong Kong is said to enjoy a high degree of autonomy from London. Usually, the claim is supported by two pieces of evidence: the first is that Britain never opposed any legislation in recent Hong Kong history, and the second is that financial autonomy was returned to Hong Kong in 1958 after almost a decade of Treasury control.[25] However, these events cannot prove the argument of autonomy because even though Britain chose not to make use of the institutional power on the colony, it does not mean that the colonial state was really autonomous. It may simply mean that Britain did not need to employ these formal mechanisms to secure compliance. Indeed, the sheer power wielded by London in the appointment and dismissal of the Governor ensured that the latter had to follow London's instructions carefully, if he did not want to jeopardize his career.[26]

The political subordination of the colony to the metropole country is one of the most important factors in accounting for the phenomenon of the colonial government's accumulation of large budget surpluses year after year, and its unwillingness to direct resources toward industrial deepening. These surpluses were kept in London as Hong Kong's sterling balance. Initially, the sterling balance accumulated as a result of the debts which Britain incurred *vis-á-vis* the colonies and Commonwealth members during the Second World War. Given Britain's very weak balance of payments after the War, repaying these balances would have further threatened the value of the sterling, because balance holders were sure to convert them quickly into US dollars for imports. The management of these balances evolved into an elaborate set of monetary and exchange controls binding colonies and independent Commonwealth countries into a Sterling Area. Sterling balances could be accumulated by various means. In the case of Hong Kong, the overwhelming majority were built up in three ways. The first was the legal requirement of full exchange backing for each Hong Kong dollar issued, and such backing, as stipulated by law, had to be in sterling. Second, the Hong Kong government was obliged to bank its budget surplus in Britain. Finally, the reserves of banks were also customarily placed in Britain.[27]

Recent debates on the liquidation of the post-war British Empire have revealed that various British governments, both Labour and Conservative, were preoccupied with maintaining sterling's international value. The relation between sterling and decolonization is too complex an issue to be dealt with here.[28] The size of Hong Kong's reserves and the role they played in the overall system still await more detailed studies and analyses. Nevertheless, it is possible to discuss the impact of Britain's sterling policy on Hong Kong's industrialization by dividing the two decades after the Second World War into three phases.

Immediately after the Second World War, Britain entered a stage of he-gemonic decline. Its weakness was manifested in a serious shortage of US dollars, and the consequent inconvertibility of sterling. Having already proved their value during the War, the colonies once again provided the relief for Britain's woes. Ernest Bevin, the Foreign Secretary of the Labour government, declared that he 'was not prepared to sacrifice the British Empire because if the Empire fell…it would mean that the standard of living of our constituents would fall'.[29] The new mission defined at that moment was to turn the colonies into a dollar-earning powerhouse by intensifying local development and expanding exports. After sterling suffered another disaster in the 1947 convertibility crisis, a full-fledged programme aimed at exploiting the export potentials of the colonies, embodied in the Colonial and Development Act, was launched. The 1949 sterling devaluation was staged with an eye to increasing the competitiveness of colonial exports.[30] Policies were also devised to conserve dollars. Apart from strict import controls, industrialization of the colonies was encouraged for the first time in imperial history because domestic production could replace imports. This attempt to remould the colonial empire is known as its 'Second Occupa-tion'.[31]

The colonial officials in Hong Kong were of course affected by Britain's crisis. Short of exportable commodities, they encouraged labour-intensive industriali-zation. Britain's new economic policy encouraged the colonial officials to take a new look at Chinese manufacturing enterprises. Neglected, belittled and condemned as vain endeavours prior to the Second World War, as Ngo shows in this volume, these industries were actively revived and promoted through policies such as the preferential allocation of raw materials, concessionary landleases, overseas export-promoting missions, etc.[32] In light of post-war contingencies, colonial industrialization was no longer viewed as causing potential competition for British industries. These colonial industries were now a valuable asset that could not only save Hong Kong from economic collapse, but also make a precious dollar contribution to the British Empire.

The Korean War was a blessing for the Sterling Area which saw export revenues soaring as a result of rising commodity prices. By the mid-1950s, thanks to the contributions from the colonies, the sterling crisis had temporarily receded. The significance of their contribution could be gauged from the changing composition of the sterling balances. Previously, major holders were ex-colonies and independent Sterling Area members such as India, Ceylon, Pakistan, Australia and South Africa. Their share had now been reduced, and that of colonies such as the Gold Coast (Ghana), Nigeria, Malaya and Hong Kong was increased.[33] With most of the balances directly under the control of British officials in the colonies, the prospect of a crisis precipitated by runs on the balances greatly diminished.

Britain's sterling crisis entered its second phase after the mid-1950s. New developments, within and outside of the empire, convinced Britain that empire and sterling were incompatible. A fateful decision was made to opt for the latter, a foregone conclusion to many observers who were aware of the domination of the finance capital, symbolized by London which is often referred to as 'the City', in British politics.[34]

Since the mid-1950s, Britain had begun to wonder about the economic value of maintaining the empire. In terms of trade, the purchasing power of the Sterling Area shrank after the collapse of commodity prices in the post-Korean War era, while trade between West European countries expanded dynamically. At the same time, the costs of running the empire became unbearable, and severely sapped Britain's limited reserves. To gain the loyalty of independent members of the Sterling Area, Britain encouraged capital investment in these countries, worsening its own external account. The cost of policing and maintaining the formal empire rose steeply in the face of challenges from nationalist movements, stirred up by the intensification of exploitation disguised as colonial development. The pivotal event that changed Britain's course was the 1956 Suez Crisis. This incident, which ignominiously terminated after the refusal of the US to extend aid, ended any lingering hope of Britain's regaining its former glory, and convinced it to accept a 'special relationship' with the US. In effect, Britain became a subordinate partner of the US in Europe. In a sequence of quickly unfolding events, it accepted US assistance in making sterling convertible in 1958. In the colonies, it exchanged political independence for the commitment of colonial leaders to manage their sterling balances 'responsibly'. A period of hasty decolonization, known as the 'Winds of Change', descended upon the colonies between late 1950s and early 1960s. And finally, Britain launched its first bid for European Community membership in 1961.[35]

The question pertinent to our study is why Britain did not give up Hong Kong, especially when it had abandoned colonies with even greater economic value. There are three plausible reasons. In the first place, the strategic value of Hong Kong as an outpost against, and an intelligence-gathering centre on, Communist China would have made the US reluctant to allow Britain to abandon the colony.[36] Second, since there was no credible threat to British rule within Hong Kong, defence expenditure was not likely to be heavy. And finally, this expenditure had to be weighed against the potential gains. Hong Kong's blooming industrial economy set it apart from other colonies relying mainly on primary commodity production. In the final phase of the sterling crisis, which started in the early 1960s, the costs of retaining Hong Kong were far outweighed by the profits.

Unfortunately, however, the dismantling of the empire did not cure the ailing sterling. Before long, Britain was hit by another series of crises: '[e]verything went wrong between 1959 and 1965', according to John Darwin.[37] Analysts have attributed the crisis in this phase to Britain's weak industrial capacity, which was hurt by an overvalued sterling. London's obsession with defending the sterling's status as an international reserve currency made it resist devaluation, thus keeping the value of sterling artificially high. All this put heavy pressure on Britain's reserves. Successive governments subsequently deflated the economy so as to reduce imports, and raised interest rates to attract larger inflows of foreign capital. After implementing these rescue measures, the value of the pound was stabilized, but not without harming industry. Triggered off by another round of low reserves shortly afterwards, the same cycle repeated itself, giving rise to a pattern called the 'stop-go' economy. Convertibility aggravated this situation because, since capital could move in and out more freely, the pound was exposed to speculation pressures.[38]

It was during this period of currency crisis, decolonization and the uncertain allegiance of former colonies to sterling, that Hong Kong's contribution acquired increasing significance. The political control over Hong Kong by British officials was the best guarantee that the mechanism for transferring Hong Kong's reserve to London would operate without hindrance. Indeed, the mechanism functioned so efficiently that, by 1967, an astonishing £350 million, which represented about one-third of Britain's total reserves had been deposited in London.[39] The sheer size of these reserves must have warranted them a place in Britian's consideration of any major policy initiatives on Hong Kong. Susan Strange commented that if 'the fat surplus' had not been of such a major concern to successive British governments, 'their policy towards Hong Kong might not have been petrified for so long into almost total immobility'.[40]

From this perspective, an altogether different interpretation can be made on the Hong Kong government's excuse of the lack of resources in promoting industrial restructuring. While it is true that the government practised a tight fiscal policy, it is far too simplistic to explain this policy purely in terms of the ideological commitment of the various Financial Secretaries to fiscal conserva- tism. In reality, tremendous benefits were reaped by Britain in keeping the Hong Kong government lean, if not mean.

Critical observers have long pointed out that the placing of Hong Kong's reserves in London represented a direct exploitation of the Hong Kong people. Joe England put forward this idea most bluntly. According to him, 'Rarely has exploitation of a colony by the metropolitan power been so direct.'[41] This, however, is in need of some qualification, since nominally, the reserves were still owned by the Hong Kong government and they earned returns on investments in securities and other financial instruments. Nevertheless, Britain did derive considerable benefits from the colony's reserves, and exercised considerable control over them. In the first place, Hong Kong was not allowed to remove these funds from Britain even if sterling was unstable. In the second place, the mere fact that Hong Kong was required to put its reserves in London rather than leave them in Hong Kong meant that its resources were 'on loan' to Britain and could not be used for its own purposes.[42] To put it in more stark terms, Britain used Hong Kong's colonial status to force a developing territory to extend a loan to a developed country. In a milder tone, the *Far Eastern Economic Review* criticized the reserve system as an imposition on Hong Kong of the 'unpleasant task' of supporting sterling, a task which 'is a potentially damaging drain on funds which Hong Kong could make fruitful use of'.[43]

The class interests of the colonial state

Because Hong Kong was designed as a trading post, an élite of British traders and bankers long dominated the colony. By the end of the nineteenth century, however, their economic position had been gradually overshadowed by the Chinese trading élite, who had become the top taxpayers supporting the colonial government.[44] Their ethnic and political connections enabled them to play an influential role in the colonial state. This remained the case even after the main form of accumulation had switched from commercial and entrepôt activities to export-oriented manufacturing.

The extent of the power of the commercial interests could be illustrated in the 1967 devaluation episode.[45] The Hong Kong dollar initially followed sterling in a full 14.3 per cent devaluation. After four days, the Hong Kong government revalued the dollar by 10 per cent, resulting in an effective devaluation of 5.7 per cent. Most incredibly, the colonial state compensated in full the loss incurred by the commercial banks on their sterling reserves with money from the Exchange Fund. This compensation, together with the loss of the Exchange Fund itself, cost the Hong Kong people a total of HK$450 million, or nearly HK$120 per person.[46]

With the colonial officials readily defending the interests of the financial and commercial sector, the colony's industrial transformation had to be carried out in an economic regime originally designed for a commercial economy. Rather than replacing the trading system, the industrial sector was superimposed onto it. Although initially, the free port regime was beneficial to the export-oriented industries, it eventually became an impediment to the latter's further development. Through their privileged access to the colonial state, the commercial élite stonewalled almost every request from the industrial élite that might have infringed the free trade system. The calls for the modification of the free port policy, the setting up of protective tariffs, and the formation of an 'industrial commission' to direct industrial and trade development all either fell on deaf ears or were dismissed out of hand.[47]

A rare glimpse into the conflicts between the industrialists and the banking élite, and the position of the colonial government, can be gleaned from a study of the debate on the setting up of an industrial bank. Undeniably, the prospect of getting inexpensive long-term loans was the primary driving force sustaining the campaign for an industrial bank for more than one and a half decades since the first call was made in the mid-1950s.[48] The industrialists argued that the bank was needed, not just for their own interests, but also for the development of a brighter and more prosperous future for Hong Kong as a whole. As a supporter remarked, '[a]n industrial bank is not merely an organization for the dissemination of financial assistance; it is also a centre for economic study and thought, and a source of guidance to the government...'[49] This vision collided with the bankers' preference for *laissez-faire*. They regarded the industrialists' demand, in the words of R.G.L. Oliplant, the deputy chief of the Hongkong and Shanghai Banking Corporation, as being a

> mere thinly disguised plea for a bank which will give loans to industry against inadequate security....It is not the duty of a bank to accept the equity risk in a new business, which is the responsibility of the proprietor and shareholders...[50]

What is interesting about these remarks is not so much Oliplant's steadfast adherence to the commercial banking principle of never borrowing short and lending long, but the implied assumption that if the Hongkong and Shanghai Bank would not take such risks, the Hong Kong state should also not do so.

The ability of the banking community to impose its will on the state was clearly indicated in the composition of the 1959 Industrial Bank Committee, whose Chairman was the deputy Financial Secretary, and which included five unofficial members of the Executive and Legislative Councils. None of them had any industrial background, but three came from the banking sector.[51] The dominance of the committee by members from the banking sector almost guaranteed a negative recommendation, because they 'resented the notion of setting up a public or semi-public financial institution that would compete with them'.[52]

In conclusion, the uncertain colonial future, the crisis of British imperialism, and the dominance of the financial and commercial class presented a formidable obstacle against industrial upgrading. Nevertheless, these structural constraints were not deterministic. If the industrial bourgeoisie had possessed the power and the resolve to change the structure, this could have significantly affected the outcome. But the industrial élite did not push for change. On the one hand, they did not want to antagonize the colonial state, and on the other hand, they were weakened by their own internal division and disorganization.

The ambivalent relationship between the industrial and commercial classes

Although the colonial state was loath to alter the free port structure, it did care for the well-being of the industrial economy. The colonial state was very willing, and also successful, within limits, in suppressing the rise of production costs and assisting the diversification of Hong Kong's overseas markets, as long as the fundamental interests of the financial and commercial bourgeoisie were left untouched.

The Hong Kong government's exceptionally active approach in trade promotion was not only an attempt to expand industrial production, but also a way of deflecting the anger of the Hong Kong people over British protectionism, and to cater directly to the interests of the commercial sector which had been marketing a large portion of its industrial products overseas.[53] The large investments in infrastructure projects, including the building of reservoirs, the ocean terminal, and new towns, and the expansion of the international airport, consumed a large part of government revenue, but with the growing tax revenue and repressed welfare costs, infrastructural expenditure was found to be a good investment within the means of a small budget.

The most important means of maintaining the low cost structure was the colonial state's apathy, if not outright hostility, towards any call to improve the livelihood of the working people. Demands for higher wages, better working conditions and improvement of social welfare were all branded as a conspiracy aimed at turning the colony into a 'welfare state', which was deemed unrealistic and unreasonable for a developing society. On this issue, the two main factions of the capitalist class reached a high degree of consensus, which reinforced the colonial state's resistance to calls for fairer redistribution of wealth.

Another pillar supporting Hong Kong's low cost structure was China. Up to the early 1970s, China supplied food and consumer goods to Hong Kong at below world market prices. Combined with the rise of price levels for Hong Kong's industrial exports due to the general inflationary tendency of the world market in the 1960s, China thus enabled Hong Kong manufacturers to make increasing profits.[54]

The dedication of the colonial state to maintaining the low cost economy is not too difficult to understand, because keeping costs low is essential for the flourishing of labour-intensive industries. What is more significant, however, is that the continued success of these industries was in the interest not only of the Chinese industrialists, but also of the British financial and commercial élite. After the imposition of the trade embargo on China by the United Nations during the Korean War, the traders and bankers reoriented themselves to serve the rapidly growing industries, either as distributors of industrial materials and machinery, exporters of finished products, financiers of loans and credits, or agents of shipping lines.

The close relationship between the two sectors can be easily gauged from the changing composition of the business of the banks and trading firms. For instance, the Hongkong and Shanghai Banking Corporation, the largest bank in the colony, extended over 30 per cent of its loans to the manufacturing sector between 1966 and 1970. Throughout this period, the manufacturing sector 'remained the largest sector in terms of credit allocated'.[55] The banks also reaped huge profits in providing foreign exchange services which fed the insatiable demand from the export-oriented industries.[56] During the industrial boom in the

1960s, manufacturing industries were such a lucrative source of business for the banks that these banks competed to open branches in industrial districts such as Tsuen Wan and Kwun Tong to serve the industries' needs.[57]

Some big *hongs*, i.e., the large expatriate-owned trading firms, not satisfied with merely serving the manufacturing industries, branched out and set up factories of their own. In 1964, Jardines joined hands with the South China Textile Mill to form a new company, the Textile Alliance, which innovatively integrated all the separate production processes from spinning to garment-making in one big operation.[58] Another big *hong*, Wheelock Merden, was also reported to have an extensive involvement in the textile and toy industries, although its main business remained shipping.[59]

The high integration between the trading and the industrial sectors is further confirmed by Victor Sit's 1979 study on small industries, which found that as many as 44.8 per cent of small firms obtained orders solely, and another 12 per cent partly, from trading firms. Sit also suggests that these percentages must have been higher in the 1960s because firms tended to develop their own marketing network once they were more established.[60]

Indeed, the business of marketing Hong Kong's industrial products became so important for traders that when textile quotas were imposed on Hong Kong in the early 1960s, the traders engaged in a fierce battle with the manufacturers for control over these quotas, which was essentially a fight over the access to export markets. They successfully persuaded the government to reject the Chinese Manufacturers' Association's (CMA) proposal to divide the quota into two equal halves, one for the traders, the other for themselves, and to accept instead a system based on past performance. The latter system worked against the manufacturers because a large number of them had relied on exporters to market their outputs overseas. Under the scheme proposed by the traders, these manufacturers were disqualified from quota entitlement.[61]

The manufacturing industries became Hong Kong's most important, and dynamic sector, and their ups and downs had a direct impact on the entire economy. But why did the sector fail to convert its economic strength into political power? The contention is that, amongst other factors, the industrial élite was a class domesticated by the colonial state.

The domesticated industrial bourgeoisie

The political weakness of the industrial bourgeoisie is noted by observers such as Henderson who points out that 'in spite of the significance of manufacturing industry to the colony's economy, the corridors of power continue to be the almost exclusive preserve of representatives of banking and commercial interests'.[62] Structural factors such as those discussed in the previous sections are crucial in accounting for the political impotence of the industrialists. However they should not be overstated. As the political development in the colony has shown, the industrial bourgeoisie did not mobilize themselves to confront these structures. Instead, they were depoliticized and demobilized by internal division, susceptibility to manipulation, and their sense of insecurity towards the capitalist system. The more organized and better endowed upper stratum was co-opted, absorbed and tamed by the colonial state. The small industrialists, deprived of leaders, were easily bought off by the colonial state which met their basic need for suppressed labour costs. As a result, the colonial state was able to domesticate the bourgeoisie, which became a class more committed to the status quo than to the active creation of the preconditions for its own development.

In order to understand the political impotence of the industrial bourgeoisie, it is important to be aware of its internal divisions and the adept way in which the colonial state manipulated these divisions to its own advantage. Contemporary observers noted the 'disunity' between the larger, better capitalized industrialists and the small manufacturers who ran labour-intensive businesses.[63] Some tended to see such internal divisions primarily in terms of a sub-ethnic conflict between the large immigrant Shanghainese spinners, and the native Cantonese small manufacturers. Although this sub-ethnic division may be real, it should not be exaggerated because the persistent rivalry was probably not due to ethnicity *per se*, but rather to the substantial differences in interests and capital needs. That ethnicity cannot in itself be a sufficient factor to account for intra-élite rivalry is shown in a study by Wong Siu-lun, who noted that the Shanghainese industrialists were on friendlier terms with the expatriates than with their Cantonese compatriots, and preferred to join the former's trade association, the General Chamber of Commerce, rather than the latter's CMA.[64]

A review of the statements made by the CMA shows that the CMA consistently advocated a more interventionist, less export-oriented, industrial policy, which was in sharp disagreement with that of the colonial government. Apart from making persistent demands for cheap land and subsidized loans, it urged the state to expand and protect the domestic market by ending the free port regime. Finding the colonial government not entirely responsive to their demands, the CMA launched a 'Buy Hong Kong Campaign', first through their Annual Exhibitions, and then through 'Hong Kong Weeks'. When Britain imposed harsher protectionist measures in the mid-1960s, the CMA annoyed the colonial government by demanding retaliation.[65] At the same time, they voiced the theory that the free port regime was the main obstacle to diversification, a policy which the Hong Kong government had actively promoted as a countermeasure to protectionism. Hsin Sutu, a vocal and articulate defender-cum-theorist of the CMA position, argued,

> In a world of protective tariffs and quotas, Hong Kong, being a free port, will be left devoid of bargaining power in trade negotiation. Hong Kong's industries are left unprotected against foreign dumping of goods in the domestic market. In the absence of tariff duties, vigorous competition by established foreign enterprises usually prevent new local industries from breaking into the fields, in spite of the fact that such

industries are ones to which Hong Kong is best adapted. There is some truth in the claim that the free port status results in Hong Kong specializing too narrowly. Hong Kong needs a certain degree of protection in order to diversify its industries and thereby add to its industrial stability.[66]

The colonial state dealt with this opposition in a classical divide-and-rule manner. It set up and subsidized the Hong Kong Federation of Industries (HKFI) as a counterweight to the CMA. Through a legal restriction confining voting rights to firms employing more than 100 workers, the government, in effect, invited large Shanghainese firms to control the HKFI. These firms did not share the same difficulties as their smaller counterparts: for example, they had better access to capital, and their land problem was less acute because they had either purchased land or secured concessionary 25-year leases from the government when they relocated to Hong Kong in the late 1940s and early 1950s.[67] Most importantly, as an immigrant community without deep political roots in Hong Kong society, the Shanghainese industrialists chose to collaborate with the colonial authority rather than to stand on the side of their native counterparts. They had a relationship with the colonial government not too unlike the one that existed between the overseas Chinese and the colonial state in pre-independent Southeast Asia.[68] Viewed from this perspective, it is no surprise that the HKFI behaved, in the words of informed critics, like a 'lap-dog' of the government.[69]

With the largest and the most organized stratum of the industrial bourgeoisie standing firmly on its side, the Hong Kong government could safely disregard the various demands of the small manufacturers without much fear of political repercussions. The political timidity of the industrial bourgeoisie was also enhanced by the China factor. The classical method employed by the national bourgeoisie to coerce the colonizer to make concessions to their demands is through a movement for self-rule or outright independence. However, in the peculiar context of Hong Kong, such a strategy was deemed unfeasible because the colonial state was regarded as a buffer against a Communist takeover. Although the weary Britain would probably not have been able to resist China if it had demanded the return of the colony, it was widely believed that if the colonial state's confidence to rule was seriously eroded, Hong Kong would certainly have been reclaimed by China.

The industrial bourgeoisie also regarded the demand for greater democracy as a way to increase their power as too risky because they believed that, if elections were held, the strong Communist unions in Hong Kong would win.[70] Given these limitations, real or imagined, the CMA favoured an exit strategy by sponsoring relocation to low cost production areas in neighbouring countries such as Taiwan and Singapore.[71] In a period of brisk economic growth, even this exit strategy posed little threat to the colonial state, which viewed the threat of exit as little more than a political nuisance.

In conclusion, internal division, external manipulation and the fear of a change in the capitalist system led the industrial bourgeoisie into political immobility. Unwilling to back their demands with credible threats, the industrial bourgeoisie became complacent with the status quo and largely ignored the needs for industrial restructuring.

Because industrial restructuring was not pursued in the 1960s, Hong Kong lost the best, if not its only, opportunity for industrial deepening. From the 1970s onward, strategic considerations led China to a gradual re-establishment of economic and political links with the capitalist world. Foreign goods and capital re-entered the Chinese market on a large scale. The reincorporation of China into the Western order led to the rapid resuscitation of Hong Kong's once eclipsed entrepôt trade, and the fast development of its financial market to serve China's insatiable need for capital. Cheap labour and land in China provided Hong Kong's labour-intensive industries with a second lease of life, and these industries have virtually turned Southern China into Hong Kong's industrial backyard. Under these conditions, it was understandable that industrial deepening did not figure prominently either on the state's agenda, or in the minds of the industrialists. In retrospect, when the colonial state belatedly started to ponder the merits of industrial restructuring by commissioning the Advisory Committee on Diversification to submit a report in 1979, the battle for the survival of industries in Hong Kong might have already been lost.

Conclusion

The above discussion shows that the developing trajectory of Hong Kong was far from being an outcome of free enterprises' response to free market conditions under colonial rule. Instead, it was a failed industrial restructuring effort that was shaped by the institutional dictum of colonial power structures. This institutional dictum included the broader Cold War conflict, the colonial crisis, and the dynamics between the industrial and commercial fractions of the bourgeoisie. The commonly perceived picture of the opposition of the Financial Secretary against the allocation of state resources to industrial restructuring was only one dimension of the larger power structures.

All in all, Hong Kong's failure to commit itself to restructuring its industrial system in the 1960s cannot be attributed solely to the domination of a financial and commercial élite over the colonial state. It is also because the industrial bourgeoisie were not willing to challenge the foundation of the colonial structure for fear of inviting Chinese communism to take over the colony. Even the most organized sectors of the working class, who had the most to gain in pursuing political activism, were hesitant to attack the colonial structure because they were primarily Beijing-oriented, and Beijing had a vested interest, manifested most visibly in the exchange earnings, in maintaining the prosperity of the industrial export sector of the colony.

In fact, a serious attempt to shift the industrial structure away from low cost, labour-intensive, export-oriented industrialization was undertaken, not by the industrial bourgeoisie, but by the working class, in the form of a mass strike in 1967.[72] By undermining the political stability of the colony, the working class delivered a clear message that they could not tolerate poor working conditions forever.[73] This message, had it been taken seriously, might well have generated some impetus to redesign the industrial system in a more capital- and technology-intensive way.[74] Unfortunately, after the end of the Cultural Revolution in mainland China, both the pro-Beijing Federation of Trade Unions, the largest labour organization in the colony, and the leaders of the strike quickly reverted to the conciliatory welfarism adopted since the early 1950s.[75] This gave the colonial government an excuse to interpret the 1967 incident as a purely externally instigated event, delaying major changes as if the socio-economic structure needed a facelift rather than surgery.[76] It was this strategy of withdrawal, reconciliation and quiet collaboration by the leftist-organized labour sector that deprived Hong Kong society of an important momentum for change.

NOTES

1 For two typical accounts, see James Riedel, *The Industrialisation of Hong Kong*, Tübingen, J.C.B. Mohr (Paul Siebeck), 1974 and Yun-wing Sung, 'Economic growth and structural change in the small open economy of Hong Kong', in Vittorio Corbo *et al.* (eds), *Export-Oriented Development Strategies: The Success of Five Newly Industrializing Countries*, Boulder, CO, Westview, 1985.

2 Two significant statist works with useful discussions on Hong Kong are Stephen Haggard, *Pathways from the Periphery: The Politics of Growth in the Newly Industrializing Countries*, Ithaca, NY, Cornell University Press, 1990; and Robert Wade, *Governing the Market: Economic Theory and the Role of Government in East Asian Industrialization*, Princeton, NJ, Princeton University Press, 1990.

3 Nicholas Owen, 'Economic policy in Hong Kong', in Keith Hopkins (ed.), *Hong Kong: The Industrial Colony*, Hong Kong, Oxford University Press, 1971.

4 Owen, 'Economic policy in Hong Kong', p. 153. Owen's definition of industrial upgrading is also the definition adopted in this Chapter.

5 Owen, 'Economic policy in Hong Kong', pp. 189–90. Original emphasis.

6 According to one author industrial deepening is 'one of the oldest topics...in the history of its industrial development', Ho Yin-ping, *Trade, Industrial Restructuring and Development in Hong Kong*, London, Macmillan, 1992, p. 161.

7 Since the late 1950s, numerous reports in the *Far Eastern Economic Review* (hereafter *FEER*) were devoted to the issue of protectionism, a typical one by Kayser Fung appearing on 18 October 1962, pp. 130–1. For a detailed analysis of the threat of protectionism, see Victor Mok, 'Trade barriers and export promotion: the Hong Kong example', in Tzong-biau Lin *et al.* (eds), *Hong Kong: Economic, Social and Political Studies in Development*, Armonk, NY, M.E. Sharpe, 1979.

8 For instance, a *FEER* report on 3 January 1963 claimed that 'Hong Kong is no longer a cheap labour economy'. In the next issue (10 January 1963), *FEER* further reported that high land costs had not only deterred foreign investment, but also forced local industrialists to consider relocation overseas.

9 The first *FEER* report that mentioned Taiwan as a competitor appeared on 13 May 1965. On 14 October 1965, a full *FEER* analysis reported that Taiwan's export processing zone offered free port facilities, cheap labour and low land cost. All these

together meant that 'Taiwan might present one of the biggest single threats to its [Hong Kong] economy in the future'. It was further reported that Taiwan made an intense effort to woo investment from 'overseas Chinese in Hong Kong'. Several months later (14 July 1966), Singapore and South Korea were added to the list of competitors in a mid-year review of Hong Kong's industries.

10 This kind of vicious competition led Nicholas Owen to argue that too much competition could retard the development of large and efficient production units, and 'the small firm usually escapes only through its extinction'. See Nicholas Owen, 'Competition and structural change in unconcentrated industries', *Journal of Industrial Economics*, 1971, vol. 19, no. 2, p. 144.

11 *FEER*, 27 December 1962.

12 *FEER*, 5 March 1964.

13 See Alexander Grantham, *Via Ports: From Hong Kong to Hong Kong*, Hong Kong, Hong Kong University Press, 1965. No more than five years later, when the industrial transformation was proceeding apace, Grantham regretted, during the 1954 budget speech, that 'we were all at one time too ready to think of Hong Kong only as an entrepôt', cited in *FEER*, 11 March 1954.

14 Ifan Habib, 'Studying a colonial economy – without perceiving colonialism', *Modern Asian Studies*, 1985, vol. 19, no. 3, p. 335.

15 The terms 'free market', 'free trade', and '*laissez-faire*' are used interchangeably in this Chapter to denote an economic structure with a high degree of openness and low degree of government intervention.

16 External factors such as the communist victory in China and the trade embargo imposed on China during the Korean War have determining effects on Hong Kong's industrial transformation. The colonial state was also active in assisting industrial production during the postwar reconstruction. See Alex H. Choi, 'Beyond market and state: a study of Hong Kong's industrial transformation', *Studies in Political Economy*, 1994, no. 45, pp. 28–64.

17 It was said that as much as 50 per cent of China's foreign exchange was earned from Hong Kong, see *FEER*, 20 June 1963. A smaller figure of 40 per cent was suggested in Alvin Rabushka, *The Changing Face of Hong Kong: New Departures in Public Policy*, Washington, DC, American Enterprise Institute for Public Policy Research; and Stanford, CA, Hoover Institution on War Revolution and Peace, Stanford University, 1973.

18 David Clayton, *Imperialism Revisited: Political and Economic Relations Between Britain and China, 1950–54*, London, Macmillan, 1997, p. 100.

19 For instance, K.C. Wong, Chairman of the pro-Beijing Hong Kong Chinese General Chamber of Commerce assured Hong Kong people in 1964 that Beijing wanted the colony's political status 'to be maintained for many years', *FEER*, 27 August 1964.

20 See the discussion on the Soviet factor in China's taking a hardline stand in the Kowloon Wall City crisis in *FEER*, 24 January 1963.

21 *FEER*, 10 February 1966.

22 *FEER*, 6 February 1964.

23 Joe England and John Rear, *Chinese Labor Under British Rule: A Critical Study of Labor Relations and Law in Hong Kong*, Hong Kong, Oxford University Press, 1975, p. 34.

24 Susan Strange, *Sterling and British Policy: A Political Study of an International Currency in Decline*, London, Oxford University Press, 1971, p. 112.

25 Hong Kong Government, *Hong Kong Annual Report 1959*, p. 51.

26 For a revealing account of London's tight control over the governor, see Brian St. Clair's article in *FEER*, 9 April 1964.

27 For detailed discussions of these mechanisms, see T.B. Lin, 'A theoretical assessment of the currency system of Hong Kong', *The New Asia College Academic Annual*, 1970, vol. 12, pp. 179–94 (in Chinese); Y.C. Jao, *Banking and Currency in Hong Kong: A Study of Postwar Financial Development*, London, Macmillan, 1974; Norman J. Miners, *The*

Government and Politics of Hong Kong, Hong Kong, Oxford University Press, 1975, p. 8; and the various papers in W.F. Crick (ed.), *Commonwealth Banking Systems*, Oxford, Clarendon, 1965.

28 For some fascinating discussions, see P.J. Cain and A.G. Hopkins, *British Imperialism: Crisis and Reconstruction 1914–1990*, London, Longman, 1993; Catherine R. Schenk, *Britain and the Sterling Area: From Devaluation to Convertibility in the 1950s*, London, Routledge, 1994; Allister H. Hinds, 'Sterling and imperial policy, 1945–1951', *Journal of Imperial and Commonwealth History*, 1986, vol. 15, no. 1, pp. 150–76; and 'Imperial policy and colonial Sterling balances, 1943–56', *Journal of Imperial and Commonwealth History*, 1991, vol. 19, no. 1, p. 38; Gerold Krozewski, 'Sterling, the "minor" territories, and the end of formal empire, 1939–1958', *Economic History Review*, 1993, vol. 46, no. 2, pp. 239–65; and 'Finance and empire: the dilemma facing Great Britain in the 1950s', *The International History Review*, 1996, vol. 18, no. 2, pp. 48–69; John Darwin, *Britain and Decolonization: The Retreat from Empire in the Post-War World*, London, Macmillan, 1988; Strange, *Sterling and British Policy*; A.N. Porter and A.J. Stockwell, *British Imperial Policy and Decolonization, 1938–1964*, vol. 2: 1951–64, London, Macmillan, 1988.

29 Peter Worsley, 'Imperial retreat', in E.P. Thompson (ed.), *Out of Apathy*, London, New Left Books, 1960, pp. 110–11. See also Mark Curtis, *The Ambiguities of Power: British Foreign Policy Since 1945*, Zed Press, 1995, p. 14; Bernard Porter, *The Lion's Share: A Short History of British Imperialism, 1850–1983*, London, Longman, 1984, p. 313; Cain and Hopkins, *British Imperialism*, p. 277.

30 Krozewski, 'Sterling, the "minor" territories', p. 250.

31 Darwin, *Britain and Decolonization*, p. 159; Krozewski, 'Sterling, the "minor" territories', p. 248.

32 Alex H. Choi, 'The industrial transformation of Hong Kong, 1945–58: market or state', M.A. thesis, Queen's University, Kingston, 1993, pp. 86–108.

33 Schenk, *Britain and the Sterling Area*, p. 26.

34 Cain and Hopkins, *British Imperialism*, p. 276. See also Perry Anderson, *English Questions*, London, Verso, 1992; Geoffrey Ingham, *Capitalism Divided: The City and Industry in British Social Development*, London, Macmillan, 1984.

35 See Geoffrey Maynard, 'Sterling and international monetary reform', in Paul Streeten and Hugh Corbet (eds), *Commonwealth Policy in Global Context*, Toronto, Ont., University of Toronto Press, 1971; Krozewski, 'Sterling, the "minor" territories', p. 254; Porter and Stockwell, *British Imperial Policy*, p. 27.

36 See James T.H. Tang, 'From empire defence to imperial retreat: Britain's postwar China policy and the decolonization of Hong Kong', *Modern Asian Studies*, 1994, vol. 28, no. 2, pp. 317–37.

37 Darwin, *Britain and Decolonization*, p. 241. See also Cain and Hopkins, *British Imperialism*, p. 292.

38 For the 'stop-go' economy, see Colin Leys, *Politics in Britain: From Labourism to Thatcherism*, rev. edn, London, Verso, 1989; Sean Glynn and Alan Booth, *Modern Britain: An Economic and Social History*, London, Routledge, 1996; Cains and Hopkins, *British Imperialism*, p. 282.

39 See *FEER*, 30 November 1967 and 4 April 1968. See also Jao, *Banking and Currency*, p. 142, Table 6.3; and Schenk, *Britain and the Sterling Area*, p. 52, Appendix to Chapter 2.

40 Strange, *Sterling and British Policy*, p. 112.

41 Joe England, *Hong Kong: Britain's Responsibility*, London, Fabian Society, 1976, p. 10. For a similar view, see Angela Wei Djao, 'Social control in a colonial society: a case study of working class consciousness in Hong Kong', Ph.D. dissertation, University of Toronto, Ont., 1976, p. 93; Gregor Benton, *The Hong Kong Crisis*, Pluto Press, 1983, p. 9; Hong Kong Research Project, *Hong Kong: A Case to Answer*, Nottingham, Spokesman Books, 1974, p. 32.

42 Lin, 'A theoretical assessment of the currency system of Hong Kong'.

43 *FEER*, 2 May 1968 and 6 June 1968.

44 An excellent analysis of the class relationship in pre-war Hong Kong is to be found in Chan Wai Kwan, *The Making of Hong Kong Society: Three Studies of Class Formation in Early Hong Kong*, Oxford, Clarendon Press, 1991.

45 This episode also indicates that the interests of Britain and resident British capital were not always in harmony. After the devaluation, Hong Kong-based British banks strongly opposed London's demand that all Hong Kong reserves be continuously deposited in sterling.

46 See Hong Kong Government, *Hong Kong Annual Report 1968*, pp. 46–67; Strange, *Sterling and British Policy*, p. 114; Jao, *Banking and Currency*, pp. 36–7; Miners, *The Government and Politics*, p. 9.

47 For an example of these requests, see *FEER*, 6 December 1962; Miners, *The Government and Politics*, pp. 227–31.

48 After the 1967 riot, the colonial regime finally conceded to the pressure of the industrialists to re-examine their demand for an industrial bank. The outcome of such review was the setting up in 1973 of a small-scale hire purchase loan scheme for small and medium-sized enterprises. For an overview of the debate on the industrial bank issue, see Victor Mok, 'Small factories in Kwun Tong: problems of strategies for development', in Ambrose Y.C. King and Rance Y.L. Lee (eds), *Social Life and Development in Hong Kong*, Hong Kong, Chinese University Press, 1981.

49 *FEER*, 12 March 1965.

50 *FEER*, 25 March 1965.

51 Stephen Chiu, 'The politics of laissez-faire: Hong Kong's strategy of industrialization in historical perspective', Hong Kong Institute of Asia Pacific Studies occasional paper no. 40, Hong Kong, Chinese University of Hong Kong, 1994, p. 82.

52 Chiu, 'The politics of laissez-faire', p. 83.

53 The market development activities were eventually centralized in 1966 under the Hong Kong Trade Development Council. *FEER*, 20 October 1966. It is also interesting to point out that, while the Chinese Manufacturers' Association argued that the main problem facing the industrial sector in the 1960s was industrial upgrading, the General Chamber of Commerce stated that it was the search and development of new markets. Its demand to the Hong Kong government was the setting up of more overseas trade representative offices, *FEER*, 4 April 1963.

54 The importance of inexpensive and stable supplies from China for the Hong Kong economy has been raised by many observers. See England and Rear, *Chinese Labour Under British Rule*, p. 41; England, *Hong Kong*, p. 24; Benton, *The Hong Kong Crisis*, p. 9; *FEER*, 9 November 1964, 10 August 1967, 14 September 1967.

55 Y.C. Jao, 'Financing Hong Kong's early postwar industrialization: the role of the Hongkong and Shanghai Banking Corporation', in Frank H.H. King (ed.), *Eastern Banking: Essays in the History of the Hongkong and Shanghai Banking Corporation*, London, Athlone Press, 1983, p. 538.

56 Jao, *Banking and Currency*, p. 94.

57 Hong Kong Government, *Hong Kong Annual Report 1960*, p. 66.

58 *FEER*, 20 March 1964.

59 *FEER*, 9 January 1964.

60 Victor Fung-Shuen Sit, 'Dynamism in small industries: the case of Hong Kong', *Asian Survey*, 1982, vol. 22, no. 4, pp. 399–409.

61 *FEER*, 17 January 1963, 7 February 1963. For the operation of the quota system, see Morris E. Markre, 'Rent-seeking and Hong Kong textile quota system', *Developing Economies*, 1979, vol. 17, no. 1, pp. 110–18.

62 J. Henderson, 'Urbanization in the Hong Kong–South China Region: an introduction to dynamics and dilemmas', *International Journal of Urban and Regional Research*,

1991, vol. 15, no. 2, p. 172. Davies made a similar observation in S.N.G. Davies, 'One brand of politics rekindled', *Hong Kong Law Journal*, 1977, vol. 7, no. 1, p. 63.

63 *FEER*, 6 June 1963, 10 December 1974, and 6 May 1965.

64 Wong Siu-lun, *Emigrant Entrepreneurs: Shanghai Industrialists in Hong Kong*, Hong Kong, Oxford University Press, 1988.

65 See *FEER*, 17 January 1963, 12 December 1963, 16 December 1965, 17 February 1966, 19 October 1967 and 14 December 1967.

66 Sutu Hsin, 'Whither Hong Kong's industry?', *United College Journal*, 1963, vol. 2, p. 10. See also Sutu Hsin, Chien-min Chang and Kin-Yu Cheng, 'A summary of industries in Hong Kong with special reference to their structure', *Journal of the Chinese University of Hong Kong*, 1977, vol. 4, no. 1, pp. 185–205.

67 Wong, *Emigrant Entrepreneurs*, p. 89.

68 On this point, see J.A.C. Mackie (ed.), *The Chinese in Indonesia: Five Essays*, Melbourne, Nelson, 1976; Arief Budiman, 'The emergence of the bureaucratic capitalist state in Indonesia', in Lim Teck Chee (ed.), *Reflections on Development in Southeast Asia*, Singapore, Institute of Southeast Asian Studies, 1988; Ruth McVey, 'The materialization of the Southeast Asian entrepreneur', in Ruth McVey (ed.), *Southeast Asian Capitalists*, Ithaca, NY, Cornell University Press, 1992.

69 *FEER*, 6 June 1963.

70 The conventional wisdom as to why Hong Kong had no democracy before the 1980s is that truly democratic reform would invite pro-communist labour unions to power. For some insightful comments refuting this view, see Benton, *The Hong Kong Crisis*, p. 29.

71 See the reports of such activities in *FEER*, 21 May 1963, and 20 March 1964.

72 For details of the 1967 riot, see Ian Scott, *Political Change and the Crisis of Legitimacy in Hong Kong*, Hong Kong, Oxford University Press, 1989, p. 89.

73 Despite the rapid economic growth, the mass majority of the workers did not feel that they enjoyed the fruit of economic progress. Even some members of the colonial government admitted that the living conditions of the working class were bad, and warned that this could breed social unrest. The Labour Commissioner, R.M. Hetherington, reported in 1961 that the working conditions of a large proportion of workers were 'the least tolerable'. They had to work twelve hours a day, seven days a week. And even so, 'all but the simplest pleasures are beyond the reach of many families'; R.M. Hetherington, 'Industrial labour in Hong Kong', *Hong Kong Economic Papers*, no. 2, 1963, pp. 31, 36. See also England and Rear, *Chinese Labour under British Rule*, p. 66.

74 In view of working class activism, a perceptive *FEER* reporter stated that the industrial future for Hong Kong was industrial deepening, because 'better products fetch better prices', and industries could then afford to pay better wages; *FEER*, 1 June 1967.

75 After a period of active unionism and anti-colonial struggle between 1947 and 1952, the FTU changed its confrontational course and adopted a strategy of withdrawal. Instead of organizing workers, it ran welfare activities like free medical clinics, discount stores and benefits programmes for the unemployed. The change in FTU strategy was so dramatic and noticeable that the 1953 edition of the *Hong Kong Annual Report* notes that there was 'a shift in policy of the FTU and its affiliates', and attributed the lack of labour incidents in that year to 'a marked stress on welfare activities rather than the acerbation [sic] of industrial disputes [by the FTU].' Hong Kong Government, *Hong Kong Annual Report 1953*, p. 32. See also Clayton, *Imperialism Revisited*, p. 104–5; and Joe England, *Industrial Relations and Law in Hong Kong*, 2nd edn, Hong Kong, Oxford University Press, 1989, pp. 110–15.

76 The government's version of the 1967 riot appeared in Hong Kong Government, *Hong Kong Annual Report 1967*, pp. 1–19.

9

FLEXIBLE MANUFACTURING IN A COLONIAL ECONOMY

Kim-Ming Lee

The Hong Kong post-war economic miracle has often been attributed to flexibility which was given full scope by the colonial government's free market policy.[1] Rabushka claims that the adaptability of Hong Kong's economy is due to the operation of an 'automatic corrective mechanism' rooted in the free market economy.[2] This alters internal costs and prices and brings them quickly in line with those of the rest of the world. Others argue that flexibility stems from the ability of manufacturers to find new market niches and respond quickly to market changes by the means of exploiting cheap labour.[3] In this Chapter, I will argue that this flexibility was not deliberately designed by the colonial government. Instead, it was the outcome of Hong Kong manufacturers' response towards the colonial government's policy bias against industry.

The flexibility of the Hong Kong economy stems from the interactions between the business strategies of Hong Kong entrepreneurs and the subcontracting networks of small and medium-sized firms (SMFs). The business strategies of Hong Kong entrepreneurs constitute a panoply of guerrilla tactics whose origins may be traced to a transient mentality developed before the Second World War. The SMF subcontracting networks, on the other hand, are a system of relationships linking SMFs and large local factories, SMFs and trading companies, and governing inter-relationships among SMFs themselves. Their interactions help the Hong Kong economy to build up a flexible manufacturing system that is capable of functioning in a fluctuating market environment. This system was actually established before the Second World War, but it has been ignored in the literature because the dominant historiography, as argued by Ngo in this volume, downplayed the contribution of the Chinese-dominated manufacturing sector to the early Hong Kong economy. The historical narrative aims, rather, at constructing a legitimation discourse on the theme, 'the good policy of *laissez-faire*'.

The first part of this Chapter discusses various kinds of flexibility provided by the interactions between the business strategy and the subcontracting networks. The second part describes the historical origin of and institutional legacies from the entrepôt period, and the international environment responsible for the emergence of the transient mentality and the subcontracting networks will be described. Finally, the limitation of the Hong Kong flexible manufacturing system will be examined.

The flexibility of Hong Kong's entrepreneurs

The Hong Kong economy is characterized by the strong and growing position of the SMFs. In 1971, 1979 and 1989 most manufacturing establishments employed fewer than fifty persons, accounting for 33.5 per cent, 36.7 per cent and 45.7 per cent of the total workforce in the manufacturing sector, respectively (see Table 9.1). There was an upward trend in the number of manufacturing SMFs from 1971 to 1989. A significant part of the industrial development of Hong Kong is attributed to the dynamism and flexibility of the SMFs. The picture is more obvious if we look at the changes in labour employment, gross output and value added.

Table 9.1 Number of establishments and labour force in the manufacturing sector (1971–89)

No. of employees	Establishment (in)			Employment (in)		
	1971	1979	1989	1971	1979	1989
1–9	62.7	62.9	71.4	11.6	11.3	16.0
10–19	17.3	15.3	12.7	8.9	9.2	10.7
20–49	10.9	12.3	9.9	13.0	16.2	19.0
50–99	4.7	5.4	3.7	12.6	15.7	15.5
100–499	3.9	3.6	2.1	30.0	29.2	24.9
500–999	0.4	0.3	0.2	9.0	8.9	6.7
1000	0.2	0.1	0.1	15.0	9.4	7.2

Source: Francois Soulard, 'The restructuring of Hong Kong industries and the urbanization of Zhujiang Delta, 1979–1989', Ph.D. dissertation, Chinese University of Hong Kong, Hong Kong, 1993, p. 66 and p. 68.

Table 9.2 shows that while the total labour force in the manufacturing sector declined slightly (0.5 per cent) from 1979 to 1989, there was an increase in employment for those establishments with fewer than fifty employees. In terms of value added, the SMFs also outperformed their larger counterparts. The rate of increase in value added indicates that economic returns have increased more rapidly in smaller establishments than larger ones. The SMF sector thus constitutes not only a most important economic sector in Hong Kong, it is also the primary source of flexibility in the economy.

163

Table 9.2 Variation rates for labour ratio, gross output, compensation, and added value in the manufacturing sector (1979–89)[a]

No. of employees	Labour ratio[b]	Gross output[c]	Compensation[d]	Added value[e]
1–9	1.42	5.32	3.86	4.93
10–19	1.17	4.54	3.68	4.51
20–49	1.17	4.68	3.75	4.71
50–99	0.99	3.88	3.36	4.11
100–199	0.86	3.36	3.04	3.72
200–499	0.84	2.87	2.97	3.36
500–999	0.75	2.92	2.75	2.89
1000	0.76	2.89	2.66	2.90
Average	0.995	3.64	3.26	3.82

Source: Soulard, 'The restructuring of Hong Kong industries', p. 70.

Note:
[a] All the figures are ratios rather than absolute figures.
[b] Labour indicates the total employment by establishment size.
[c] Gross output indicates total value of the sales of goods, industrial work and services.
[d] Compensation describes wages and salaries paid to operatives and other employees.
[e] Added value is obtained by deducting the consumption of materials, supplies and industrial work, services, rents and other operating expenses from the gross output.

In this context, the business strategy employed by Hong Kong industrialists hinges on guerrilla tactics that evolved from a transient mentality but also share much in common with those of small enterprises throughout East Asia. Lam and Lee observe that small Chinese firms in East Asia

> ...seek out an opportunity for high profit margins in a particular good, develop a formula, exploit it by rapidly flooding the market before the established firms can respond, make profits over the short term, and then leave the market for another one before competition forces the prices down to the point where firms from newly industrializing countries are no longer profitable without large-scale investments in technology or infrastructure.[4]

With regard to receiving orders, small Chinese firms seldom consider their own production capacity as a constraint. They bid for as many orders as possible and then subcontract the part exceeding their capacity.[5]

In terms of capital equipment, they tend to see their machines capable of producing a wide range of commodities rather than being restricted to specific items. For instance, owners of metal stamping machines will not turn down business stamping computer casings or automobile parts if they still have surplus capacity.[6] Hong Kong entrepreneurs normally prefer not to be locked in a particular production technology for a long time. They commonly buy machinery with a view to a four-year payback period.[7] Capital is usually invested in multi-purpose factories that can accommodate various product lines. The decline of the wig industry demonstrates how flexibly Hong Kong industrialists view their machines. By 1970 the wig industry accounted for 8 per cent of Hong Kong's domestic exports, and employed 39,000 people, but employment fell to only fifty-nine employees in 1977. Despite such a dramatic decline, many entrepreneurs of wig factories did not abandon their machines, because they found that the machinery was particularly suitable for scaling fish![8]

This adaptability exemplifies the responsive flexibility of the Hong Kong entrepreneurs. But the effective functioning of the guerrilla strategy requires a corresponding institutional system. This corresponding institutional system is the SMF subcontracting networks.

Most of the manufacturing firms in Hong Kong have concentrated on light industries, like clothing, electronics, toys and watches. These products are subject to seasonal demand changes and fashions. Thus the markets on which Hong Kong entrepreneurs depend are highly fluctuating both in volume and the nature of the products demanded. Under this condition, firm owners carefully guard against over-expansion of capacity. They do not hesitate, however, to accept orders well beyond their capacity, meeting deadlines and delivering products punctually by means of a subcontracting network. Subcontracting is a substitute for net investment, which, on the one hand, reduces the risk incurred when demand declines.[9] In a survey on SMFs, Sit and Wong find that most SMFs contract out their orders, mainly because of insufficient capacity and labour shortage.[10] Sit and Wong also find that the contractors seldom engage just one subcontractor. Half of their sample firms engage two or three subcontractors while one-third of them have four to ten subcontractors. Half of them claimed that subcontracts accounted for 1–19 per cent of their total sales,while 38.2 per cent of them claimed it was 20–49 per cent.

Subcontracting can also reduce capital requirements for setting up a business and for day-to-day operations because inventory can be kept to a minimum. Another mechanism that helps to enhance flexibility in handling operational capital is the credit system, developed among subcontracting partners. Payment for goods can always be delayed for a certain period of time depending upon the relationship among the subcontracting partners. The informality in subcontracting relationships among SMFs provides flexibility for individual entrepreneurs to deal with changes in the business environment, while the formality provides a last resort to handle breached contracts. All these, in turn, stimulate the growth of SMFs even when industrialists are confronted with an unhelpful government and the reluctance of banks to lend them money.[11]

The flexibility of the SMF subcontracting system

The most notable characteristic of the SMF subcontracting system is its high degree of organizational flexibility. Morroni defines the organizational flexibility of a firm as its ability to organize rigid machines and equipment in a way most fit to produce current mixes.[12] However, what does organizational flexibility mean for an economic sector? By extending Morroni's definition, the organizational flexibility of an economic sector is the ability of the sector to organize its production factors in such a way to produce an output mix that meets the changes of the economic environment. One important property of organizational flexibility is on-time delivery. In Hong Kong's garment industry, the order-to-delivery cycle time is 14 days for small firms and 30 days for large firms.[13] Typical lead times for knitwear production are 17.5 days for small firms and 35 days for large firms.[14] This indicates that Hong Kong's SMF subcontracting networks are able to minimize the organizational obstacles.

In order to pinpoint the organizational flexibility of the SMF sector, a number of factors that inhibit the smooth flow of information and resources have to be identified: (1) bottlenecks in some production subprocesses due to transportation difficulties and co-ordination problems; (2) poor supplier relations; (3) improper performance criteria set up for subcontractors; (4) overly complicated business processes; and (5) inadequate production scheduling.[15] In the Hong Kong SMF sector, success in addressing these problems hinges on the following factors. First, subcontracting allows a high degree of specialization by SMFs. In a survey of 174 SMFs, Sit finds that less than 40 per cent were involved in the complete process of making finished goods.[16] Most SMFs were involved in only one aspect of the whole production process. Hong Kong entrepreneurs are quite successful in dividing a supposedly integrated production process into subprocesses and making finished products through subcontracting. This is further illustrated by Lam and Lee, who say,

> an assembling factory for electronic circuit boards built on the Western model would own a group of machines that undertook board masking and etching, drilling, perhaps automated component inserters, wave soldering machines, and even possibly a computerized testing machine at the end of the line. Conversely, in the Chinese NICs [newly industrializing countries], each of these pieces of equipment would be owned by a separate entrepreneur.[17]

Thus subcontracting permits the owners of SMFs to specialize in what they are most familiar with and capable of.[18] As a result, the production run for each subprocess is shortened.

Second, since SMFs are located closely together, transportation will not create a bottleneck. Third, SMF owners can always find some other subcontractors to produce the goods that exceed their firm's capacity in order to meet the delivery time. Fourth, contractors frequently provide raw materials for the SMFs to use subcontracted goods.[19] Most of the contractors are trading companies that have extensive international networks with the overseas suppliers. Beside the contractors, most subcontracting firms rely on intermediaries for raw material supply. These intermediaries have substantial international connections to ensure adequate supply. Furthermore, even when there is a problem of supply, trading companies or SMFs are able to mobilize other trading companies or SMFs to lend them the necessary materials. This is possible because of their quasi-familial ties that provide reciprocity and mutual help. Sit and Wong note that other manufacturers play a significant role as sources of raw materials in the textiles and plastics industries.[20]

Fifth, the authority structure of SMFs is often dominated by a single individual, the owner. The major strength of this single person-dominated structure is the speed of response towards markets. In large firms, business decisions involve extensive processes of rationalization, like the study of market statistics, or the employment of analysts and advisers. But in SMFs, the business owners rely on intuition honed during years of experience, and personal networks, in making decisions.[21].

Sixth, more often than not, subcontracting relationships among SMFs are informal. Their business relationships are based on trust rather than on contract. As a result, the subcontracting partners can easily bargain for a mutually acceptable quality standard and production schedule without much transaction cost being incurred. Finally, Hong Kong is a market economy in which competition is keen. So if an SMF cannot demonstrate its ability to meet delivery time, it will soon fail. In Hong Kong, most contract breaches are delays in delivery.[22]

The flexibility of the Hong Kong economy

The whole Hong Kong economy also exhibits a kind of organizational flexibility. The organizational flexibility of an economy refers to its ability to organize its factor endowment to meet the changing international economic environment. Subcontracting is a method of handling the ups and downs of a fluctuating market without expanding the individual firm's capacity. If the market is continuously diminishing, the SMF subcontracting networks play a part in cushioning the impact by gradually phasing out the lowest tier of subcontracting firms. Since most subcontracting firms are small, in terms of capital investment as well as employment, the impact on the Hong Kong economy is still manageable. At the same time, failure in a diminishing industry is often balanced by another expanding industry. The decline in the number of small firms in the declining industry is matched by a growth of small firms in the expanding industry. The speedy reallocation of capital and labour from the declining to the expanding industry is possible because of the smallness of the firm size and the lower skill requirement of light industry.

Another more significant and direct factor is the flexible labour market strategy employed by the SMF owners.[23] This flexible labour market strategy is an active response to non-interventionism of the colonial government in industry, the non-manufacturing-oriented banking strategy and the guerrilla strategy of Hong Kong's entrepreneurs.[24] The flexible labour market entails the use of cheap unskilled labour, which is provided by a minimally regulated competitive labour market, to produce labour-intensive goods.

Since organizational flexibility at the economy level implies the ease of shifting from a 'sunset' sector to a 'sunrise' sector, the more homogeneous the factors of production between the two manufacturing sectors are, the easier is the shift. In the post-war period, Hong Kong experienced a variety of restructuring in the manufacturing sector. The textile industry was dominant in the 1950s; it was replaced by the garment industry as the most important industry in the 1960s. The electronics industry became the new star in the 1970s though the garment industry remained the largest sector. However, all these changes were confined to the light industry rather than to capital-intensive or heavy industries. Unskilled labour can thus be easily transferred from one light industry to another. As a result, although the Hong Kong economy exhibits a high degree of organizational flexibility, this flexibility is limited to light industries.

The flexibility of the subcontracting system and the business strategies of Hong Kong entrepreneurs evolved within a context shaped by Hong Kong's history and changes in the world economy. The following sections discuss the historical origins and the international conditions that gave rise to the flexibility of the post-war Hong Kong manufacturing sector.

Transient mentality and guerrilla business strategy

Why is the Hong Kong economy dominated by SMFs? A conventional answer is that Hong Kong's inhabitants are highly motivated to be their own boss rather than work for others. However, if we push the question further – asking why Hong Kong people are so eager to be their own boss – we have to examine the historical contingencies that preceded the manufacturing boom. Recasting the Weberian thesis of the spirit of capitalism, I will argue that the transient mentality of Hong Kong people induces a kind of entrepreneurship in line with a gambler's mentality.

Hong Kong is often described as an immigrant city. According to the 1961 census and the 1966 by-census, the proportion of the population born in Hong Kong in 1921, 1931, 1961 and 1966 were 26.7 per cent, 32.5 per cent, 47.7 per cent and 53.8 per cent respectively.[25] The first influx was caused by the Taiping uprising in the 1850s. The second wave occurred during the 1911 Revolution. The third happened in 1938 when the Japanese attacked Guangdong. However, during the period of the Japanese occupation in Hong Kong (1941–5), large numbers of people returned to China. The restoration of British rule resulted in another wave of immigration to Hong Kong. The biggest wave occurred during the period of the communist takeover in mainland China.[26]

These immigrants had little political expectation of the colonial government, nor did they believe that the government would provide them with social and economic assistance. Most of them came to Hong Kong seeking economic opportunities. Whenever an opportunity arose elsewhere, they would not hesitate to move there. As a result, a transient mentality developed among these opportunistic immigrants. Hong Kong was regarded as a temporary place for making money. The immigrants seized material rewards as fast as possible, and left once the opportunity was gone.

Such a materialistic orientation also has institutional and historical foundation. Occupational advancement and social mobility in imperial China were achieved largely by climbing up the political ladder through the civil service system. However, for the Hong Kong Chinese, social status was mainly determined by the possession of wealth, as discussed by Carroll in Chapter 2 of this volume. This implies a shift of value priorities: from political reputation to wealth as the main criterion for status.[27]

This peculiar state of living is characterized by the impulse of exit and risk-taking. The impulse of exit manifests a strong desire for survival by emigrating elsewhere while risk-taking exhibits a desire for profit.[28] Under the tensions of insecurity, uncertainty and physical survival, the Hong Kong people were driven to earn as much money as possible and to save some of it even at the expense of necessary consumption.[29] In sum, the entrepreneurial Hong Kong spirit, characterized by their highly active guerrilla tactics in doing business, was nurtured by specific historical and institutional circumstances.

International commercial networks

The performance of the SMF subcontracting networks depends upon the effective supply of materials and orders, acquisition of market information, and connections with foreign buyers. However, the owners of SMFs are mainly concerned with production processes, and lack marketing ability. In this aspect, the international commercial networks that have been built up by Chinese merchants since the entrepôt period play a significant part in ensuring the proper functioning of the SMF subcontracting system.

The Hong Kong economy had integrated into the global market as a regional business centre since the nineteenth century. The abolition of slavery in most countries by the latter half of the nineteenth century was one factor contributing to high demand for cheap labour from China. As a free and modern seaport, Hong Kong became the major centre for Chinese emigration abroad, as well as the major port for returning Chinese.[30] The emigration business was very profitable and was responsible for the growth of shipping firms, brokers and labour recruiters.[31] More importantly, the emigration business helped link Hong

Kong to the Chinese communities overseas, which retained close ties with their homeland in China.[32] As Tsai remarks, 'Hong Kong became the centre of a flourishing commercial network encompassing China, Southeast Asia, Australia, and America'.[33] There were about 1,700 Chinese commercial firms listed on the Hong Kong directory of 1915 engaged in the import-export business.[34] Table 9.3 shows the number of Chinese trading firms and their international networks. These import-export firms not only consolidated, but also extended, the business networks between Hong Kong and the rest of the world.[35] In sum, the emigration business in the entrepôt period helped build the basis for the international commercial networks which is important to the post-war industrial boom.

Apart from these institutional factors, international conditions played an important part in ensuring the adequate supply of orders for Hong Kong's SMFs. The first was the emergence of the new international division of labour. Fröbel, Heinrichs and Kreye stated that world economic conditions changed in the twentieth century: a practically inexhaustible reservoir of disposable labour; the decomposition of production processes; and the development of transport, communications and organizational technology overcoming the problem of geographical distances.[36] Under these conditions, a new international division of labour was created.

> This new international division of labour is an "institutional"…innovation of capital itself necessitated by changed conditions…It is a consequence and not a cause of these new conditions that various countries and companies have to tailor their policies and profit-maximising strategies to these new conditions (that is, to the requirements of the world market for industrial sites). [37]

International subcontracting is a major strategy employed in the advanced countries. Landsberg listed three reasons for the major growth of international subcontracting: (1) The tremendous increase of the demand for labour-intensive consumer goods in the advanced capitalist countries propelled capital to mass production. (2) The increased competition from Japan and West Germany in the mid-1960s urged American transnational capital to meet this challenge by means of international subcontracting. In turn, this forced Japan and Germany into a similar strategy. (3) The growing class struggles in the advanced countries further compelled capitalists to employ much cheaper Third World labour.[38] The conflicts between the international manufacturers and mass merchandisers initiated the process of international subcontracting. The pre-war international cartel arrangements among the big European and United States consumer electronics manufacturers were still intact in the post-war years. They traditionally refused to supply to mass merchandisers whose pricing policies they could not control. As a result, mass merchandisers sought overseas suppliers for producing cheap but quality low-end products.[39] The mass merchandisers placed

Table 9.3 Number of different types of import and export firms in 1915

Nam Pak Hong (General Exporters and Importers to Southern & Northern Ports, and to Southeast Asian Ports)	84
Kam Shan Chung (Exporters & Importers to Melbourne, Sydney, San Francisco and Honolulu)	239
Exporters & Importers to Peru, Havana and Panama	9
Exporters & Importers to Spain and Southeast Asia (including Manila, Haiphon, Annam, Cambodia, Siam, Sandakan, Java, Penang and Singapore)	186
Exporters & Importers to Japan	30
Exporters & Importers to Calcutta and South Africa	2

Source: Jung Fang Tsai, *Hong Kong in Chinese History: Community and Social Unrest in the British Colony, 1842–1913*, New York, Columbia University Press

large contracts with East Asian producers by supplying designs, specifications and quality control. In response to the aggressive strategies of mass merchandisers, American and European manufacturers moved significant production to East Asian countries.[40] As Gregory remarked, 'East Asian electronics manufacturers were surrogates in a continuing competitive struggle between mass merchandisers and manufacturers in the principal markets of North America and Europe'.[41]

Hong Kong was one of the fastest developing economies which exported subcontracted products to the United States: it contributed 68.4 per cent of the total imports from the developing countries under the tariff item 807.00 in 1966, 24.0 per cent in 1970 and 10.4 per cent in 1974. The total value rose from US$41.4 million in 1966 to US$200.1 million in 1974.[42] Although no official statistics are available, international commercial subcontracting is widely practised in Hong Kong, and it is very common for a locally manufactured product to bear an overseas company's brand name.

The second factor is the international political environment created after the Second World War, especially during the Cold War period. The Korean War and the Cold War heightened the hostility already existing between the United States and China. Consequently, the United Nations imposed a trade embargo on China. This not only compelled Hong Kong capital to develop manufacturing, but also made China tolerate colonial rule because Hong Kong became indispensably the only place where China could earn hard currency. Trade between Hong Kong and China also kept the cost of living in Hong Kong stable because most necessities, especially foodstuffs, were imported cheaply from China. This indirect subvention from China contributed to the competitiveness of Hong Kong's products in the world market.[43]

Government policies and flexible manufacturing

As previously mentioned, subcontracting is one of the industrialists' responses to the government's unfavourable policy. The *laissez-faire* policy of the government was a product of its colonial origin, and later the policy became institutionalized and adopted as the official ideology of the government in the post-war era.

There are two related historical factors shaping the policy. The first is the constraints from the merchants, bankers and property developers. The establishment of Hong Kong as a Crown Colony was mainly the response of the British government to the demands of British merchants and traders for a settlement on the South China coast from which they might trade freely and safely. Because of that, the Hong Kong-based British merchants expected to influence the government to protect their interests. They closely scrutinized the ruling of the government, opposed any measures which they perceived to be against their interests, and even petitioned back to London if necessary.[44] Any policy that involved 'unnecessary' expenditure or did not directly contribute to trading activities would be vetoed by the merchants.

Second, there was a lack of commitment on the part of Britain to develop Hong Kong other than as an entrepôt. As early as 1849, the British authority put pressure on the colonial government to meet its own expenditure in order to avoid burdening the British taxpayers.[45] The British government had subsidized the colonial government till 1855, from then on the colonial government had to self-finance its own expenditure.[46]

Against this background, a particular state–business relationship evolved: a coalition between the colonial government and the big merchant houses, bankers and property developers was formed, in which manufacturers were excluded. Notwithstanding the domination of commerce over industry, there was an ambivalent relationship between the industrial and commercial interests, as Choi argues in Chapter 8. After the victory of the Chinese Communist Party in 1949, the British *hongs* lost their business opportunities in China. The decline of the entrepôt trade, because of the 1951 UN embargo on China, struck a further blow to their business in Hong Kong. As a result, many small *hongs* closed. However, the remaining *hongs* were able to capitalize on the manufacturing boom and shift their business to import-export trade.[47] As suggested by Endacott, '[r]aw materials had to be imported and manufactures exported, and as the import-export entrepôt machinery was already there, its adaptation to the new commerce was relatively easy'.[48]

Hence, the merchant houses, which originally acted as intermediaries for trade between China and the West, served as a ready-made bridge between local manufacturers and foreign importers. Indeed, in the early years, the trading houses captured a significant portion of the benefits which resulted from post-war export-oriented industrialization. Most of the manufacturers, who mainly produced for export, possessed no knowledge of marketing. They had to depend solely upon orders from the local export houses. As a result, the local export houses were apt to take advantage of their weakness by getting one manufacturer to cut prices against the other merely by calling for several quotations for the same article.[49]

In these aspects, the manufacturing interests were quite compatible with the trade-related interests. Moreover, the tremendous demand for space required for industrial development further enhanced the interests of land and real estate developers. As a result, all the vested interests founded in the entrepôt period, as Ngo describes in this volume, were incorporated in the new economic structure.

How does this economic background help to create a passive industrial policy, if not an absence of it? Immediately after the UN embargo on China, the British government recognized that Hong Kong was China's only gateway to the West. China would tolerate Hong Kong's colonial status as long as Hong Kong maintained a growing economy. Since the transition from an entrepôt to an industrialized city was fairly smooth, and the colonial government did not put much effort into promoting industrialization, the government did not risk launching more interventionist industrial policies whose effects were uncertain.

Moreover, given the inexperience of the colonial government in intervening in industry, the effectiveness of carrying out an active industrial policy was highly questionable. Faced with great uncertainty in formulating new industrial policies, the safest way for the colonial government was to continue its passive policy of the past hundred years. Another reason for the absence of an active industrial policy is that the major bodies that the colonial government could consult came from the trade-finance alliance. Although the trade-related interests were compatible with the industrial interests, this did not mean that the trade-related interests would not attempt to obtain a bigger share of the profit generated from industrialization. As a result, though the trade-related interests would suggest ways to promote industrialization, the policy remained biased against the industrialists.

Basically, the colonial government still maintained its free market policy because it best served dominant trade-related interests. The option of providing state financial support for industries was not considered. The government provided mainly service-based support. In the 1960s, the government set up three statutory bodies, two of which were trade-related, to promote industrialization: the Trade Development Council, the Hong Kong Export Credit Insurance Corporation and the Hong Kong Productivity Council. However, their effect on upgrading Hong Kong's manufacturing technology was quite limited. The government never helped industrial firms to expand or to develop technology in the long run. In the absence of any government assistance, the most efficient business strategy for Hong Kong industrialists was to build up business networks and remain alert to all kinds of economic opportunities without any rigid commitment.

The limitation of flexible manufacturing

The flexibility provided by Hong Kong's SMF subcontracting system is actually a kind of responsive flexibility which is confined to labour-intensive and standardized products. The system itself has no internal mechanism for encouraging industrialists to upgrade their technological level. The nature of international subcontracting also precludes the Hong Kong manufacturers from developing their own brand name products. Since the 1980s, they have mainly relied on intensifying their flexible labour market strategy by relocating their production to mainland China in response to the intense foreign competition. By examining the foreign trade statistics in the period 1963–82, Chen comments that '[t]echnological intensity and capital intensity are slowly increasing in Hong Kong manufacturing, but the speed does not seem to be adequate for the maintenance of Hong Kong's economic position'.[50] The increase in technological and capital intensity can be partly explained by direct foreign investment which transfers technical know-how to Hong Kong, especially for the electronics industry.[51]

With regard to diversification, the subcontracting system does not encourage product differentiation, but imitation. There is no innovative flexibility inherent within the subcontracting system. Industrialists will pool all their resources to produce the goods for which demand is high, and then turn to other goods when the demand falls. They lack the ability to create demand for their products. Chen and Li find that Hong Kong industrialists do try to differentiate their products from those of their competitors and move upmarket, but the effect is limited, because most Hong Kong products lack brand names.[52] Consumer loyalty cannot be generated, and Hong Kong's competitiveness can be easily lost to another country.

Industrial diversification is in an even worse state. Without a sophisticated technological base and lacking many supporting industries to enhance the further development of traditional industries like electronics and plastics,[53] Hong Kong's industrial diversification lags far behind Taiwan, South Korea and Singapore.[54] In 1977, the government appointed a high-level commission to study the possibility of industrial diversification. The report was released in 1979. The commission put forward a number of recommendations to reorient and upgrade Hong Kong's industry. However, under great pressure from other Asian competitors, most of the industrialists relocated their manufacturing operation to Guangdong.[55] As a result, the government did not adopt these recommendations because there was no need for it to undertake risks by implementing uncertain policies.

Another weakness of the guerrilla business strategy and the subcontracting network system is that they do not provide adequate industrial training. As a result, there is always a shortage of skilled industrial labour. This not only increases wages, but also impedes technological development. As the Hong Kong industrialists need to produce more quality products in order to compete with other Asian competitors, they have to recruit skilled labour. Since most of the industrial firms are small and the manufacturers are reluctant to provide long-term training for their workers, when faced with a shortage of skilled labour, the industrialists will recruit the needed labour from other firms by paying higher wages. As a result, the initial manpower shortage will prompt competition which generates high labour turnover. This labour turnover in turn discourages training. This interaction between turnover and shortage creates a vicious circle from which the Hong Kong manufacturing sector is unlikely to extricate itself without the intervention of the government.[56] Although the government did establish a number of vocational training schools, these schools are quite inefficient and ineffective in providing suitable and adequate manpower for the industries. This is because the government lacks vision about the direction Hong Kong industries should take. The manpower deficiency caused by the lack of industrial training greatly hinders Hong Kong manufacturing from moving upmarket.

The competitive advantage of Hong Kong manufacturing is conditional upon the low wages and minimal diversification which gave rise to a production structure with low design and technology content. As wages rose, competitiveness gradually eroded. In response, Hong Kong industrialists continue their labour-intensive production strategy by relocating their factories to China, especially Guangdong where there is an abundance of cheap labour and cheap land. By mid-1988, there were about 2,400–2,700 enterprises in China that had direct investment from Hong Kong-based companies, with most of them undertaking manufacturing. The total investment made by Hong Kong companies was estimated between US$4.7 and US$5.1 million. It is estimated that over 30 per cent of Hong Kong's manufacturing has moved to the mainland. For some of them, like electronics and plastics, this amounts to as much as 70–80 per cent.[57] This industrial relocation provokes the comeback of the re-export trade. The direct investment of Hong Kong manufacturers in China and the indirect trade relations between China and Taiwan have caused Hong Kong's re-exports to exceed its own domestic exports since 1988. Consequently, a structural change in Hong Kong has taken place where the service sector has replaced the manufacturing sector as the biggest economic sector, especially after 1987.[58]

Most of Hong Kong's direct investment is in the form of sole proprietorships, producing by means of original equipment manufacture, and subcontracting substantial parts of the manufacturing processes.[59] There are a number of problems caused by the outward processing. As observed by Tuan and Ng, although most of the outward processors still confine their operations to pure fabrication and production processes, the material management and sourcing (upper stream process) and shipping and exporting (lower stream process) of 20–40 per cent of the firms take place in China.[60] If the trend were to continue and grow, crucial parts of the service content operations, such as overseas market connections, and other higher value-added operations would eventually move out of Hong Kong. Hsueh and Woo argue that outward processing activities may crowd out domestic investment in manufacturing leading to lower employment and wage income in Hong Kong, though higher profits would accrue to the investors.[61] Another side-effect of outward processing is that the increase in the re-export trade, caused by outward processing, makes some services sectors more profitable than manufacturing. As a result, Hong Kong manufacturers may be more willing and financially able to pursue an inter-sectoral shift business strategy. Both scenarios will cause structural unemployment. Hsueh and Woo further argue that even if there is no 'crowding out' of domestic manufacturing, the participants of the outward processing trade in Hong Kong will spend more in Hong Kong because of the higher profits gained from trade. Consequently, their spending will intensify inflation, which is also detrimental to the poor. Despite these problems, outward processing has become an irreversible trend.

Conclusion

As a response to the government policy bias against industry, industrialists have developed a particular kind of system that can ensure their survival by producing labour-intensive goods with a short production run time. The guerrilla business strategy induces an individual flexibility that ensures a quick response to market changes. However, it also inhibits entrepreneurs from developing a commitment to technological upgrading. Even more damaging, these entrepreneurs would possibly leave manufacturing production if other business opportunities, like the property market, proved to be more profitable.

The guerrilla business has its historical roots in the transient mentality that prevailed in the whole colonial period and intensified after the Second World War, because of the uncertainty about the colonial status of Hong Kong. Subcontracting networks were created and maintained because of the predominate SMF manufacturing sector and the guerrilla business strategy. The SMF subcontracting networks not only resolve the problems of lack of capital and under-capacity for individual firms, but also provide a mechanism that can smooth the process of re-allocating resources when adjustment of the economy has to be made in response to changes in the international economic environment. The success of this flexible production system, however, depends upon a number of historical and international factors. They are the international commercial networks that have been built up by Chinese merchants since the entrepôt period, the new international division of labour and the international political environment created after the Second World War.

From the 1980s onwards, the favourable international conditions that had given rise to the Hong Kong manufacturing sector disappeared. Hong Kong manufacturers now have to deal with increasingly keen competition from other developing countries, Western protectionism and rising domestic wages. Most of the SMFs in Hong Kong responded to these challenges by moving their production to China, in order to take advantage of cheap labour.

NOTES

1 For examples, see Yun-wing Sung, 'The Hong Kong development model and its future evolution: neoclassical economics in a Chinese society', in Y.C. Jao *et al.* (eds), *Economic Development in Chinese Societies; Models and Experience*, Hong Kong, Hong Kong University Press, 1989.

2 Alvin Rabushka, *The Changing Face of Hong Kong: New Departures in Public Policy*, Washington, DC, American Enterprise Institute for Public Policy Research; and Stanford, CA, Hoover Institution on War Revolution and Peace, Stanford University, 1973, pp. 3–5.

3 Tai-lok Lui and Stephen W.K. Chiu, 'A tale of two industries: the restructuring of Hong Kong's garment-making and electronics industries', *Environment and Planning A*, 1994, vol. 26, pp. 53–70.

4 Danny Kin-Kong Lam and Ian Lee, 'Guerrilla capitalism and the limit of statist theory: comparing the Chinese NICs' in Cal Clark and Steve Chan (eds), *The Evolving Pacific Basin*, Boulder, CO, LynneRienner Publishers, 1992, pp. 107–24.

5 Lam and Lee, 'Guerrilla capitalism', p. 111.

6 Lam and Lee, 'Guerrilla capitalism', p. 113.

7 Gordon R. Redding, *The Spirit of Chinese Capitalism*, Berlin, Walter de Gruyter, 1990, p. 222.

8 See Alwyn Young, 'Hong Kong and the art of landing on one's feet: a case study of a structurally flexible economy', Ph.D. dissertation, Fletcher School of Law and Diplomacy, Tufts University, Medford, Massachusetts 1989, pp. 47–8.

9 For subcontracting as a substitute for net investment see Charles-Albert Michalet, 'International sub-contracting: a state-of-the-art', in Dimitri Germidis (ed.), *International Subcontracting: A New Form of Investment*, Paris, OECD, 1980, p. 57.

10 Victor Fung-Shuen Sit and Siu-lun Wong, *Small and Medium Industries in an Export-Oriented Economy: The Case of Hong Kong*, Hong Kong, Centre of Asian Studies, University of Hong Kong, 1989, p. 186.

11 Cf. Gunar Evcimen, Mehmet Kaytaz and E. Mine Cinar, 'Subcontracting, growth and capital accumulation in Turkey', *The Journal of Development Studies*, 1991, vol. 28, pp. 130–49. They find that in Turkey non-subcontracting textile firms have a higher average profit than subcontracting firms. The success of Hong Kong's subcontracting firms depends upon historical factors that are unique to Hong Kong.

12 Mario Morroni, 'Production flexibility', in Geoffrey M. Hodgson and Ernesto Screpanti (eds), *Rethinking Economics: Markets, Technology and Economic Evolution*, Hants, Edward Elgar, 1991, pp. 69–70.

13 Most of the subcontracting orders of small firms come from either trading companies or other small firms, rather than from large firms. Hence, the figures used here can be proxy measures for the cycle time between subcontracting firms and non-subcontracting firms within Hong Kong. See Young, 'Hong Kong', p. 174.

14 Lui and Chiu, 'A tale of two industries', p. 62.

15 The list is modified from R. Michael Donovan, 'Improving manufacturing cycle time', *Productivity Digest*, 1995, December, pp. 14–16. Donovan mainly discussed cycle time at the firm level.

16 Victor Fung-Shuen Sit, 'The informal manufacturing sector in small-scale firms in the textile industry', in Victor Fung-Shuen Sit (ed.), *Urban Hong Kong*, Hong Kong, Summerson Eastern Publishers Ltd, 1981, p. 111.

17 Lam and Lee, 'Guerrilla capitalism', p. 113.

18 Young, 'Hong Kong', p. 173.

19 Young, 'Hong Kong', p. 173.

20 Sit and Wong, *Small and Medium Industries*, p. 156.

21 Redding, *The Spirit of Chinese Capitalism*, pp. 223–4.

22 Sit and Wong, *Small and Medium Industries*, p. 188.

23 Tai-lok Lui and Stephen W.K. Chiu, 'Industrial restructuring and labour-market adjustment under positive noninterventionism: the case of Hong Kong', *Environment and Planning A*, 1993, vol. 25, pp. 63–79.

24 The relationships between the flexible labour market strategy, positive non-interventionism and non-manufacturing-oriented banking strategy are well documented in Stephen W.K. Chiu and Tai-lok Lui, 'Hong Kong: unorganized industrialism', in Gordon Clark and Won-bae Kim (eds), *Asian NIEs and the Global Economy: Industrial Restructuring and Corporate Strategy in the 1990s*, Baltimore, MD, Johns Hopkins University Press, 1995, pp. 85–111; Stephen Chiu, 'The politics of laissez-faire: Hong Kong's strategy of industrialization in historical perspective', Hong Kong Institute of Asia-Pacific Studies occasional paper no. 40, Hong Kong, Chinese University of Hong Kong, 1994; and Lui and Chiu, 'Industrial restructuring and labour-market adjustment' and 'A tale of two industries'. I will not repeat them here. With regard to the guerrilla strategy, maintaining investment flexibility by employing expensive equipment is not a good idea. It is easier to employ or dismiss a worker than a machine.

25 David Podmore, 'The population of Hong Kong', in Keith Hopkins (ed.), *Hong Kong: The Industrial Colony*, Hong Kong, Oxford University Press, 1971, p. 37.

26 Podmore, 'The population of Hong Kong', pp. 23–5.

27 Yu Shengwu and Liu Cunkuan (eds), *Shijiu shiji de Xianggang* (Nineteenth-Century Hong Kong), Hong Kong, Qilin shuye, 1994, pp. 186–91; William T. Liu, 'Chinese value orientations in Hong Kong', *Sociological Analysis*, 1996, vol. 27, no. 2, p. 57.

28 N.Q. Tse, 'Industrialization and social adjustment in Hong Kong', *Sociology and Social Research*, 1968, vol. 52, no. 3, p. 239.

29 Marjorie Topley, 'The role of savings and wealth among Hong Kong Chinese', in I.C. Jarvie (ed.), *Hong Kong: A Society in Transition*, London, Routledge & Kegan Paul, 1969, p. 209.

30 Elizabeth Sinn, 'Emigration from Hong Kong before 1941: general trends'; 'Emigration from Hong Kong before 1941: organization and impact'; and 'Emigration from Hong Kong, 1945–1994: the demographic lead-up to 1997', in Ronald Skeldon (ed.), *Emigration from Hong Kong: Tendencies and Impacts*, Hong Kong, Chinese University Press, 1995.

31 Jung-fang Tsai, *Hong Kong in Chinese History: Community and Social Unrest in the British Colony, 1842–1913*, New York, Columbia University Press, 1993, pp. 23–6.

32 See Yuan Bangjian, *Xianggang shilue* (A Brief History of Hong Kong), Hong Kong, Zhongliu chubanshe, 1988, pp. 113–15.

33 Tsai, *Hong Kong in Chinese History*, p. 27.

34 Tsai, *Hong Kong in Chinese History*, p. 33.

35 K.C. Fok, *Lectures on Hong Kong History: Hong Kong's Role in Modern Chinese History*, Hong Kong, The Commercial Press 1990, pp. 104–5.

36 Folker Fröbel, Jürgen Heinrichs and Otto Kreye, *The New International Division of Labour*, Cambridge, Cambridge University Press, 1980, pp. 34–6.

37 Fröbel *et al.*, *The New International Division of Labour*, p. 46.

38 Martin Landsberg, 'Export-led industrialization in the Third World: manufacturing imperialism', *The Review of Radical Political Economics*, 1979, vol. 11, no. 4, p. 57.

39 Gene Gregory, 'Asia's electronics revolution', *Euro-Asia Business Review*, 1982, vol. 1, no. 1., p. 45.

40 Gregory, 'Asia's electronic revolution', p. 42–55.

41 Gregory, 'Asia's electronic revoltuion', p. 48.

42 Asian Productivity Organization, *International Sub-Contracting: A Tool of Technological Transfer*, Tokyo, Asian Productivity Organization, 1978, p. 6.

43 Alvin So, 'The economic success of Hong Kong: insights from a world-system perspective', *Sociological Perspectives*, 1986, vol. 29, no. 2, p. 245.

44 For details, see Ian Scott, *Political Change and the Crisis of Legitimacy in Hong Kong*, Hong Kong, Oxford University Press, 1989, pp. 55–9.
45 Scott, *Political Change*, p. 56.
46 Yu and Liu, *Shijiu shiji de Xianggang*, p. 239.
47 Feng Bang-yan, *Xianggang yingzi caituan* (Hong Kong British Corporations), Hong Kong, Joint Publication Co. Ltd, 1996, p. 144.
48 G.B. Endacott, *A History of Hong Kong*, rev. edn, Hong Kong, Oxford University Press, 1973, p. 317.
49 K.S. Ko, 'Hong Kong's small-scale industries', *Hong Kong Manager*, 1967, vol. 3, p. 21.
50 Edward K.Y Chen, 'Foreign trade and economic growth in Hong Kong: experience and prospects', in Collin, I Bradford, Jr and William H. Branson (eds), *Trade and Structural Change in Pacific Asia*, Chicago University of Chicago Press, pp. 364–5.
51 For details, see Edward K.Y. Chen, 'Multinational corporations and technical diffusion in Hong Kong manufacturing', *Applied Economics*, 1983, vol. 15, pp. 309–21; and J. Henderson, 'The political economy of technological transformation in the Hong Kong electronics industry', in Edward K.Y. Chen *et al.* (eds), *Industrial and Trade Development in Hong Kong*, Hong Kong, Centre of Asian Studies, 1991, pp. 57–115.
52 Edward K.Y. Chen and K.W. Li, 'Industry', in H.C.Y. Ho and L.C. Chau (eds), *The Economic System of Hong Kong*, Hong Kong, Asian Research Service, 1992, pp. 113–39.
53 For an early discussion of how the non-intervention policy of the colonial government failed to create a capital goods sector, see M. Fransman, 'Learning and the capital goods sector under free trade: the case of Hong Kong, *World Development*, 1982, vol. 10, no. 11, pp. 991–1014. For a counter-argument, see John S. Henley and Mee-Kau Nyaw, 'A reappraisal of the capital goods sector in Hong Kong: the case for free trade', *World Development*, 1985, vol. 13, no. 6, pp. 737–48.
54 Despite all these difficulties, the export performance in the mid-1980s was fairly good. This was mainly because of the pegging of the Hong Kong dollar to the US dollar in 1983. The weak US dollar in fact made the Hong Kong dollar depreciate relative to other competing countries. As a result, the competitiveness gained in the US market, the largest export destination of Hong Kong, over this period is mainly a historical accident.
55 Suzanne Berger and Richard K. Lester, *Made by Hong Kong*, Hong Kong, Oxford University Press, 1997, pp. 21–2.
56 See Nicholas Owen, 'Manpower deficiencies and industrial training', *Hong Kong Economic Papers*, 1972, no. 7, pp. 45–59.
57 Feng Bang-yan, 'The role of Hong Kong in China's economic modernization', in Chen *et al.* (eds), *Industrial and Trade Development in Hong Kong*, p. 499.
58 Chyan Tuan and Linda F.Y. Ng, 'Manufacturing evolution under passive industrial policy and cross-border operations in China: the case of Hong Kong', *Journal of Asian Economics*, 1995, vol. 6, no. 1, p. 81.
59 Chyan Tuan and Linda F.Y. Ng, 'The turning point of the Hong Kong manufacturing Sector', *The Journal of International Trade and Economic Development*, 1995, vol. 4, no. 2, p. 155.
60 Tuan and Ng, 'Manufacturing evolution', p. 76.
61 T.T. Hsueh and T.O. Woo, 'The development of Hong Kong–China economic relationship', in Benjamin K.P. Leung and Teresa Y.C. Wong (eds), *25 Years of Social and Economic Development in Hong Kong*, Hong Kong, University of Hong Kong, 1994.

REFERENCES

Ai Ming, 'Lun Xianggang huaqiao gongye zhi diwei' (On the status of Chinese industry in Hong Kong), *Changshang yuekan* (Manufacturers' Monthly Bulletin), 1948, March, pp. 9–10.

Aijmer, Göran, 'Migrants into Hong Kong's New Territories: on the background of outsider vegetable farmers', *Ethnos*, 1973, vol. 38, pp. 57–70.

——, 'An enquiry into Chinese settlement patterns: the rural squatters of Hong Kong', *Man*, 1975, vol. 10, pp. 559–70.

——, *Economic Man in Sha Tin: Vegetable Gardeners in a Hong Kong Valley*, London, Curzon Press, 1980.

——, *Atomistic Society in Sha Tin: Immigrants in a Hong Kong Valley*, Gothoburgensis, Acta Universitatis Gothoburgensis, 1986.

Alabaster, E., *Notes and Commentaries on Chinese Criminal Law*, London, Luzac & Co., 1899.

Alatas, Syed Husein, *The Myth of the Lazy Native: A Study of the Image of the Malays, Filipinos and Javanese from the 16th to the 20th Centuries and Its Function in the Ideology of Colonial Capitalism*, London, Frank Cass, 1977.

Anderson, Perry, *English Questions*, London, Verso, 1992.

Asian Productivity Organization, *International Sub-Contracting: A Tool of Technological Transfer*, Tokyo, Asian Productivity Organization, 1978.

Bachrach, Peter and Baratz, Morton S., 'Two faces of power', *American Political Science Review*, 1962, vol. 56, no. 4, December, pp. 947–52.

Baker, Hugh D.R., 'The five great clans of the New Territories', *Journal of Hong Kong Branch of Royal Asiatic Society*, 1966, vol. 11, pp. 25–47.

Balandier, G., 'The colonial situation: a theoretical approach', in Immanuel Wallerstein (ed.), *Social Change: The Colonial Situation*, New York, John Wiley & Sons, 1966.

Bard, Solomon, *Traders of Hong Kong: Some Foreign Merchant Houses, 1841–1899*, Hong Kong, Urban Council, 1993.

Benton, Gregor, *The Hong Kong Crisis*, London, Pluto Press, 1983.

Berger, Suzanne and Lester, Richard K., *Made by Hong Kong*, Hong Kong, Oxford University Press, 1997.

Bloch, Marc, *The Historian's Craft*, Manchester, Manchester University Press, 1954.

Blussé, Leonard, *Strange Company: Chinese Settlers, Mestizo Women and the Dutch in VOC Batavia*, Dordrecht, Foris, 1986.

Blyth, Sally and Wotherspoon, Ian, *Hong Kong Remembers*, Hong Kong, Oxford University Press, 1996.

Braudel, Fernand, *The Wheels of Commerce*, New York, Harper & Row, 1982.

REFERENCES

——, *The Perspective of the World*, New York, Harper & Row, 1984.

British Parliamentary Papers: China 25: Correspondence, Dispatches, Reports, Returns, Memorials and Other Papers Relating to the Affairs of Hong Kong 1862–81, Shannon, Irish University Press, 1972.

Bristow, M.R., *Land Use Planning in Hong Kong*, Hong Kong, Oxford University Press, 1984.

Brown, David, *The State and Ethnic Politics in Southeast Asia*, London and New York, Routledge, 1994.

Brown, Rajeswary Ampalavanar, *Capital and Entrepreneurship in South-East Asia*, New York, St Martin's Press, 1994.

Budiman, Arief, 'The emergence of the bureaucratic capitalist state in Indonesia', in Lim Teck Chee (ed.), *Reflections on Development in Southeast Asia*, Singapore, Institute of Southeast Asian Studies, Canton Press, 1988.

Butcher, John, 'Revenue farming and the changing state in Southeast Asia', in John Butcher & Howard Dick (eds), *The Rise and Fall of Revenue Farming*, New York, St Martin's Press, 1993.

——, 'Loke Yew', in John Butcher & Howard Dick (eds), *The Rise and Fall of Revenue Farming*, New York, St Martin's Press, 1993.

Cain, P.J. and Hopkins, A.G, *British Imperialism: Crisis and Reconstruction 1914—1990*, London, Longman, 1993.

Canton Press, various issues.

Carr, E.H., *What is History?*, 2nd edn, London, Penguin Books, 1987.

Castells, Manuel, 'Four Asian tigers with a dragon head: a comparative analysis of the state, economy, and society in the Asian Pacific rim', in Richard P. Appelbaum and Jeffrey Henderson (eds), *States and Development in the Asian Pacific Rim*, Newbury Park, Sage, 1992.

Chan, Kai-cheung, 'History', in Choi Po-king and Ho Lok-sang (eds), *The Other Hong Kong Report 1993*, Hong Kong, Chinese University Press, 1993

Chan, Ming K., 'Introduction: Hong Kong's precarious balance – 150 years in an historic triangle', Ming K. Chan with John D. Young (ed.), *Precarious Balance: Hong Kong Between China and Britain, 1842–1992*, Hong Kong, Hong Kong University Press, 1994.

——, 'All in the family: the Hong Kong–Guangdong link in historical perspective', in Reginald Yin-Wang Y. Kwok and Alvin Y. So (eds), *The Hong Kong–Guangdong Link: Partnership in Flux*, Armonk, NY, M.E. Sharpe, 1995.

——, 'The legacy of the British administration of Hong Kong: a view from Hong Kong', *China Quarterly*, 1997, no. 151, September, pp. 567–82.

Chan, Tai Tung and Chan, Man Yuen (eds), *Bainian shangye* (A Century of Commerce), Hong Kong, Guangming wenhua shiye gongsi, 1941.

Chan, Wai Kwan, *The Making of Hong Kong Society: Three Studies of Class Formation in Early Hong Kong*, Oxford, Clarendon Press, 1991.

Chan, Yat-san, 'The British government should keep up with the times in the administration over the New Territories', speech delivered on 17 February 1981, mimeograph.

Chang, Chung-li, *The Chinese Gentry: Studies on Their Role in Nineteenth Century Chinese Society*, Seattle, WA, University of Washington Press, 1955.

Chang, Pin-tsun, 'The first Chinese diaspora in Southeast Asia in the fifteenth century', in Roderich Ptak and Dietmar Rothermund (eds), *Emporia, Commodities and Entrepreneurs in Asian Maritime Trade, C. 1400–1750*, Stuttgart, Franz Steiner Verlag, 1991.

Changshang yuekan (Manufacturers' Monthly Bulletin), various issues.

Chau, Lam-yan and Lau, Siu-kai, 'Development, colonial rule, and intergroup conflict in a Chinese village in Hong Kong', in *Human Organization*, 1982, vol. 41, no. 2, pp. 139–46.

Chen, Edward K.Y., 'Multinational corporations and technical diffusion in Hong Kong manufacturing', *Applied Economics*, 1983, vol. 15, pp. 309–21.

——, 'Foreign trade and economic growth in Hong Kong: experience and prospects', in Collin I. Bradford, Jr and William H. Branson (eds), *Trade and Structural Change in Pacific Asia*, Chicago, University of Chicago Press, 1987.

Chen, Edward K.Y. and Li, K.W., 'Industry', in H.C.Y. Ho and L.C. Chau (eds), *The Economic System of Hong Kong*, Hong Kong, Asian Research Service, 1992.

Chen Qian, 'Xianggang jiushi jianwen lu (1)' (Recollections of old Hong Kong, Part 1), *Guangdong wenshi ziliao* (Studies in Guangdong Literature and History), 1984, vol. 41, pp. 1–34.

Chen, Qiaozhi, 'Dongnanya huaren ziben de tedian yu dongxiang' (The characteristics and directions of Southeast Asian Chinese capital), in Wang Muheng (ed.), *Dongnanya huaren jingji* (The Economy of the Chinese in Southeast Asia), Fuzhou, Fujian renmin chubanshe, 1989.

Chen, Shijun, 'Lun yapian zhanzheng qian de maiban he jindai maiban zhichan jieji de chansheng' (On the compradors before the Opium War and the origin of the modern comprador bourgeoisie), in Ning Jing (ed.), *Yapian zhanzheng shi lunwen zhuan ji xuanbian* (A Collection of Articles on the History of the Opium War), Beijing, Renmin chubanshe, 1984.

Chen, Zexian, 'Shijiu shiji shengxing de qiyue huagong zhi' (The prevailing 'contract labor' system in the nineteenth century), in Cuncui Xueshe (ed.), *Zhongguo jin sanbainian shehui jingji shilunji* (A Collection of Articles on the Socio-Economic History of China in the Last Three Hundred Years), vol. 2, Hong Kong, Chongwen shudian, 1972.

Cheng, Joseph (ed.), *Hong Kong: In Search of a Future*, Hong Kong, Oxford University Press, 1984.

Cheng Zhi, 'Xianggang jianshi' (Brief history of Hong Kong), in Li Jinwei (ed.), *Xianggang bainianshi* (Centenary History of Hong Kong), Hong Kong, Nanzhong chubanshe, 1948.

Cheung, Anthony B.L., 'Xin zhongchan jieji de maoqi yu zhengzhi yingxiang' (The new middle-class: its emergence and political influence), *Mingbao yuekan* (Ming Pao Monthly), 1987, no. 253, pp. 10–15.

Cheung, Anthony B.L. and Louie, K.S., 'Social conflicts in Hong Kong, 1975–1986', Hong Kong Institute of Asia-Pacific Studies occasional paper no. 3, Chinese University of Hong Kong, 1991.

Cheung, Tsui Ping, 'The opium monopoly in Hong Kong, 1844–1887', unpublished M.Phil. thesis, University of Hong Kong, Hong Kong, 1986.

The China Directory for 1867, Hong Kong, A. Shortrede, 1867.

China Mail, various issues.

China Mail, *The Hong Kong Almanack and Directory for 1846*, Hong Kong, China Mail, 1846.

Chiu, Stephen W.K., 'The politics of laissez-faire: Hong Kong's strategy of industrialization in historical perspective', Hong Kong Institute of Asia Pacific Studies occasional paper no. 40, Hong Kong, Chinese University of Hong Kong, 1994.

——, 'Unravelling Hong Kong's exceptionalism: the politics of laissez-faire in the industrial takeoff', *Political Power and Social Theory*, 1996, vol. 10, pp. 229–56.

Chiu, Stephen W.K. and Hung, Ho-fung, 'Engineering rural stability: the New Territories in Hong Kong's colonial history', paper presented at the International Workshop on 'Hong Kong: Society, Polity and Economy under Colonial Rule', Sinological Institute, Leiden University, the Netherlands, 22–24 August 1996.

Chiu, Stephen W.K. and Levin, David., 'Contestatory unionism', in Stephen W.K. Chiu and Tai-lok Lui (eds), *The Dynamics of Social Movement in Hong Kong*, Hong Kong, Hong Kong University Press, forthcoming.

Chiu, Stephen W.K. and Lui, Tai-lok, 'Hong Kong: unorganized industrialism', in Gordon Clark and Won-bae Kim (eds), *Asian NIEs and the Global Economy: Industrial Restructuring and Corporate Strategy in the 1990s*, Baltimore, MD, John Hopkins University Press, 1995.

Chiu, T.N., *The Port of Hong Kong: A Survey of Its Development*, Hong Kong, Hong Kong University Press, 1973.

Choi, Alex H., 'The industrial transformation of Hong Kong, 1945–58: market or state', MA thesis, Queens University, Kingston, 1993.*I*

——, 'Beyond market and state: a study of Hong Kong's industrial transformation', *Studies in Political Economy*, 1994, no. 45, pp. 28–64.

Chui, Ernest and Lai, On Kwok, 'Patterns of social conflicts in Hong Kong in the period 1981 to 1991', mimeograph, 1994.

Chun, Allen J., 'Land is to Live: A Study of the Concept of Tsu in a Hakka Chinese Village, New Territories, Hong Kong', unpublished Ph.D. dissertation, Chicago University, Illinois, 1985.

——, 'The land revolution in twentieth century rural Hong Kong', *Bulletin of the Institute of Ethnology Academia Sinica*, 1987, no. 61, pp. 1–40.

Clayton, David, *Imperialism Revisited: Political and Economic Relations Between Britain and China, 1950–54*, London, Macmillan, 1997.

Coatsworth, John H., 'The limits of colonial absolutism: the state in eighteenth century Mexico', in Karen Spalding (ed.), *Essays in the Political, Economic and Social History of Colonial Latin America*, Newark, DE, Latin American Studies Program, University of Delaware, 1982.

Commercial and Industrial Hong Kong: A Record of 94 Years Progress of the Colony in Commerce, Trade, Industry, and Shipping (1841–1935), Hong Kong, Bedikton Co., 1935.

Commission of Inquiry, *Kowloon Disturbances 1966: Report of Commission of Inquiry*, Hong Kong, Government Printer, 1967.

Cooke, George Wingrove, *China: Being the Times' Special Correspondence from China in the Years 1857–1858*, London, Routledge, 1858.

Cooper, Frederick, 'Conflict and connection: rethinking colonial African history', *American Historical Review*, 1994, vol. 99, no. 5, December, pp. 1516–45.

Cooray, Anton, 'Asian customary laws through Western eyes: a comparison of Sri Lankan and Hong Kong colonial experience', in Louis A. Knafla and Susan W.S. Binnie (eds), *Law, Society, and the State: Essays in Modern Legal History*, Toronto, Ont., University of Toronto Press, 1995.

Courtauld, Caroline and Holdsworth, May, *The Hong Kong Story*, Hong Kong, Oxford University Press, 1997.

Cree, Edward H., *The Cree Journals: The Voyages of Edward H. Cree, Surgeon R.N., as Related in His Private Journals, 1837–1856*, edited by Michael Levien, Exeter, England, Webb & Bower, 1981.

Crick, W.F. (ed.), *Commonwealth Banking Systems*, Oxford, Clarendon, 1965.

Crisswell, Colin N., *The Taipans: Hong Kong's Merchant Princes*, Hong Kong, Oxford University Press, 1981.

Cunynghame, Arthur, *The Opium War; Being Recollections of Service in China*, London, Saunders & Otely, 1844.

Curtin, Philip D., *Cross-Cultural Trade in World History*, Cambridge, MA, Cambridge University Press, 1984.

Curtis, Mark, *The Ambiguities of Power: British Foreign Policy Since 1945*, Zed Press, 1995.

Darwin, John, *Britain and Decolonization: The Retreat from Empire in the Post-War World*, London, Macmillan, 1988.

Davies, S.N.G., 'One brand of politics rekindled', *Hong Kong Law Journal*, 1977, vol. 7, no. 1, pp. 44–84.

Dick, Howard, 'Fresh approach to Southeast Asian history', in John Butcher & Howard Dick (eds), *The Rise and Fall of Revenue Farming*, New York, St Martin's Press, 1993.

Ding You, *Xianggang chuqi shihua* (Early Hong Kong), Beijing, Lianhe chubanshe, 1983.

Dirks, Nicholas B., 'Introduction: colonialism and culture', in Nicholas B. Dirks (ed.), *Colonialism and Culture*, Ann Arbor, MI, University of Michigan Press, 1992.

Djao, Angela Wei, 'Social control in a colonial society: a case study of working class consciousness in Hong Kong', Ph.D dissertation, University of Toronto, Ont., 1976.

Donckels, Rik and Lambrecht, Johan, 'Networks and small business growth: an explanatory model', *Small Business Economics*, 1995, vol. 4 , pp. 273–89.

Donovan, R. Michael, 'Improving manufacturing cycle time', *Productivity Digest*, 1995, December, pp. 14–16.

Duff, Peter; Findlay, Mark; Howarth, Carla; and Chan, Tsang-fai, *Juries, a Hong Kong Perspective*, Hong Kong, Hong Kong University Press, 1992.

Eckert, Carter J., *Offspring of Empire: The Koch'ang Kims and the Colonial Origins of Korean Capitalism, 1876–1945*, Seattle, WA, University of Washington Press, 1991.

Eitel, E.J., *Europe in China: The History of Hong Kong from the Beginning to the Year 1882*, London, Luzac & Co., 1895.

Endacott, G.B., *A Biographical Sketch-Book of Early Hong Kong*, Singapore, Eastern Universities Press, 1962.

—— (ed.), *An Eastern Entrepôt: A Collection of Documents Illustrating the History of Hong Kong*, London, Her Majesty's Stationery Office, 1964.

——, *A History of Hong Kong*, Hong Kong, Oxford University Press, 1964; rev. edn., 1973.

——, *Government and People in Hong Kong 1841–1962: A Constitutional History*, Hong Kong, Hong Kong University Press, 1964.

England, Joe, *Hong Kong: Britain's Responsibility*, London, Fabian Society, 1976.

——, *Industrial Relations and Law in Hong Kong*, 2nd edn, Hong Kong, Oxford University Press, 1989.

England, Joe and Rear, John, *Chinese Labor Under British Rule: A Critical Study of Labor Relations and Law in Hong Kong*, Hong Kong, Oxford University Press, 1975.

Evans, Dafydd Emrys, 'Chinatown in Hong Kong: the beginnings of Taipingshan', *Journal of the Hong Kong Branch of the Royal Asiatic Society*, 1970, vol. 10, pp. 69–78.

——, 'The foundation of Hong Kong: a chapter of accidents', in Marjorie Topley (ed.), *Hong Kong: The Interaction of Traditions and Life in the Towns*, Hong Kong, Hong Kong Branch of the Royal Asiatic Society, 1975.

Evcimen, Gunar; Kaytaz, Mehmet; and Mine Cinar, E., 'Subcontracting, growth and capital accumulation in small-scale firms in the textile industry in Turkey', *The Journal of Development Studies*, 1991, vol. 28, no. 1, pp. 130–49.

REFERENCES

Fairbank, John King, *Trade and Diplomacy on the China Coast: The Opening of the Treaty Ports, 1842–1854*, 2 vols, 1953, repr. (2 vols in 1), Cambridge, MA, Harvard University Press, 1964.

Far Eastern Economic Review, various issues.

Feng, Bang-yan, 'The role of Hong Kong in China's economic modernization', in Edward K.Y. Chen, Mee-Kau Nyaw and Teresa Y.C. Wong (eds), *Industrial and Trade Development in Hong Kong*, Hong Kong, Centre of Asian Studies, 1991.

——, *Xianggang yingzi caituan* (Hong Kong British Corporations), Hong Kong, Joint Publication Co. Ltd, 1996.

Fisch, J., *Cheap Lives and Dear Limbs: The British Transformation of the Bengal Criminal Law 1769–1817*, Wiesbaden, Steiner, 1983.

Fok, K.C., *Lectures on Hong Kong History: Hong Kong's Role in Modern Chinese History*, Hong Kong, The Commercial Press, 1990.

Fortune, Robert, *Three Years' Wanderings in the Northern Provinces of China, including a Visit to the Tea, Silk, and Cotton Countries: With an Account of Agriculture and Horticulture of the Chinese, New Plants, etc.*, London, J. Murray, 1847.

Fransman, M., 'Learning and the capital goods sector under free trade: the case of Hong Kong', *World Development*, 1982, vol. 10, no. 11, pp. 991–1,014.

Freedman, Maurice, 'Shifts of power in the Hong Kong New Territories', *Journal of Asian and African Studies*, 1966, no.1, pp. 3–12.

Friend of China, various issues.

Fröbel, Folker; Heinrichs, Jürgen; and Kreye, Otto, *The New International Division of Labour*, Cambridge, Cambridge University Press, 1980.

Gatrell, V.A.C. and Hadden, T.B., 'Criminal statistics and their interpretation', in E.A. Wrigley (ed.) *Nineteenth-Century Society: Essays in the Use of Quantitative Methods for the Study of Social Data*, Cambridge, Cambridge University Press, 1972.

Glynn, Sean and Booth, Alan, *Modern Britain: An Economic and Social History*, London, Routledge, 1996.

Gongshang ribao bianjibu, *Xianggang huazi gongchang diaochalu* (A Survey of Chinese-Capital Factories), Hong Kong, Gongshang ribao yingyebu, 1934.

Grant, Charles J., *The Soils and Agriculture of Hong Kong*, Hong Kong, Government Printer, 1962.

Grantham, Alexander, *Via Ports: From Hong Kong to Hong Kong*, Hong Kong, Hong Kong University Press, 1965.

Great Britain, Public Record Office, *Colonial Office Records*, CO 129, Dispatches from the Governor of Hong Kong.

——, CO 131, Minutes of Executive Council meetings and administrative reports.

——, CO 537, Supplementary.

——, CO 1030, Original Correspondence.

——, CO 885/HO XC/A29033, Report of the Inter-Departmental Committee on the Industrial Development of the Colonial Empire, March 1934.

Great Britain, Public Record Office, *Foreign Office Records*, FO 17, China Correspondence.

——, FO 233, Records of letters between the Plenipotentiary and the High Provincial Authorities, and proclamations by H.E. the Governor and Chief Magistrate, 1844–9.

Great Britain, SOAS Library, South China and Ultra Ganges, Box 5, London Missionary Society/CWM, 1843–72, Hirschberg to Tidman, 5 September 1853.

Gregory, Gene, 'Asia's electronics revolution', *Euro-Asia Business Review*, 1982, vol. 1, no.1, pp. 42–55.

REFERENCES

Groves, R.G., 'Militia, market and lineage: Chinese resistance to the occupation of Hong Kong's New Territories in 1899', *Journal of Hong Kong Branch of Royal Asiatic Society*, 1969, vol. 9, pp. 31–64.

Guha, Ranajit, 'The prose of counter-insurgency', in Ranajit Guha (ed.), *Selected Subaltern Studies*, New York, Oxford University Press, 1988.

Habib, Irfan, 'Studying a colonial economy – without perceiving colonialism', *Modern Asian Studies*, 1985, vol. 19, no. 3, pp. 335–58.

Haggard, Stephen, *Pathways from the Periphery: The Politics of Growth in the Newly Industrializing Countries*, Ithaca, NY, Cornell University Press, 1990.

Halliday, Jon, 'Hong Kong: Britain's Chinese colony', *New Left Review*, 1974, nos 87–8, September–December, pp. 91–112.

Hao, Yen-p'ing, *The Comprador in Nineteenth Century China: Bridge between East and West*, Cambridge, MA, Harvard University Press, 1970.

Harris, Peter, *Hong Kong: A Study of Bureaucratic Politics*, Hong Kong, Heinemann Asia, 1978.

——, *Hong Kong: A Study of Bureaucracy and Politics*, Hong Kong, Macmillan, 1988.

Havinden, Michael and Meredith, David, *Colonialism and Development: Britain and Its Tropical Colonies, 1850–1960*, London, Routledge, 1993.

Hay, Douglas, 'Property, authority and the criminal law', in Douglas Hay, Peter Linebaugh, John G. Rule, E.P. Thompson, Cal Winslow, *Albion's Fatal Tree: Crime and Society in Eighteenth-Century England*, Harmondsworth, Penguin Books, 1977.

Hayes, James, 'The nature of village life', in David Faure, J. Hayes and A. Birch (eds), *From Village to City: Studies in the Traditional Roots of Hong Kong Society*, Hong Kong, Centre of Asian Studies, 1984.

——, *Friends and Teachers: Hong Kong and Its People 1953–87*, Hong Kong, Hong Kong University Press, 1996.

Henderson, J., 'The political economy of technological transformation in the Hong Kong electronics industry' in Edward K.Y. Chen, Mee-Kau Nyaw and Teresa Y.C. Wong (eds), *Industrial and Trade Development in Hong Kong*, Hong Kong, Centre of Asian Studies, 1991, pp. 57–115.

——, 'Urbanization in the Hong Kong–South China region: an introduction to dynamics and dilemmas', *International Journal of Urban and Regional Research*, 1991, vol. 15, no. 2, pp. 169–79.

Henley, John S. and Nyaw, Mee-Kau, 'A reapraisal of the capital goods sector in Hong Kong: the case for free trade', *World Development*, 1985, vol. 13, no. 6, pp. 737–48.

Hetherington, R.M., 'Industrial labour in Hong Kong', *Hong Kong Economic Papers*, no. 2, 1963.

Hinds, Allister E., 'Sterling and imperial policy, 1945–1951', *Journal of Imperial and Commonwealth History*, 1986, vol. 15, no. 1, pp. 150–76.

——, 'Imperial policy and colonial Sterling balances, 1943–56', *Journal of Imperial and Commonwealth History*, 1991, vol. 19, no. 1, pp. 24–44.

Historical and Statistical Abstract of the Colony of Hong Kong, 1841–1930, Hong Kong, Noronha, 1932.

Ho, Yin-ping, *Trade, Industrial Restructuring and Development in Hong Kong*, London, Macmillan, 1992.

Hong Kong, Public Record Office, HKRS 100, Correspondence received by the Chief Police Magistrate from the Colonial Secretary, 2 Feb. 1844 – 31 Dec. 1846.

Hong Kong Chinese Manufacturers' Union, *Xianggang Zhongguo huopin zhanlanhui* (Pictorial Record of the Exhibition of Hong Kong Chinese Products), Hong Kong, Hong Kong Chinese Manufacturers' Union, various years.

Hong Kong Chinese Manufacturers' Union (ed.), *Xianggang Zhonghua changshang chupin zhinan* (A Guide to the Products of Chinese Factories in Hong Kong), Hong Kong, Hong Kong Chinese Manufacturers' Union, 1936.

Hong Kong Council of Social Service, *Community Development Resource Book*, various years.

Hong Kong Daily Press, various issues.

Hong Kong Federation of Students, *Xianggang xuesheng yundong huigu* (A Review of the Hong Kong Student Movement), Hong Kong, Wide Angle Publications, 1983.

Hong Kong Financial Times, 28 November 1990.

Hong Kong General Chamber of Commerce, *Hong Kong General Chamber of Commerce Report*, various years.

Hong Kong Government, *Administrative Report*, various years.

——, *Hong Kong Annual Report*, various years.

——, *Hongkong Government Gazette*, various years.

——, *Hongkong Hansard*, various years.

——, *White Paper: The Urban Council*, 1971.

——, Census Commissioner, *Report of the Census 1961*, 1962.

——, District Commissioner, New Territories, *Annual Department Report*, various years.

——, Hong Kong Trade Development Council, *Survey on Hong Kong Domestic Exports, Re-exports, and Triangular Trade*, 1991.

Hong Kong Register, various years.

Hong Kong Research Project, *Hong Kong: A Case to Answer*, Nottingham, Spokesman Books, 1974.

Hsueh, T.T. and Woo, T.O., 'The development of Hong Kong–China economic relationship', in Benjamin K.P. Leung and Teresa Y.C. Wong (eds), *25 Years of Social and Economic Development in Hong Kong*, Hong Kong, University of Hong Kong, 1994.

Huang, Yifeng, 'Diguo zhuyi qinlue Zhongguo de yige zhongyao zhizhu – maiban jieji' (The comprador class – an important support for the imperialist invasion of China), in Cuncui xueshe (eds), *Zhongguo jin sanbainian shehui jingji shi lunji* (A Collection of Articles on the Socio-Economic History of China in the Last Hundred Years), vol. 4., Chongwen shudian, 1974.

Hughes, Richard, *Borrowed Place Borrowed Time: Hong Kong and Its Many Faces*, 2nd rev. edn, London, André Deutsch, 1976.

Hung, Ho-fung, 'The colonial state and rural protest in Hong Kong: a historical and sociological analysis', M.Phil. thesis, Chinese University of Hong Kong, Hong Kong, 1998.

Hyde, Francis E., *Far Eastern Trade 1860–1914*, London, Adam & Charles Black, 1973.

Ingham, Geoffrey, *Capitalism Divided: The City and Industry in British Social Development*, London, Macmillan, 1984.

Jansen, Marius B., *China in the Tokugawa World*, Cambridge, MA, Harvard University Press, 1992.

Jao, Y.C., *Banking and Currency in Hong Kong: A Study of Postwar Financial Development*, London, Macmillan, 1974.

——, 'Financing Hong Kong's early postwar industrialization: the role of the Hongkong and Shanghai Banking Corporation', in Frank H.H. King (ed.), *Eastern Banking: Essays in the History of the Hongkong and Shanghai Banking Corporation*, London, Athlone Press, 1983.

Jenkins, Craig J. and Klandermans, Bert (eds), *The Politics of Social Protest*, London, UCL Press, 1995.

Jingji ziliaoshe (Economic Information Agency) (ed.), *Xianggang gongshang shouce* (Hong Kong Industry and Commerce Directory), Hong Kong, Jingji ziliaoshe, 1946.

Jomo, Kwame Sundaram, *A Question of Class: Capital, the State, and Uneven Development in Malaysia*, Singapore, Oxford University Press, 1986.

Jones, Catherine, *Promoting Prosperity: The Hong Kong Way of Social Policy*, Hong Kong, Chinese University Press, 1990.

Kahn, Ellison, *Trial by Jury*, Hong Kong, University of Hong Kong Law Working Paper Series no. 6, 1992.

King, Ambrose Y.C., 'Administrative absorption of politics in Hong Kong: emphasis on the grassroots level', in Ambrose Y.C. King and Rance P.L. Lee (eds), *Social Life and Development in Hong Kong*, Hong Kong, Chinese University Press, 1981.

——, 'The political culture of Kwun Tong', in Ambrose Y.C. King and Rance P.L. (eds), *Social Life and Development in Hong Kong*, Hong Kong, Chinese University Press, 1981.

King, Anthony D., 'Colonial cities: global pivots of change', in Robert Ross and Gerald J. Telkamp (eds), *Colonial Cities: Essays on Urbanism in a Colonial Context*, Leiden, Martinus Nijhoff, for Leiden University Press, 1985.

Kirby, Stuart E, 'Developing small industries in Hongkong', *Far Eastern Economic Review*, 1961, vol. 32, pp. 216–19.

Ko, K.S. 'Hong Kong's small-scale industries', *Hong Kong Manager*, 1967, vol. 3, no. 1, pp. 19–21.

Krozewski, Gerold, 'Sterling, the "minor" territories, and the end of formal empire, 1939–1958', *Economic History Review*, 1993, vol. 46, no. 2, pp. 239–65.

——, 'Finance and empire: the dilemma facing Great Britain in the 1950s', *The International History Review*, 1996, vol. 18, no. 2, pp. 48–69.

Kuan, Hsin-chi, 'Political stability and change in Hong Kong', in Tzong-biau Lin, Rance P.L. Lee and Udo-Ernst Simonis (eds), *Hong Kong: Economic, Social and Political Studies in Development*, New York, M.E. Sharpe, 1979.

Kuan, Hsin-chi and Lau, Siu-kai, 'Development and the resuscitation of rural leadership in Hong Kong: the case of neo-indirect-rule', CUHK Social Research Centre occasional paper no. 81, Hong Kong, Chinese University of Hong Kong, 1979.

——, 'Planned development and political adaptability in rural areas, in Ambrose Y.C. King and Rance P.L. Lee (eds), *Social Life and Development in Hong Kong*, Hong Kong, Chinese University Press, 1981.

Kuhn, Philip A., *Rebellion and Its Enemies in Late Imperial China: Militarization and Social Structure, 1796–1864*, Cambridge, MA, Harvard University Press, 1970.

Lam, Danny Kin-Kong and Lee, Ian, 'Guerrilla capitalism and the limit of statist theory: comparing the Chinese NICs', in Cal Clark and Steve Chan (eds), *The Evolving Pacific Basin*, Boulder CO, LynneRienner Publishers 1992.

Landsberg, Martin, 'Export-led industrialization in the Third World: manufacturing imperialism', *The Review of Radical Political Economics*, 1979, vol. 11, no. 4, pp. 50–63.

Latham, A.J.H., 'The dynamics of intra-Asian trade 1868–1913: the great entrepôts of Singapore and Hong Kong', in A.J.H. Latham and H. Kawakatsu (eds), *Japanese Industrialization and the Asian Economy*, London and New York, Routledge, 1994.

REFERENCES

Lau, Siu-kai, *Utilitarianistic Familism: An Inquiry into the Basis of Political Stability in Hong Kong*, Hong Kong, Chinese University of Hong Kong Social Research Centre, 1977.

——, 'Utilitarianistic familism: the basis of political stability in Hong Kong', CUHK Social Research Centre occasional paper no. 74, Hong Kong, Chinese University Press, 1978.

——, *Society and Politics in Hong Kong*, Hong Kong, Chinese University of Hong Kong, 1982.

Lau, Siu-kai, and Kuan Hsin-chi, *The Ethos of the Hong Kong Chinese*, Hong Kong, Chinese University Press, 1988.

Lee, Ming-kwan, 'The evolution of the Heung Yee Kuk as a political institution', in David Faure, J. Hayes and A. Birch (eds), *From Village to City: Studies in the Traditional Roots of Hong Kong Society*, Hong Kong, Centre of Asian Studies, 1984.

——, 'Yali tuanti yu zhengdang zhengzhi (Pressure groups and party politics)', in Lee Ming-kwan, *Bianqian zhong de Xianggang zhengzhi he shehui* (Hong Kong Politics and Society in Transition), Hong Kong, Commercial Press, 1987.

——, 'Hong Kong identity – past and present', in S.L. Wong and T. Maruya (eds), *Hong Kong Economy and Society: Challenges in the New Era*, Tokyo, Institute of Developing Economies, 1998.

Leeming, Frank, 'The earlier industrialisation of Hong Kong', *Modern Asian Studies*, 1975, vol. 9, no. 3, pp. 337–42.

Lethbridge, Henry J., 'Caste, class, and race in Hong Kong before the Japanese occupation', in Marjorie Topley (ed.), *Hong Kong: The Interaction of Traditions and Life in the Towns*, Hong Kong, Royal Asiatic Society, Hong Kong Branch, 1975.

Leung, Benjamin K.P., 'Power and politics: a critical analysis', in Benjamin K.P. Leung (ed.), *Social Issues in Hong Kong*, Hong Kong, Oxford University Press, 1990.

——, *Perspectives on Hong Kong Society*, Hong Kong, Oxford University Press, 1996.

Leung, Benjamin K.P. and Chiu, Stephen W.K., 'A social history of industrial strikes and the labour movement in Hong Kong, 1946–1989', Social Sciences Research Centre occasional paper no. 3, Hong Kong, University of Hong Kong, 1991.

Leung, C.B., 'Community participation: the decline of residents' organizations', in Joseph Cheng (ed.), *Hong Kong in Transition*, Hong Kong, Oxford University Press, 1986.

Leys, Colin, *Politics in Britain: From Labourism to Thatcherism*, rev. edn, London, Verso, 1989.

Liang, Qianwu, 'Xianggang huaqiao gongye zhi niaokan' (A bird's eye view of Chinese industry in Hong Kong), in Hong Kong Chinese Manufacturers' Union (ed.), *Xianggang Zhonghua changshang chupin zhinan* (A Guide to the Products of Chinese Factories in Hong Kong), Hong Kong, Hong Kong Chinese Manufacturers' Union, 1936.

Lin, T.B., 'A theoretical assessment of the currency system of Hong Kong', *The New Asia College Academic Annual*, 1970, vol. 12, pp. 179–94 (in Chinese).

Lin, Yuanhui and Zhang, Yinglong, *Xinjiapo Malaixiya huaqiao shi* (History of Overseas Chinese in Singapore and Malaysia), Guangzhou, Guangdong gaodeng jiaoyu chubanshe, 1991.

Liu, Guoliang, *Zhongguo gongyeshi (jindaijuan)* (Chinese Industrial History (Modern Period)), Jiangsu, Jiangsu Science and Technology Publisher, 1992.

Liu, Shuyong, 'Hong Kong: a survey of its political and economic development over the past 150 years', *China Quarterly*, 1997, no. 151, September, pp. 583–92.

Liu, William T, 'Chinese value orientations in Hong Kong', *Sociological Analysis*, 1966, vol. 27, no. 2, pp. 53–66.

Lo, C.P., *Hong Kong*, London, Belhaven Press, 1992.

Lo, Wai Luen, *Xianggang gushi* (Hong Kong Story), Hong Kong, Oxford University Press, 1996.

Lockhart, J.H.S., *Extracts From Papers Relating to the Extension of the Colony of Hong Kong*, Hong Kong, Hong Kong Government, 1899.

Lowe, Kate, and McLaughlin, Eugene, ' "An El Dorado of riches and a place of unpunished crime": the politics of penal reform in Hong Kong, 1877–1882', *Criminal Justice History*, 1993, vol. 14, pp. 57–89.

Lu Yan *et al.*, *Xianggang zhanggu* (Hong Kong Anecdotes), 12 vols, Hong Kong, Guangjiao-jing chubanshe, 1977–89.

Lui, Tai-lok, 'Yali tuanti zhengzhi yu zhengzhi canyu' (Pressure group politics and political participation), in Jospeh Cheng (ed.), *Guoduqi de Xianggang* (Hong Kong in the Transitional Period), Hong Kong, Joint Publications, 1989.

——, 'Fanpu guizhen' (Back to basics: rethinking the roles of residents' organizations), in Hong Kong Council of Social Service, *Community Development Resource Book 1989 & 1990*, 1990.

——, 'Two logics of community politics', in Lau Siu-kai and K.S. Louie (eds), *Hong Kong Tried Democracy*, Hong Kong, Hong Kong Institute of Asia-Pacific Studies, 1993.

——, 'Mishi yu jiju zhuanbian zhengzhi huanjing de Xianggang minzhong yundong' (The path of development of Hong Kong's popular movements), *Xianggang shehui kexue xuebao* (Hong Kong Journal of Social Sciences), 1994, no.4, pp. 67–78.

Lui, Tai-lok and Chiu, Stephen W.K., 'Industrial restructuring and labour-market adjustment under positive noninterventionism: the case of Hong Kong', *Environment and Planning A*, 1993, vol. 25, pp. 63–79.

——, 'A tale of two industries: the restructuring of Hong Kong's garment-making and electronics industries', *Environment and Planning A*, 1994, vol. 26, pp. 53–70.

Lui, Tai-lok and Kung, James K.S., *Chengshi zongheng* (City Unlimited: Community Movement and Urban Politics in Hong Kong), Hong Kong, Wide Angle Publications, 1985.

Luo, Xianglin, *Yiba sier nian yiqian zhi Xianggang jiqi duiwai jiaotong* (Hong Kong's Overseas Relations Before 1842), Hong Kong, Zhongguo Xueshe, 1959.

Mackie, J.A.C. (ed.), *The Chinese in Indonesia: Five Essays*, Melbourne, Nelson, 1976.

Mallon, Florencia E., 'The promise and dilemma of subaltern studies: perspectives from Latin American history', *American Historical Review*, 1994, vol. 99, no. 5, December, pp. 1,491–515.

Markre, Morris E., 'Rent-seeking and Hong Kong textile quota system', *Developing Economies*, 1979, vol. 17, no. 1, pp. 110–18.

Mathews, Gordon, 'Heunggongyahn: on the past, present, and future of Hong Kong identity', *Bulletin of Concerned Asian Scholars*, 1997, vol. 29, no. 3, p. 5.

Mayers, F. William; Dennys, N.B.; and King, Charles, *The Treaty Ports of China and Japan: A Complete Guide to the Open Ports of those Countries, Together with Peking, Yedo, Hongkong and Macao*, Hong Kong, A. Shortrede, 1867.

Maynard, Geoffrey, 'Sterling and international monetary reform', in Paul Streeten and Hugh Corbet (eds), *Commonwealth Policy in Global Context*, Toronto, Ont., University of Toronto Press, 1971.

McAdam, Doug; McCarthy, John; and Zald, Mayer, *Comparative Perspectives on Social Movements*, Cambridge, Cambridge University Press, 1996.

McVey, Ruth, 'The materialization of the Southeast Asian entrepreneur', in Ruth McVey (ed.), *Southeast Asian Capitalists*, Ithaca, NY, Cornell University Press, 1992.

Mei, June, 'Socioeconomic origins of emigration: Guangdong to California, 1850–1882', *Modern China*, 1979, vol. 5, no. 4, pp. 463–501.

Meredith, David, 'The British government and colonial economic policy, 1919–39', *Economic History Review*, 1973, vol. 28, no. 3, pp. 484–99.

Michalet, Charles-Albert, 'International sub-contracting: a state-of-the-art', in Dimitri Germidis (ed.), *International Subcontracting: A New Form of Investment*, Paris, OECD, 1980.

Migdal, Joel S., *Peasants, Politics, and Revolution: Pressures toward Political and Social Change in the Third World*, New Jersey, Princeton University Press, 1974.

Mills, Lennox A., *British Rule in Eastern Asia: A Study of Contemporary Government and Economic Development in British Malaya and Hong Kong*, London, Oxford University Press, 1942.

Miners, Norman J., *The Government and Politics of Hong Kong*, Hong Kong, Oxford University Press, 1975.

——, *Hong Kong Under Imperial Rule, 1912–1941*, Hong Kong, Oxford University Press, 1987.

——, 'The use and abuse of emergency powers by the Hong Kong government', *Hong Kong Law Journal*, 1996, vol. 26, part 1, pp. 47–57.

Mok, Victor, 'Trade barriers and export promotion: the Hong Kong example', in Tzong-biau Lin, Rance P.L. Lee and Udo-Ernst Simonis (eds), *Hong Kong: Economic, Social and Political Studies in Development*, Armonk, NY, M.E. Sharpe, 1979.

——, 'Small factories in Kwun Tong: problems of strategies for development', in Ambrose Y.C. King and Rance Y.L. Lee (eds), *Social Life and Development in Hong Kong*, Hong Kong, Chinese University Press, 1981.

Morroni, Mario, 'Production flexibility', in Geoffrey M. Hodgson and Ernesto Screpanti (eds), *Rethinking Economics: Markets, Technology and Economic Evolution*, Hants, Edward Elgar, 1991.

Munn, Christopher, 'The Chusan episode: Britain's occupation of a Chinese island, 1840–46', *Journal of Imperial and Commonwealth History*, 1997, vol. 25, no. 1, pp. 82–112.

Ng, Peter Y.C. and Baker, Hugh D.R., *New Peace County: A Chinese Gazetteer of Hong Kong Region*, Hong Kong, Hong Kong University Press, 1983.

Nie, Baozhang, 'Yang hang maiban yu maiban zhichan jieji' (Foreign companies, compradors, and comprador bourgeoisie), in Sun Jian (ed.), *Zhongguo jingji shi lunwen ji* (Collection of Articles on China's Economic History), Beijing, Zhongguo renmin daxue chubanshe, 1987.

Norton-Kyshe, J.W., *The History of the Laws and Courts of Hong Kong, Tracing Consular Jurisdiction in China and Japan, and including Parliamentary Debates, and the Rise, Progress, and Successive Changes in the Various Public Institutions of the Colony from the Earliest Period to the Present Time* (1898), 2 vols, Hong Kong, Vetch & Lee, 1971.

Olson, Alison Gilbert, *Making the Empire Work: London and American Interest Groups, 1690–1790*, Cambridge, MA, Harvard University Press, 1992.

Ouchterlony, John, *The Chinese War: An Account of All the Operations of the British Forces from the Commencement to the Treaty of Nanking*, London, Saunders & Otley, 1844.

Owen, Nicholas, 'Competition and structural change in unconcentrated industries', *Journal of Industrial Economics*, 1971, vol. 19, no. 2, pp. 133–47.

——, 'Economic policy in Hong Kong', in Keith Hopkins (ed.), *Hong Kong: The Industrial Colony*, Hong Kong, Oxford University Press, 1971.

——, 'Manpower deficiencies and industrial training', *Hong Kong Economic Papers*, 1972, no. 7, pp. 45–59.

Palmer, Michael, 'The surface-subsoil form of divided ownership in late imperial China: some examples from the New Territories of Hong Kong', *Modern Asian Studies*, 1987, vol. 21, pp. 1–119.

Patten, Christopher, *Hong Kong: Transition – The 1996 Policy Address*, Hong Kong, Government Printer, 1996.

Peng, Jiali, 'Shijiu shiji xifang qinlüezhe dui Zhongguo laogong de lulue' (The seizure of Chinese labor by western invaders in the nineteenth century), in Chen Hansheng (ed.), *Huagong chuguo shi ziliao huibian*, vol. 4, Beijing, Zhonghua shuju, 1981.

Phang, A. Boon Leong, *The Development of Singapore Law*, Singapore, Butterworths, 1990.

Podmore, David, 'The population of Hong Kong', in Keith Hopkins (ed.) *Hong Kong: The Industrial Colony*, Hong Kong, Oxford University Press, 1971.

Polanyi, Karl, *The Great Transformation*, Boston, MA, Beacon Press, 1957.

Porter, A.N. and Stockwell, A.J., *British Imperial Policy and Decolonization, 1938–1964*, vol. 2: 1951–64, London, Macmillan, 1988.

Porter, Bernard, *The Lion's Share: A Short History of British Imperialism, 1850–1983*, London, Longman, 1984.

Potter, Jack M., *Capitalism and the Chinese Peasant: Social and Economic Change in a Hong Kong Village*, Berkeley and Los Angeles, CA, University of California Press, 1968.

Prakash, Gyan, 'After colonialism', in Gyan Prakash (ed.), *After Colonialism: Imperial Histories and Postcolonial Displacements*, Princeton, NJ, Princeton University Press, 1995.

Rabushka, Alvin, *The Changing Face of Hong Kong: New Departures in Public Policy*, Washington, D.C., American Enterprise Institute for Public Policy Research; and Stanford, CA, Hoover Institution on War Revolution and Peace, Stanford University, 1973.

——, *Hong Kong: A Study in Economic Freedom*, Chicago, IL, University of Chicago Press, 1979.

Rear, John, 'One brand of politics', in Keith Hopkins (ed.), *Hong Kong: The Industrial Colony*, Hong Kong, Oxford University Press, 1977.

Redding, Gordon R., *The Spirit of Chinese Capitalism*, Berlin, Walter de Gruyter, 1990.

Registrar of Trade Unions, *Annual Departmental Report*, Hong Kong, Government Printer, 1972, 1982.

Reid, Anthony, 'The seventeenth century crisis in South-East Asia', *Modern Asian Studies*, 1990, vol. 24, pp. 639–59.

——, 'The origins of revenue farming in Southeast Asia', in John Butcher & Howard Dick (eds), *The Rise and Fall of Revenue Farming*, New York, St Martin's Press, 1993.

'Report of the commission appointed by His Excellency the Governor of Hong Kong to enquire into the causes and effects of the present trade depression in Hong Kong and make recommendations for the amelioration of the existing position and for the improvement of the trade of the colony', *Hong Kong Legislative Council Sessional Papers 1935–36*, pp. 64–131.

Riedel, James, *The Industrialisation of Hong Kong*, Tübingen, J.C.B. Mohr (Paul Siebeck), 1974.

Robinson, Ronald, 'Non-European foundations of European imperialism: sketch for a theory of collaboration', in Roger Owen and Bob Sutcliffe (eds), *Studies in the Theory of Imperialism*, London, Longman, 1972.

——, 'European imperialism and indigenous reactions in British West Africa', in H.L. Wesseling (ed.), *Expansion and Reaction: Essays in European Expansion and Reactions in Asia and Africa*, Leiden, Leiden University Press, 1978.

Rodan, Gary, *The Political Economy of Singapore's Industrialization: National State and International Capital*, Kuala Lumpur, Forum, 1989.

Rush, James, *Opium to Java*, Ithaca, NY, Cornell University Press, 1990.

Sayer, Geoffrey Robley, *Hong Kong: Birth, Adolescence, and Coming of Age*, London, Oxford University Press, 1937.

Schenk, Catherine R., *Britain and the Sterling Area: From Devaluation to Convertibility in the 1950s*, London, Routledge, 1994.

Schiffer, Jonathan R., 'State policy and economic growth: a note on the Hong Kong model', *International Journal of Urban and Regional Research*, 1991, vol. 15, no. 2, pp. 180–96.

Scott, Ian, *Political Change and the Crisis of Legitimacy in Hong Kong*, Hong Kong, Oxford University Press, 1989.

Sender, Henry, 'Inside the overseas Chinese network', *Institutional Investor*, 1991, vol. 25, no. 10, September, pp. 37–42.

Sing, Ming, 'Mobilisation for political change: the pro-democracy movement in Hong Kong (1980s–1994)', in Stephen W.K. Chiu and Tai-lok Lui (eds), *The Dynamics of Social Movement in Hong Kong*, Hong Kong, Hong Kong University Press, forthcoming.

Sinn, Elizabeth, *Power and Charity: The Early History of the Tung Wah Hospital, Hong Kong*, Hong Kong, Oxford University Press, 1989.

——, 'Emigration from Hong Kong before 1941: general trends', in Ronald Skeldon (ed.), *Emigration From Hong Kong: Tendencies and Impacts*, Hong Kong, Chinese University Press, 1995.

——, 'Emigration from Hong Kong before 1941: organization and impact', in Ronald Skeldon (ed.), *Emigration From Hong Kong: Tendencies and Impacts*, Hong Kong, Chinese University Press, 1995.

——, 'Emigration from Hong Kong, 1945–1994: the demographic lead-up to 1997', in Ronald Skeldon (ed.), *Emigration From Hong Kong: Tendencies and Impacts*, Hong Kong, Chinese University Press, 1995.

Sit, Victor Fung-Shuen, 'The informal manufacturing sector', in Victor Fung-Shuen Sit (ed.), *Urban Hong Kong*, Hong Kong, Summerson Eastern Publishers Ltd, 1981.

——, 'Dynamism in small industries: the case of Hong Kong', *Asian Survey*, 1982, vol. 22, no. 4, pp. 399–409.

Sit, Victor Fung-Shuen and Wong, Siu-lun, *Small and Medium Industries in an Export-Oriented Economy: The Case of Hong Kong*, Hong Kong, Centre of Asian Studies, University of Hong Kong, 1989.

Skocpol, Theda, *States and Social Revolutions: A Comparative Analysis of France, Russia, and China*, New York, Cambridge University Press, 1979.

Smith, Carl T., 'The Chinese settlement of British Hong Kong', *Chung Chi Bulletin*, 1970, vol. 48, pp. 26–32.

——, *Chinese Christians: Elites, Middlemen, and the Church in Hong Kong*, Hong Kong, Oxford University Press, 1985.

——, *A Sense of History: Studies in the Social and Urban History of Hong Kong*, Hong Kong, Hong Kong Educational Publishing Co., 1995.

Smith, Rev. G., *A Narrative of an Exploratory Visit to Each of the Consular Cities of China and to the Islands of Hong Kong and Chusan, In Behalf of the Church Missionary Society in the Years 1844, 1845, 1846*, London, Seeley, Burnside & Seeley, 1847.

So, Alvin, 'The economic success of Hong Kong: insights from a world-system perspective', *Sociological Perspectives*, 1986, vol. 29, no. 2, pp. 241–58.

Soulard, Francois, 'The restructuring of Hong Kong industries and the urbanization of Zhujiang Delta, 1979–1989', Ph.D. dissertation, Chinese University of Hong Kong, Hong Kong, 1993.

South China Morning Post, 'The MacLehose years 1971–1982', *South China Morning Post Supplement*, April 1982.

Sprenkel, Sybille van der, *Legal Institutions in Manchu China: A Sociological Analysis*, London, University of London Press, 1962.

Steinberg, David Joel, *In Search of Southeast Asia: A Modern History*, Honolulu, University of Hawaii Press, 1987.

Strange, Susan, *Sterling and British Policy: A Political Study of an International Currency in Decline*, London, Oxford University Press, 1971.

Strauch, Judith, 'Middle peasants and market gardeners, the social context of the 'Vegetable Revolution' in a small agricultural community in New Territories, Hong Kong', in David Faure, J. Hayes and A. Birch (eds), *From Village to City: Studies in the Traditional Roots of Hong Kong Society*, Hong Kong, Centre of Asian Studies, 1984.

Sung, Yun-wing, 'Economic growth and structural change in the small open economy of Hong Kong', in Vittorio Corbo, Ann O. Krueger and Fernando Ossa (eds), *Export-Oriented Development Strategies: the Success of Five Newly Industrializing Countries*, Boulder, CO, Westview, 1985.

——, 'The Hong Kong development model and its future evolution: neoclassical economics in a Chinese society', in Y.C. Jao, Victor Mok and Lok-sang Ho (eds), *Economic Development in Chinese Societies: Models and Experience*, Hong Kong, Hong Kong University Press, 1989.

Sutu, Hsin, 'Whither Hong Kong's industry?', *United College Journal*, 1963, vol. 2, p. 1–15.

Sutu, Hsin; Chang, Chien-min; and Cheng, Kin-Yu, 'A summary of industries in Hong Kong with special reference to their structure', *Journal of the Chinese University of Hong Kong*, 1977, vol. 4, no. 1, pp. 185–205.

Szczepanik, Edward, *The Economic Growth of Hong Kong*, London, Oxford University Press, 1958.

Tang, James T.H., 'From empire defence to imperial retreat: Britain's postwar China policy and the decolonization of Hong Kong', *Modern Asian Studies*, 1994, vol. 28, no. 2, pp. 317–37.

Tang, Stephen, 'The power structure in a colonial society: a sociological study of the Legislative Council in Hong Kong', unpublished senior B.Soc.Sci. thesis, Sociology Department, Chinese University of Hong Kong, Hong Kong, 1973.

Tarrant, William, 'History of Hong Kong', *Friend of China*, 23 November 1860.

——, 'History of Hong Kong', *Friend of China*, 9 November 1861.

Tate, D.J.M., *The Making of Modern South-East Asia*, Kuala Lumpur, Oxford University Press, 1979.

Telkamp, Gerard J., *Urban History and European Expansion: A Review of Recent Literature Concerning Colonial Cities and a Preliminary Biography*, Leiden, Leiden Centre for the History of European Expansion, 1978.

Ting, Joseph Sun Pao, 'Xianggang zaoqi zhi huaren shehui, 1841–1870' (Early Chinese community in Hong Kong, 1841–1870), Ph.D. dissertation, University of Hong Kong, 1989.

——, 'Native Chinese peace officers in British Hong Kong, 1841–1861', in Elizabeth Sinn (ed.), *Between East and West: Aspects of Social and Political Development in Hong Kong*, Hong Kong, Centre of Asian Studies, University of Hong Kong, 1990.

'The districts of Hong Kong and the name Kwan Tai Lo', *China Review 1873*, vol. 1, pp. 333–4.

Topley, Majorie, 'Capital, saving and credit among indigenuous rice farmers and immigrant vegetable farmers in Hong Kong's New Territories', in Raymond Firth and B.S. Yamey (eds), *Capital, Saving and Credit in Peasant Societies*, London, George Allen & Unwin Ltd, 1964.

——, 'The role of savings and wealth among Hong Kong Chinese', in I.C. Jarvie (ed.), *Hong Kong: A Society in Transition*, London, Routledge & Kegan Paul, 1969.

Trocki, Carl A., *Opium and Empire: Chinese Society in Colonial Singapore, 1800–1910*, Ithaca, NY, Cornell University Press, 1990.

——, 'The collapse of Singapore's great syndicate', in John Butcher & Howard Dick (eds), *The Rise and Fall of Revenue Farming*, New York, St Martin's Press, 1993.

Tsai, Jung-fang, *Hong Kong in Chinese History: Community and Social Unrest in the British Colony, 1842–1913*, New York, Columbia University Press, 1993.

Tsang, Shu-ki *et al.*, *Wuxingqi xia de Xianggang* (Hong Kong Under the Red Flag), Hong Kong, Twilight Books, 1982.

Tsang, Steve (ed.), *Government and Politics: A Documentary History of Hong Kong*, Hong Kong, Hong Kong University Press, 1995.

Tse, N.Q. 'Industrialization and social adjustment in Hong Kong', *Sociology and Social Research*, 1968, vol. 52, no. 3, pp. 237–51.

Tuan, Chyan and Ng, Linda F.Y., 'Manufacturing evolution under passive industrial policy and cross-border operations in China: the case of Hong Kong', *Journal of Asian Economics*, 1995, vol. 6, no. 1, pp. 71–88.

——, 'The turning point of the Hong Kong manufacturing sector', *The Journal of International Trade and Economic Development*, 1995, vol. 4, no. 2, pp. 153–70.

Tung, Chee Hwa, 'A future of excellence and prosperity for all', speech by the Chief Executive the Honourable Tung Chee Hwa at the ceremony to celebrate the establishment of the Hong Kong Special Administrative Region of the People's Republic of China, 1 July 1997.

Turner, H.A. *et al.*, *The Last Colony: But Whose?* Cambridge, Cambridge University Press, 1980.

Uchida, Naosaku, *The Overseas Chinese*, Stanford, Hoover Institution, Stanford University, 1959.

Wade, Robert, *Governing the Market: Economic Theory and the Role of Government in East Asian Industrialization*, Princeton, NJ, Princeton University Press, 1990.

Wah Kiu Yat Po, various issues.

Wang, Chuying (ed.), *Xianggang gongchang diaocha* (Survey of Hong Kong Factories), Hong Kong, Nanqiao News Enterprise, 1947.

Wang, Jingyu, *Shijiu shiji xifang ziben zhuyi dui Zhongguo de jingji qinlüe* (The Nineteenth-century Western Capitalist Economic Invasion of China), Beijing, Renmin chubanshe, 1983.

Welsh, Frank., *A History of Hong Kong*, London, HarperCollins, 1993.

Wesley-Smith, Peter, 'Anti-Chinese legislation in Hong Kong', in Ming K. Chan (ed.), *Precarious Balance: Hong Kong Between China and Britain, 1842–1992*, Armonk, NY, M.E. Sharpe, 1994.

Wong, Gilbert, 'Business groups in a dynamic environment: Hong Kong 1976–1986', in Gary Hamilton (ed.), *Business Networks and Economic Development in East and Southeast Asia*, Hong Kong, Centre of Asian Studies, University of Hong Kong, 1991.

Wong, K.C., *Zhonghua shangye zhinan* (China Commercial Directory), Hong Kong, 1933.

Wong, Lin Ken, 'Singapore: its growth as an entrepôt port, 1819–1941', *Journal of Southeast Asian Studies*, 1978, vol. 4, no. 1, pp. 50–84.

Wong, P.W. 'The pro-Chinese democracy movement in Hong Kong, 1976–95', in Stephen W.K. Chiu and Tai-lok Lui (eds), *The Dynamics of Social Movement in Hong Kong*, Hong Kong, Hong Kong University Press, forthcoming.

Wong, Siu-lun, *Emigrant Entrepreneurs: Shanghai Industrialists in Hong Kong*, Hong Kong, Oxford University Press, 1988.

Wong, Thomas, 'Discourses and dilemmas: 25 years of subjective indicators studies in Hong Kong', in Lau Siu-kai, Wan Po-san, Lee Ming-kwan and Wong Siu-lun (eds), *Indicators of Social Development: Hong Kong 1990*, Hong Kong, Hong Kong Institute of Asia-Pacific Studies, 1992.

World Bank, *The East Asian Miracle: Economic Growth and Public Policy*, New York, Oxford University Press, 1993.

Woronoff, Jon, *Hong Kong: Capitalist Paradise*, Hong Kong, Heinemann Asia, 1980.

Worsley, Peter, 'Imperial retreat', in E.P. Thompson (ed.), *Out of Apathy*, London, New Left Books, 1960.

Wu, Chung-Tong, 'Societal guidance and development: a case study of Hong Kong', Ph.D. thesis, University of California, Los Angeles, 1973.

Wu, Tianqing, *Xianggang jingji yu jingji zhengce* (The Hong Kong Economy and Economic Policy), Hong Kong, Zhonghua shuju, 1990.

Wu Hao, *Huaijiu Xianggangdi* (Longing for Old Hong Kong), Hong Kong, Boyi, 1988.

Yan, Zhongping; Xu, Yisheng; Yao, Xiangao; Sun, Yutang; Wang, Jingyu; Nie, Baozhang; Li, Wenzhi; Zhang, Youyi; and Luo, Ergang, *Zhongguo jindai jingji shi tongji ziliao xuanji* (Selection of Statistical Data on the Economic History of Modern China), Beijing, Kexue chubanshe, 1955.

Young, Alwyn, 'Hong Kong and the art of landing on one's feet: a case study of a structurally flexible economy', Ph.D. dissertation, Fletcher School of Law and Diplomacy, Tufts University, Medford, Massachusetts, 1989.

Young, Crawford, *The Colonial State in Comparative Perspective*, New Haven, CT, Yale University Press, 1994.

Youngson, A.J., *Hong Kong Economic Growth and Policy*, Hong Kong, Oxford University Press, 1982.

Yu, Shengwu and Liu, Cunkuan (eds), *Shijiu shiji de Xianggang* (Nineteenth-Century Hong Kong), Hong Kong, Qilin shuye, 1994.

Yu Lou, 'Xianggang chuqi haidaoshi' (Piracy in early Hong Kong), in Li Jinwei, *Xianggang bainianshi* (Centenary History of Hong Kong), Hong Kong, Nanzhong chubanshe, 1948.

Yuan, Bangjian, *Xianggang shilue* (A Brief History of Hong Kong), Hong Kong, Zhongliu chubanshe, 1988.

Yuandong shiwu pinglun she (Observers of Far Eastern Affairs) (ed.), *Xueyun chunqiu* (The Student Movement), Hong Kong, Yuandong shiwu pinglun she, 1982.

Zhang, Xiaohui, 'Jindai Xianggang de huazi gongye' (Chinese industry in modern Hong Kong), *Jindaishi yanjiu* (Studies in Modern History), 1996, vol. 91, no. 1, pp. 140–64.

Zhang Yueai, 'Xianggang, 1841–1980' (Hong Kong, 1841–1980), in Lu Yan *et al.*, *Xianggang zhanggu* (Hong Kong Anecdotes), vol. 4, Hong Kong, Guangjiaojing chubanshe, 1981.

REFERENCES

Zheng, Deliang, *Xianggang jingji wenti chutan* (A Preliminary Review of Hong Kong's Economic Problems), Guangdong, Zhongshan daxue chubanshe, 1984.

Zheng, Youkui, 'Zhuzhuai de lüesuo ji qi lirun' (The seizure of 'coolies' and the resulting profits), in Chen Hansheng (ed.), *Huagong chuguo shi ziliao huibian* (Anthology of Materials Concerning the Export of Chinese Labor), vol. 4., Zhonghua shuju, 1981.

Zhu, Zongyu; Yang, Yuanhua; and Dou, Hui, *Cong Xianggang gerang dao nuwang fanghua* (From the Loss of Hong Kong to Her Majesty's Visit to Hong Kong), Fuzhou, Fujian renmin chubanshe, 1990.

Zhuang, Guotu, *Zhongguo fengjian zhengfu de huaqiao zhengce* (The Chinese Feudal Government's Policies Towards Overseas Chinese), Xiamen, Xiamen daxue chubanshe, 1989.

——, 'Lun Ming ji haiwai Zhongguo sichou maoyi (1567–1643)' (On China's overseas silk trade during the late Ming period (1567–1643)), in Xiamen daxue nanyang yanjiusuo (ed.), *Nanyang yanjiu lunwenji* (Anthology of Nanyang Studies), Xiamen, Xiamen daxue chubanshe, 1992.

Zhuang, Wenqing, 'Ming Qing Guangzhou zhongxi maoyi yu Zhongguo jindai maiban de qiyuan' (Sino–Western trade in Ming-Qing Canton and the origin of modern Chinese compradors), in Guangdong lishi xuehui (ed.), *Ming Qing Guangdong shehui jingji xingtai yanjiu* (A Study of the Social and Economic Situation in Ming-Qing Guangdong), Guangzhou, Guangdong renmin chubanshe, 1985.

Zürcher, Erik, ' "Western expansion and Chinese reaction" – a theme reconsidered' in H.L. Wesseling (ed.), *Expansion and Reaction: Essays in European Expansion and Reactions in Asia and Africa*, Leiden, Leiden University Press, 1978.

INDEX

INDEX